Pellucid Paper

Bureaucratic Media And Poetry In Early Modern Spain

Technographies

Series Editors: Steven Connor, David Trotter and James Purdon

How was it that technology and writing came to inform each other so extensively that today there is only information? Technographies seeks to answer that question by putting the emphasis on writing as an answer to the large question of 'through what?'. Writing about technographies in history, our contributors will themselves write technographically.

Pellucid Paper

Bureaucratic Media And Poetry In Early Modern Spain

Adam Wickberg

OPEN HUMANITIES PRESS

London 2018

First edition published by Open Humanities Press 2018

Freely available at:

http://www.openhumanitiespress.org/books/titles/pellucid-paper/

Print ISBN 978-1-78542-054-2

PDF ISBN 978-1-78542-055-9

OPEN HUMANITIES PRESS

Open Humanities Press is an international, scholar-led open access publishing collective whose mission is to make leading works of contemporary critical thought freely available worldwide. More at http://openhumanitiespress.org

Contents

Quod non est in actis, non est in mundo

Philip II of Spain

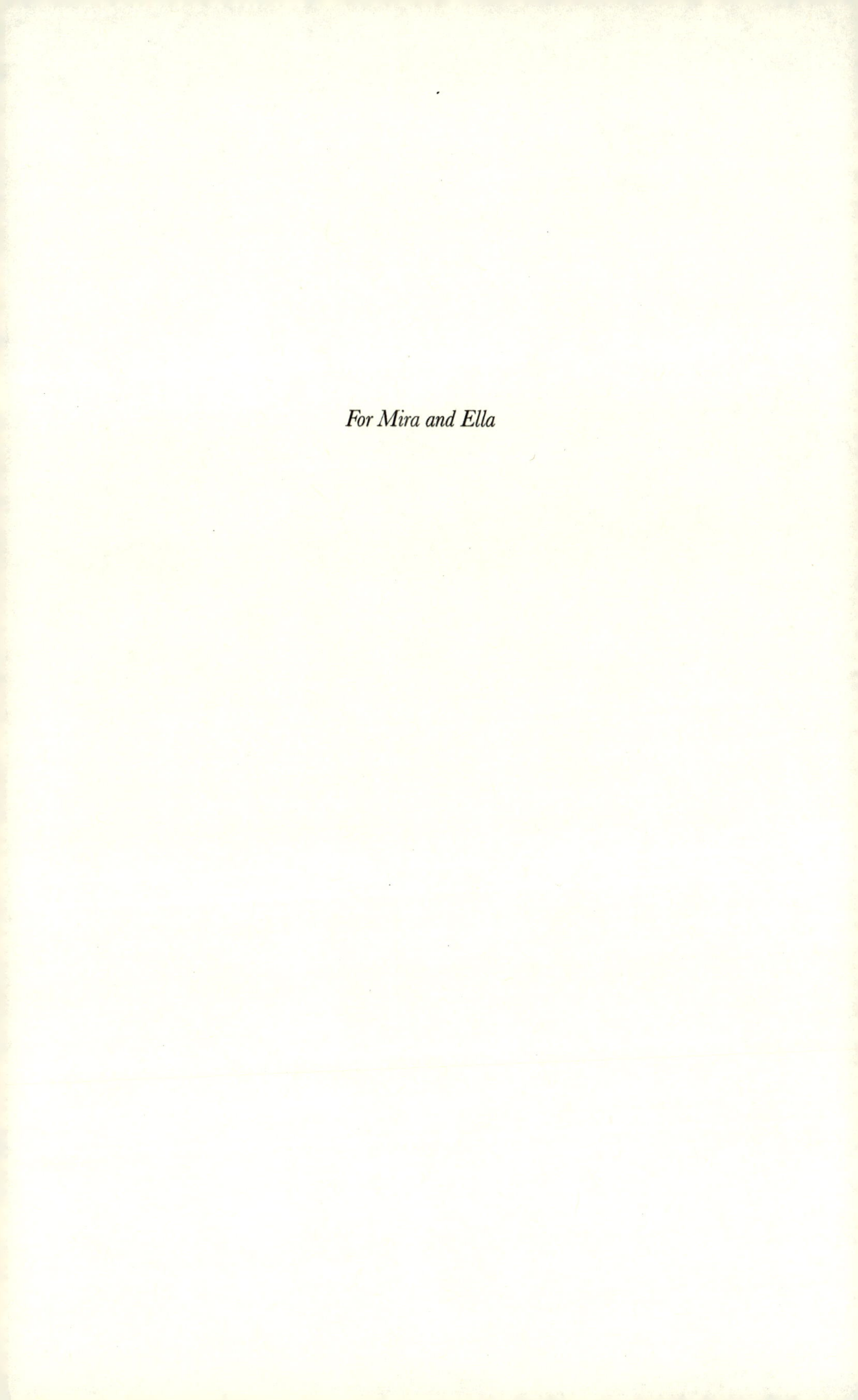

For Mira and Ella

Acknowledgements

There are many people I should thank for contributing to the coming into existence of this book following the five years of research that lie behind it. But as academic acknowledgements tend to get very long, I will try to keep it as short as possible. I want to thank Anders Cullhed for supervising me during my PhD years and all my colleagues at Stockholm University. I thank Mercedes Blanco for coming to Stockholm and providing an excellent opposition at my thesis defence. I also want to thank Hans Ulrich Gumbrecht for supervising my dissertation for a year at Stanford University. I want to thank John Durham Peters for many valuable comments and encouragement in the process of turning the dissertation into a book. I also owe thanks to my brilliant editors at Open Humanities Press, James Purdon, Steven Connor, and David Trotter, for working so generously with the manuscript. Above all, I want to thank my partner Mira Stolpe Törneman, also a scholar of media history, who generously has provided me with the most ingenious and exciting ideas from beginning to end, many of which now form part of this book. It is a huge understatement to say that without her, this book would never have been written.

Introduction: Paper Fever

On 12 December 1628 Don Antonio Chacon handed over a luxuriously produced manuscript of calfskin parchment to its dedicatee, the Count-Duke of Olivares. This meticulously calligraphed manuscript in three volumes brought together the complete poems of the poet Luis de Góngora, who had died the year before. In it, the poet and the collector had arranged the poems chronologically and according to genre, and had provided the circumstances of composition for each poem. Olivares, who was the First Minister of Philip IV, had desired the works of Góngora for his exclusive library. By the time of his death Góngora had become the most sought-after poet of the Spanish Golden Age without ever having had his poetry printed. Thus the existence of this material object raises a number of questions with regard to early modern media and cultural techniques. If the only book fully supervised by the poet was destined for a private library and only produced after his death, where and how did this poetry exist for contemporary readers? This material aspect of Golden Age poetry has primarily attracted editors and philologists who have carried out the important task of making it available today through critical editions. The conceptual object of poetry, however, has often been taken for granted, as if its existence as linguistic entity were self-evident, universal, and transhistorical. In reality, the opposite is true. Every poem needs to be perpetually stored in such a manner that its user can access it: a particular problem if the author has refrained from producing any such object.

The aim of this book is to investigate Góngora and the cultural production of his time by analyzing media as cultural techniques, which logically precede the symbolic and conceptual objects that can subsequently be extracted from them (such as an intentional authorial meaning). The media and materiality of early modern Spain are not used to explain the poetry of the time, nor is the poetry employed to explain historical circumstances. Indeed, the distinction between 'poetry' and other 'contexts' is rejected from the very outset as a product of a modern epistemology which the study seeks to overcome. In understanding poetic writing as 'technography', *Pellucid Paper* traces poetry back to its material conditions, both in terms of storage and in terms of a general material culture of which it inevitably forms part, and sheds new light on early modern cultural techniques. The Chacon manuscript is an important actor in this network, providing a point of departure for the three main chapters.

A further motivation for a materially-oriented understanding of early modern culture is the importance that is continually ascribed to material objects in historical sources. Issues of storage and perpetuation were urgent around 1600 in Spain, and, as will be shown, were related to the concepts of *vanitas* and *memento mori*. *Vanitas* is Latin for vanity, and refers in early modern culture to the transient nature of earthly existence. *Memento mori*, literally 'remember you shall die', is an associated (medieval Christian) reflection on mortality. The issue of the ephemeral quality of human existence and its relation to time, which found its symbolic expression in *Stilleben* paintings of skulls and hourglasses, can be understood in relation to the urge to use material media to store words and images in perpetuity. The book will thus unveil a dynamic relationship between the death-oriented aesthetics of *vanitas*, techniques and media of storage, and a form of mediated presence that permeates the inseparable spheres of the political and the aesthetic.

The early modern Spanish monarchy, which can be described as the first global empire, relied thoroughly on media for its existence and extension. The printing press had by 1600 become quite influential, but it was by no means regarded as unproblematic. Rather, it was heavily regulated and co-existed with the older medium of the manuscript, as did the relatively newer medium of paper and the older medium of parchment. Poetic writing formed an integral part of a network which also encompassed political memorials, legislation, historical documents, religious acts, and other material objects, all of which played a part in ascribing and ordering human subjectivity, or rather the cultural techniques of subject constitution.

The medium of paper is significantly older than the printing press, which has often been associated with modernity. The use of paper is also broader than the constraints of the printed book. As Harold Innis pointed out, at a time when parchment was being employed in the decentralized governance of European monasteries, paper already supported a centralised bureaucracy in China (Innis 1986: 115). In loose sheets, forms, acts, documents, and letters – to mention but a few uses – paper later became the decisive material foundation of western modernity. Paper has been such an omnipresent product that it has been hard to recognise it as such, and throughout history one finds a great number of examples of how paper, both metaphorically and physically, has interacted with thought. Today, the dominance of the medium of paper seems to be challenged by digital communication and some even predict a paperless future. However that might be, we still measure written communication by the page, and on computer screens and tablets paper is remediated as the default format of information (Bolter and Grusin 1999). This relationship between old and new media is an expression of how media always exist as practice, rather than in abstract terms or as fixed entities, and of how the material medium of paper affects thought. The history of paper is long and widespread, and in recent years a significant scholarly interest in this ever-present medium has arisen, perhaps as a consequence of its apparently imminent disappearance as a default medium of writing (Müller 2012; Kafka 2012; Krajewski 2011; Gitelman 2014; Vismann 2000).

The use of the medium of paper around 1600 – for the Spanish Empire 1570-1630 are the pivotal years – marks the beginning of an epoch that is now said to be approaching its end with the advent of digital media. Dreams of a paperless society, where information is no longer stored in cellulose but in virtual clouds, have appeared over the last few decades. This new media situation is still very much affected by our habitual use of old media such as paper, and it is therefore imperative to understand these current changes in a longer historical perspective. Thus media history can shed new light on current changes, where issues of memory, storage and copying are recurrently renegotiated with the introduction of new media technologies. At the same time, it is the imminent disappearance of paper-based media that allows them to be seen as such. In this sense, digitisation provides a perspective by which one can investigate the past.

Paper came into Europe from the Arab world in the twelfth century; it was introduced through Spain, and more particularly Córdoba, the most important base for Islamic culture in the West (Müller 2012: 44). Paper had been used to copy the Quran for some time and was then brought to the Iberian Peninsula by the large number of Moors and Jews inhabiting the southern parts of Spain. By the end of the fifteenth century, the Catholic kings decided to expel all non-Christian citizens, particularly Jews and Moors, from their territory (Peters 2003). A consequence of this violent expulsion was that while the culture was seething with paper-based cultural products around 1600, the kingdom suffered from a constant lack of high-quality paper for the simple reason that most people with the knowledge of paper production had been expelled (Carmen Hidalgo Brinquis 2006: 200). Paper thus came to be a sought-after and crucial product for the emerging bureaucracy of King Philip II, as well as for cultural and religious communication during his rule.

The Paper King

In the same epoch that the Catholic kings united Spain and expelled Moors and Jews, the Spanish Empire began colonizing what came to be known as the New World. Thus Spain grew enormously during the sixteenth century: it came to comprise, as well as the Iberian Peninsula, Italy, Belgium and the Netherlands in Europe, colonies on all the known continents. So when Philip II inherited the Spanish crown from his father Charles V in 1556, it came with an enormous geographical territory that could be described as the first global empire (Parker 1998: 47). Unable to be physically present in all parts of his kingdom at the same time, Philip had to deal with the problems of distance and communication. He came to rely on early modern media, and more particularly, on the medium of paper. Paper enabled him to communicate quickly over greater distances, and he was soon ruling the empire from his office. This historically new means of executing power meant that Spain saw the transition from sword to pen, as the modern bureaucratic way of exercising power by signatures on paper was born. Philip's new strategy soon earned him the epithet 'The Paper King', and he was reputed to be an absent king with no time for warfare, or for love, since he spent his days at his desk writing letters and orders (Bouza 1994: 58). *Quod non est in actis, non est in mundus* – 'what is not in the files is not in the world', the motto that originally referred to the written legal formation of Roman court proceedings – is said to have been a favourite of Philip's. Cornelia Vismann strikingly analyzes how the double negation of the proverb reveals 'the performative operation of the law in constructing reality' (Vismann 2008: 56). She explains that the burden of proof that something indeed exists is thereby placed on the world rather than the archive, an obvious advantage for bureaucratic rule.

The Paper King would often sign large volumes of papers every day. In March 1571 he personally worked through more than 1250 petitions, meaning he signed about forty per day. In March 1576 he informed his secretary that he could not be disturbed, as he had more than four hundred papers to sign. Philip embodied the prototype of the early modern ruler and his technique of power can be understood as an origin of modern bureaucratic media (Brendecke 2006). Forms and surveys were sent across the vast empire and archives were created in order to organise the massive flow of information, while synoptic representations from maps demonstrated its circulation, imposing a necessary distance for the execution of power and letting the ruler reign in peace without distractions or questions (Müller 2012: 58). Numerous testimonies exist about how Philip buried himself in paper day and night (Campos y Fernández de Sevilla 2009: 21). An impenetrable barrier of paper was forged between the ruler and the ruled, removing physical presence from the exercise of power. Even at audiences, Philip used paper to gain control, often bringing along a stack of papers at which he pointed to indicate that he possessed more information than he expressed orally (Müller 2012: 59). The opposition between cognitive memory and material storage through writing that had existed since antiquity, notably expressed by Plato, was thereby revived in the early modern media practice of the Paper King. In Foucauldian terms, the historical transition from orality to literacy enabled new possibilities for the exercise of power in a bureaucratic *apparatus* (Foucault 1980: 194; Agamben 2009). By using paper as a silent actor that could not be questioned, Philip improved and simplified the execution of power in his vast empire. The place of power thereby became anonymous (Gumbrecht 1990: 359). And this feature of paper has come to be the quintessential function of modern bureaucracy. As Vismann insists, 'the unlimited capacity for addition and circulation turns files into a medium of presence. It endows them with the same characteristics as speech, with the result that they appear to be up-to-date, live, ever changing, acting and inexhaustible. Files take on ontological qualities' (Vismann 2009: 10).

Philip's media practice can further be understood in accordance with Michel Serres's concept of the *quasi-object* (Serres 1982: 224). The inanimate object may seem devoid of life, but in practice it functions as an actor with agency, and with the ability to affect other entities. Paper instantiates the human subject as sovereign and subjectivity is ascribed through the circulation of paper, thereby establishing a network wherein the *quasi-object* circulates and turns subjects (as conscious and living entities) into subjects (as subjected to power). Large parts of the King's administration were handled by himself, rather than by writers or copyists (Bouza 1994: 61). The medium of paper enabled Philip to rule through the written word rather than on the battlefield, and, according to a contemporary witness, he achieved as much with his pen as his predecessors had done with their swords. By constantly focussing on reading and writing as his primary tasks, Philip could overcome the great physical distances of his empire and protect the peace and quiet of his office from disturbing elements. One of the essential features of paper was thus its non-responsive silence. With time the stacks of paper would grow, since Philip insisted on handling a lot of paperwork personally. As his office filled up with papers, the empire became paralysed; complaints about inefficiency started to be heard, while the economy was ruined in the first great economic crisis in Europe. The silence of the orders that were sent out and signed was mirrored by the silence that met people who sent in letters of complaint. The Paper King would simply avoid the oral audience that was habitual at court and instead let the silent paper bear the responsibility for executing orders as well as listening to problems. Hence silent paper replaced speech as well as hearing. The feeling of crisis that has often been associated with the seventeenth century in Spain can, from this perspective, be understood as an effect of a historically specific media practice.

While this proposition may seem controversial, there is mounting evidence that the seventeenth-century 'crisis' was to some extent due to wars following the climate change of the little Ice Age, as Geoffrey Parker has recently demonstrated (Parker 2013). That change in the earth's ecological system can in turn be related to the mass deaths of fifty million people and the following reforestation of their farmed lands that occurred in the process of the Spanish colonisation of the Americas, as has been shown by geographers attempting to define the geological epoch of the Anthropocene (Lewis & Maslin 2015: 171-80). The Spanish colonial project and its massive infrastructure for moving humans, non-humans and other objects around, were to a large extent dependent upon the bureaucratic media that the Paper King and his secretaries and councillors developed (Siegert 2003: 65-110). From the palace of El Escorial to the distant New Spain across the Atlantic, the paper-based bureaucracy administered every aspect of its subjects' lives.

In the Kingdom of Secretaries

The concept of the Spanish Empire as a 'kingdom of secretaries' comes from Bernhard Siegert's proposition in *Passage des Digitalen* (2003) that Philip II's intimate relationship with media marks the end of the medieval 'travel kingdom' and the beginning of a new mode of power which relies on paper and writing instead of bodies and voices. The notion of a kingdom of secretaries is adopted here to explore the interrelation of bureaucratic media practices and those texts that are usually labelled poetic. As Roger Chartier explains, writing came to be the fundamental instrument of the 'Moderns':

> Beginning in the fifteenth century and perhaps earlier, recourse to writing played an essential role in several major evolutions within western societies. The first of these was the construction of a state based on justice and finance, which supposes the creation of bureaucracies, the construction of archives, and the development of administrative and diplomatic communication. (Chartier 2013: 10)

In Spain around 1600 a large number of people earned a living from writing and copying without having any claim to the status of authors. Copyists and scribes multiplied the written word by hand, even though the technique of print was well established. Underground copying by students and temporary employment as a scribe at a church were commonplace (Bouza 2001: 35). The same state apparatus that expelled non-Christian citizens around 1500 now carried out large-scale control of the information flow in manuscripts and printed papers. The Spanish Inquisition had prohibited a large number of writings, for example translations of the Bible into vernacular languages, meaning that copying by hand emerged as a way to escape censorship and legal actions. Manuscript books and loose papers of drama and poetry also circulated throughout the country. The absence of copyright meant that people in the audience could copy a play from hearing and then sell or circulate it further, without the author's knowledge. These texts often found their way to print shops, and playwrights such as Lope de Vega and Calderón de la Barca could find their plays heavily corrupted in a *librería* without having had anything to do with the material products or having any means of taking action against the phenomenon. Calderón called the people who practised this type of unauthorised copying 'little thieves', and Lope tried his best to maintain control over his works. In the prologue to the thirteenth part of his collected works, Lope talks about these copyists in terms of big and small memory: 'People call them the small memory and the big memory, because with a few verses that they memorise they add an infinite number of their own barbaric ones, with which they make a living, selling them to villages and authors outside of the walls' (Vega 1965: 120). Lope then adds that these thieves answer accusations of theft by arguing that the playwright has sold the performance to the audience, and what remains in their memory rightfully belongs to them. To the issue of memory is thus added that of the material storage of spoken words, an issue that runs throughout the cultural production of the era.

The widespread use of paper as a medium on which one could quickly annotate, fabricate, and disseminate written material gave rise to a problem that is familiar today in the age of digital reproduction: the relatively large scale and uncontrolled dissemination of information with the aid of new technology (Blair 2010: 303-16). The difference is that around 1600 there existed no legal copyright, nor any legislation establishing the ownership of words as what we would now term 'intellectual property' distinct from its material storage (Rose 1995). The regulation of print was a matter of state control, designed not primarily to protect authors but to protect the general public from information considered dangerous. The only things a playwright like Lope could do were to complain, and to write even more. In another prologue from the same year he claims to have written 'Nine hundred comedies, twelve books on various topics in verse and prose and so many loose papers that the printed will never catch up with what is left to print' (Vega 1965: 120). His production grew tremendously and his collected works, published in his lifetime, comprise no fewer than 25 books. His strategy was thus to counter the troubling material multiplication of his works by multiplying his own writing himself. Lope thereby appears as a companion to the Paper King in his constant multiplying of paper. Cervantes called him a 'monstruo de la naturaleza' precisely due to his tremendous speed of production – a scribal velocity he apparently shared with Philip II – and not because of any quality of his texts (Sanchez-Jiménez 2006: 81).

Lope's writing frenzy can also be understood in connection with his function within this kingdom of secretaries. From 1607 to 1628, Lope served as a secretary for the Duke of Sessa, for whom he primarily produced love letters (Weber 2005: 406). While being a successful playwright in high demand, Lope spent a lot of time composing letters for the influential Duke. The explanation for this is that Lope, who came from a simple family without any noble connection, tried to achieve a position within the court and establish himself as a poet and intellectual rather than the 'vulgar' playwright he was considered by many to be. The secretary of a nobleman could, if the patron had influence, achieve a position that guaranteed a certain amount of wealth and power. Lope's attempts were frustrated, but his vocation was strong enough for him to compose one of the thirteen poems that open Gabriel Pérez del Barrio's *Dirección de Secretarios de Señores*, published in 1613. Pérez del Barrio opens his book on the practice of the secretary with a note to the curious reader, where he explains that:

> Having found myself relieved of affairs and papers in the wilderness, where I tried to exchange their commerce for the

> pleasures of hunting and agriculture, I was taken over by the natural inclination to pass some time in ordering and writing papers of various matters. (Barrio 1613: 17)

Relieved of his duties, the secretary turns to the woods for leisure, only to be taken over once again by the 'natural' inclination to return to the order of papers. The front matter of the book contains an emblem of a silent minotaur in the midst of an agricultural labyrinth, holding a paper in one hand while making a sign of silence by putting the index finger to its lips with the other (see Figure 1). The Latin motto of the emblem reads *Labore et silentio fortuna vincit*: 'Fortune is victorious by means of work and silence'. The minotaur became a symbol for the perfect secretary in the seventeenth century, associated with the virtues of silence and paperwork in the labyrinth of the Court (Álvarez-Ossorio 1999: 21).

Pérez del Barrio's book contains important information with regard to the execution of power, as is underlined in another laudatory sonnet by Antonio Hurtado de Mendoza: 'For of a true man it is not less honourable to tame the rebel, honour the wise, reward the quill, than to conduct the sword' (Barrio 1613: 25). Mendoza's lines testify to the importance placed on the cultural technique of writing for the practice of sovereignty, and resonate with the abovementioned testimony that Philip II achieved as much with his quill as his father had with his sword.

Pérez del Barrio's recurring references to agriculture in explaining the importance of the secretary is perhaps not incidental. As Cornelia Vismann points out, the practice of cultural techniques is as old as culture itself, which derives from the Latin word *colere*, to cultivate:

> To start with an elementary and archaic cultural technique, a plough drawing a line in the ground: the agricultural tool determines the political act; and the operation itself produces the subject, who will then claim mastery over both the tool and the action associated with it. Thus, the *Imperium Romanum* is the result of drawing a line – a gesture which, not accidentally, was held sacred in Roman law. (Vismann 2013: 84)

Quod non est in actis, non est in mundo, as the Paper King liked to repeat, and so the drawing of lines by means of quill on paper came to be instrumental for the moderns. The importance conferred upon paper and writing in early modern Spain is integral to its geopolitical situation of empire building. Pérez del Barrio insists from the first page of his book, with an agricultural metaphor, on the need for rules and guidelines for the practice of the secretary. He concurs that even if Philip II, the Paper King, had done well in trying to reform this profession, the need for his six-volume book was urgent, not least to 'distinguish among the diversity of papers' (Barrio 1613: 38). A

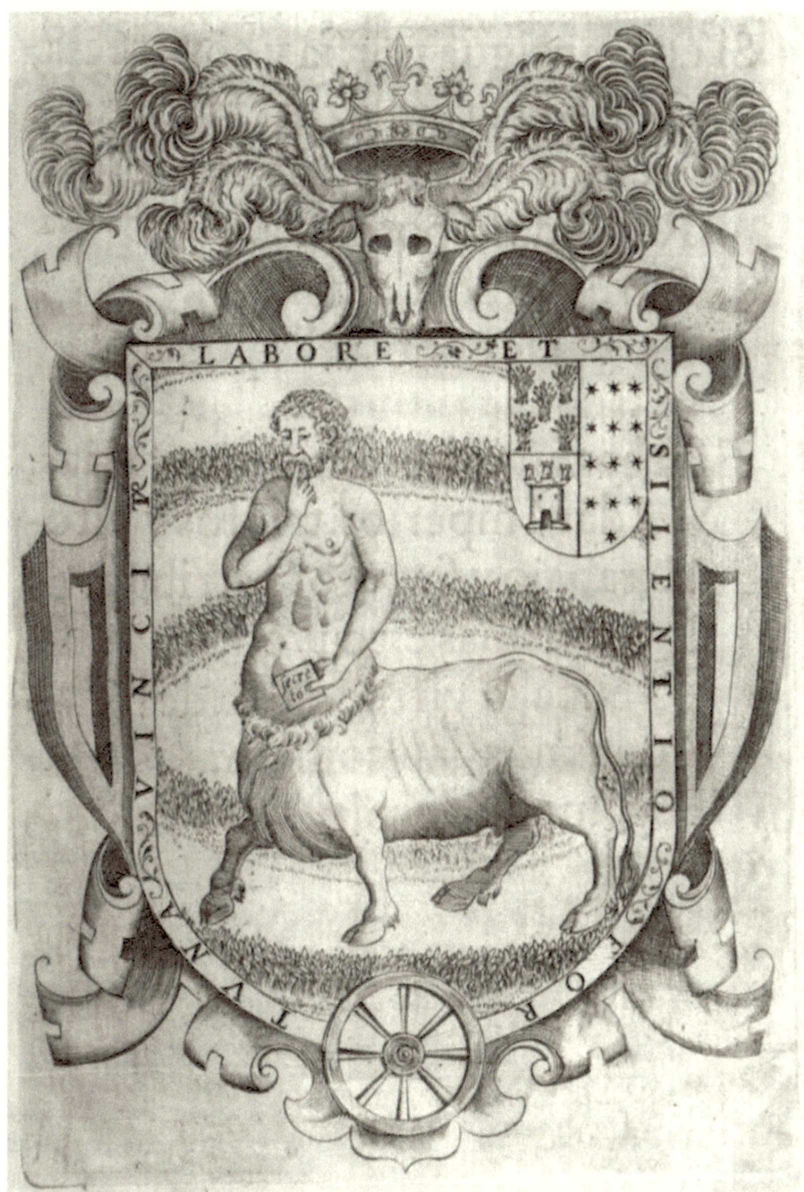

Figure 1. Gabriel Pérez de Barrio, *Dirección de Secretarios* (1613). Source: Europeana.

royal secretary working with the Paper King would generally work through about a thousand letters a month, so the paperwork extended far beyond Philip´s desk (Bouza 1996: 2-15). After naming a number of essential political functions, Pérez del Barrio places secretaries at the centre of the functioning of the global empire, because they 'care for the punctuality and assistance, order and functioning that is needed, and the promptitude and harmony among the bustle and multitudes of people, and present a wonderful theatre of much admiration' (Barrio 1613: 42).

In stressing the importance of the secretary as the one who keeps the 'wonderful theatre' running, he also gives a hint of the interconnected administrative institutions which exercise the power of the sovereign. The cultural technique of writing and associated bureaucratic media are thus explicitly linked to the functioning of this global empire, in which poets often functioned as secretaries, librarians, or postmasters (Lope de Vega, Francisco de Rioja, Conde de Villamediana, for example) if not as chaplains (Góngora), to mention but a few of the media-oriented professions (Sieber 1998: 86). In this context, poetry was not separate from, but integral to, the practice of power and sovereignty. Pérez del Barrio goes on to explain that the secretary of a lord or king is 'the memory and consultant of the suits, cases and things that are offered and are in waiting, and ready to take care of them, as well as in demand, in order to conduct their dispatch to good ends' (Barrio 1613: 41). The cultural technique of acting as secretary consists in reducing the human body to an intermediary point between the hand of the master and the papers that constitute the execution of power, and thus produce the subjects (cf. Kraijewskij 2013).

When the diplomat Diego de Saavedra Fajardo published his influential emblem book *Political Maxims: The Idea of a Political Christian Prince* in 1640, the function of the secretary assumed a privileged position. The emblem of the secretary (see Figure 2) depicts a hand writing on paper with a compass, since, as he explains, the task of the secretary is not only to write, but to 'measure and adjust resolutions, compare events and times, so that the executions are correctly timed: a profession so united with that of the Prince, that if permitted, his majesty would turn to no one else, because if the secretary is not a part of the Majesty, it is its reflection' (Saavedra Fajardo 1642: 409). Above the hand is placed a Latin motto that reads *Qui a Secretis ab Omnibus*: 'Who has secrets of everything'. To Saavedra Fajardo, the secretary matters more than the minsters, since a king can govern with bad ministers but cannot do with an incompetent secretary. In Spanish political metaphors of the time, the secretary is not only the throat supporting the head of state (the King) over the body politic, but the stomach through which everything passes. In Saavedra Fajardo's words, if the secretary-stomach does not properly digest the affairs of the state and they come out undigested, the government will be short-lived (410).

Gaspar de Guzmán, Count-Duke of Olivares and first minister of Philip IV, is an actor of particular importance for the governance of the 1620s and 1630s. As Philip IV, who assumed the throne in 1621, was not so inclined to beauracratic media practices as his grandfather, he left the administrative function to Olivares, who thereby became the de facto ruler of the empire.

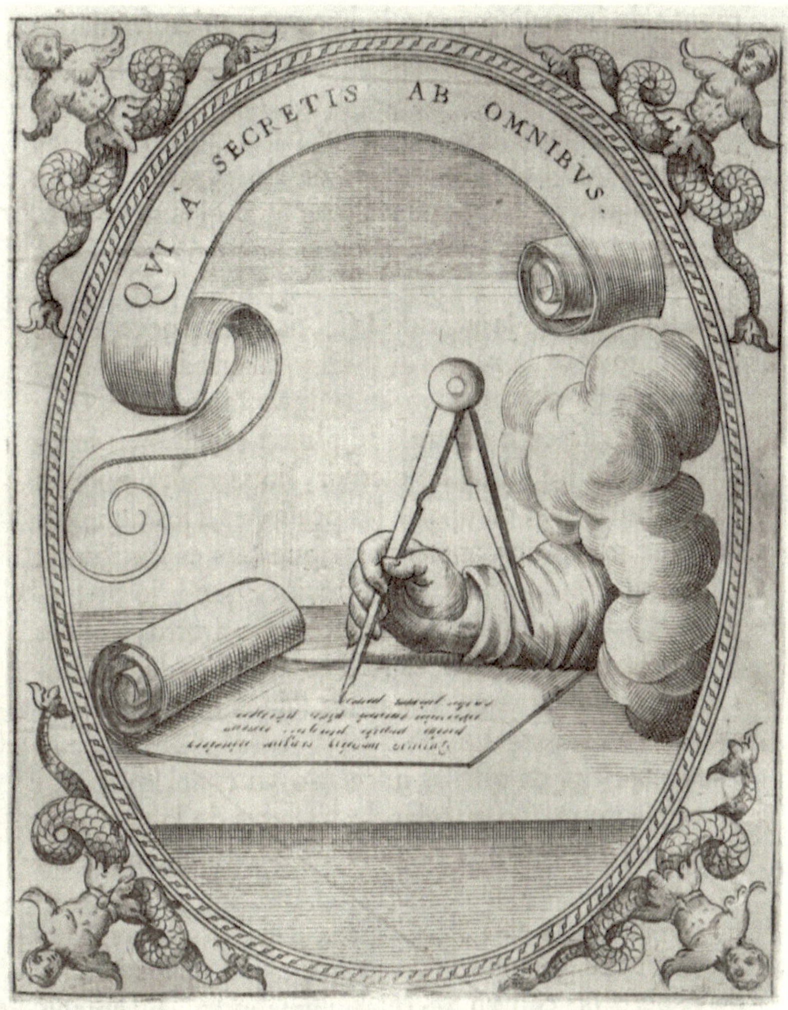

Figure 2. Diego de Saavedra Fajardo, *Empresas politicas* (1640). 'Emblem of the Secretary'. Source: Europeana.

The Count-Duke's father, Enrique de Guzmán, had become known as 'El Papelista', for his vast production of written papers as ambassador to Rome during the reign of Philip II (Marañon 1935: 677). Olivares himself earned the epithet 'Archduke of Writers' and spent a lot of his time as minister in his office, at his writing desk, working through papers (Marañon 1936: 169). He even had royal permission (*cédula real*) to take any documents, papers or books of the state and keep them in his own private library and archive (434).

The epithet 'Papelista' was used in a pejorative sense, as an expression of complaint about the practice of ruling through paper. When the Count of Luna writes of Philip II that the kings are *papelistas*, he is pointing toward the shift in the practice of sovereignty from sword to pen: 'The ministers [...] make use of these media, which are prevalent in our time when the Kings are *papelistas* and friends of hearing it all and enemies of being involved in the practice of their armies' (Marañon 1936: 169, n. 8). A contemporary account of Olivares helps to consolidate this image of the reign of paper. Victorio Siri, an Italian historian who published fifteen volumes on contemporary history between 1644 and 1682, describes in his first book how Philip IV occupied himself only with pastimes such as hunting, leaving the actual execution of power to Olivares. While this fact is today well known, the description of Olivares depicts him as the inheritor of Philip II, the Paper King:

> Because he never presented himself in front of the King without an abundance of petitions in the pockets of his robe, and his hands full of different papers; that is how he achieved the name of Archduke of Writers and Prince of Writings: in the end he worked hard always to appear occupied with affairs of Government, and when he went on a small trip, or even just took a walk, he took in his wagon a small table and lots of registers, to be able to write even there, or dictate to one of his secretaries. (Siri 1722: 107)

As Bernhard Siegert points out, the reign of Philip II can be understood as a 'kingdom of secretaries', where power was centralised in the capital Madrid and heavily regulated by means of documents, forms, registers and other papers. Following Hans Ulrich Gumbrecht, Siegert points out how the place of power became anonymised. Instead of connecting power to the body of the King (which in this case was rarely seen), the abundance of written documentation itself became a site of power. As Siegert puts it, 'Information media – that is a spatially powerful bureaucracy – takes in the Hispano-American kingdom the place of the sovereign' (Siegert 2003: 68). During Philip II's time the archive of Simancas became an enormous and secret depository of all the information on which his power rested; a written document signed by the King could exercise his will without his physical presence. Indeed, many of the printed books of this time contain a notice of authorization from the ruler himself, signed 'I, the King', as a testament to his control over subjects and information. This new regime of paper power becomes especially clear when considering Spain's control over the Americas, the subject of Siegert's two contributions to the field, wherein Seville as city and archive forms the absolute centre of control over both human and non-human actors who cross the sea and so enter into the cosmographic order (Siegert 2003, 2006). Siegert and Vogl's *Europa: Kultur der Sekretäre* offers further evidence of how European nation-states consolidated their new large-scale power through bureaucracies in which the secretary is the primary actor, and, sometimes the King himself. Although, as Gumbrecht has explained, this conflation of King and secretary may also be an act of deception from a master of the *disimulo* (Siegert 2003b: 71).

As the two emblems above indicate, the notion of the 'secretary' was intimately linked to the word's etymological roots in secrecy. The term is derived from the Latin word *secernere*, meaning to set apart, and in the early modern era it took on the connotation of setting private and confidential matters apart. The secretary is thus the person who sets apart sensitive information on written record, and it is easy to see why this particular position became so important in a society like the Spanish Empire, which cultivated a fierce culture of secrecy. The subtitle of this book – 'Poetry and Bureaucratic Media' – points to the fact that the poetic writings of early modern Spain, which would later be labelled 'baroque', were in fact produced by the same actors and through the same networks as those constituting this bureaucracy.

Pellucid Paper and Eternal Parchment

Luis de Góngora navigated early modern media by refusing to print any poems, even though the demand to read him was great, especially after his longer poems *Soledades* (*Solitudes*) and *La Fabula de Polyfemo y Galatea* (*The Fable of Polyphemus and Galatea*) started circulating in manuscript in 1613. Góngora himself claimed to have kept no copies of his own poetry, which he knew by heart. After finishing his poems and handing them over to a copyist, he got rid of the material storage in paper (Carreira 1998: 77). The loose papers or manuscript codices circulated from hand to hand in Madrid, and a growing number of aficionados collected his poetry. One of these aficionados, Don Antonio Chacon, who was also a friend of Góngora, convinced him at the end of his life, in 1627, to produce a manuscript copy of his collected works. Many influential men had asked Góngora to publish his poetry dedicated to them (dedications were habitual for writers in search of support) but he had so far refrained from doing so. The manuscript that he finally produced with Chacon was dedicated to Gaspar de Guzman, Count-Duke of Olivares, and first minister of the kingdom. It was skillfully calligraphed on calfskin parchment, the most expensive, exclusive, and reliable form of media at the time. This manuscript was destined for the Count-Duke's library, to be stored for future readers. The fact that parchment can last for thousands of years while paper has a significantly shorter life span shows that the choice of medium had to do with technical means of material storage. Harold Innis insists that the medium of parchment was associated with time (durability) while paper was connected to issues of space (dissemination) (Innis 1986: 134). The parallel use of paper and parchment in medieval Europe also had to do with the difference between charter and files (Müller 2012: 58). Medieval charters were stored in parchment because they were considered eternal. In a similar gesture, the use of calfskin parchment for Góngora's collected poetry indicates an emerging notion of ownership of the words, which were to be stored for the future in material form. Furthermore, it effectively set them apart from paper, the bureaucratic medium of distributed control.

Góngora's *Soledades* started circulating in 1613. Moving from hand to hand, copied and sent through the newly-established postal system which he made frequent use of, the poem soon turned its author into the most discussed and sought-after poet in the kingdom of secretaries. Copies of the poem were always the result of individual hands moving individual feather quills across newly-pressed paper. The visual impression of reading it was therefore not standardised, but rather involved variation and constant movement, with black or red inkdots spattered around elaborately formed calligraphic letters or words quickly scribbled, as if copied in a hurry. The relatively numerous manuscripts surviving to this day in various depositories, and primarily in the National Library of Spain in Madrid, gives such an impression. Today the paper is yellowed of course, and the distinct archival smell of four hundred-year-old dust has been added, but the visual appearance has not changed much. The poem narrates the destiny of a shipwrecked pilgrim (the Spanish word *peregrino* can also mean 'foreigner') as he lands on a beach and ascends the mountains where he meets the local community of farmers. The pilgrim is also a *cortesano*, a court-dweller from the city, and his experience of encountering nature for the first time, as it were, constructs a limited perspective, which has led several influential critics like António Carreira and Mercedes Blanco to associate his poetic writing with pictorial techniques of the time (Carreira 1998; Blanco 2004).

Lines 602-611 describe one such interesting natural landscape which invites comparisons with seventeenth-century Flemish painters. The *peregrino* observes how, among ash trees and poplars, a group of mountain-dwellers are on their way to a wedding. This movement of human bodies in the mountains leads to an interesting expanded metaphor that effectively intermingles nature and culture:

And so they all passed by, and in good order
as at the equinox we see furrowing
through oceans of open air
not flights of galley ships
but flocks of swift-sailing cranes,
moons perhaps waxing, perhaps on the wane
their most distant extremes,
perhaps forming letters on the pellucid
paper of the sky with
the quill feathers of their flight.

[Pasaron todos, pues, y regulados
cual en los equinoccios surcar vemos
los piélagos del aire libre algunas

volantes no galeras,
sino grullas veleras,
tal vez creciendo, tal menguando lunas
sus distantes extremos,
caracteres tal vez formando alados
en el papel dïáfano del cielo
las plumas de su vuelo]
(Góngora 2000: 382)

This rich passage is emblematic of Góngora's poetics; metaphors of mundane matters expanded into cosmic images, effectively blurring the lines between nature and culture, and between the imaginary and the real. The movement of the mountain-dwellers is compared to the migratory movement of cranes and their movement across the sky is very suggestive of writing as they dissolve and regroup in *V*-formations. The reference in the second line to the equinox recalls the fact that these birds migrate and pass over the Iberian Peninsula in late spring and autumn. Lines three and four then expand the metaphor by way of negation using the formula 'not *b* but *a*', in which the birds are brought over to the human realm in being compared to galleys sailing the sky 'through oceans of open air', and again it is typical that Góngora speaks of flights of ships and sailing cranes. These two particular lines were quoted in the most famous attack on Góngora, the *Antidote Against the Pestilent Poetry of the Solitudes*, whose author Juan de Jáuregui refers to them as being used with 'frivolous disgrace'. Góngora's Andalusian friend, Pedro Diaz de Rivas, defended him in a manuscript saying Jauregui's idea was bizarre, because 'poets often refer to ships as having wings. Now the poet refers to birds as having sails'. To substantiate the claim he adds the observation that galley ships, like cranes, are often grouped in particular formations as they move across the ocean or sky (Díaz de Ribas c.1616: 151-2). The interrelation of the concepts of sailing and flying as human and animal is based on the cultural technique of maritime navigation; by means of sails or wings bodies human and non-human are brought into movement using the element of air and the power of winds.

The next two lines introduce the moon, referring to the lunar cycle in which it appears to wax and wane. Forty years before Góngora wrote the poem, the Cosmographer of the Casa de la Contratación in Seville had sent extensive questionnaires to the administrators of the American colonies to gather relevant data, in which one of the questions concerned the observation of lunar eclipses. The first Cosmographer, Juan López de Velasco, implemented the method of observing lunar eclipses to solve the longstanding and pressing problem of accurately determining the longitude of the new overseas territories. In 1600 Antonio de Herrera's *Descripción de las Indias Occidentales*, which drew on López de Velasco, was published to great acclaim. Góngora's poetic rendering of ships, migratory birds and lunar cycles therefore points to an important theme of the time (Blanco 2012; Dünne 2011).

Lines 366-502 of the first *Solitude* contain a much-discussed passage in which the pilgrim meets an old man who relates the history of navigation as driven by greed from the earliest times through Columbus and the search for 'murderous metal' (gold), ending with the story of his own shipwreck in the East Indies where he lost his son. In the last three lines quoted above the poetic rendering takes off into the cosmic dimension, yet still retains the theme of humans and their cultural techniques. After the description of the moon cycles, the cranes are said to be forming letters (such as the letter *V*) on the 'pellucid / paper of the sky with / the quill feathers of their flight'. As many critics have observed, this section refers to the act of writing, understood as an effort to remake the book of the world (Sanchez Robayana: 1983). But more than just an aspect of metapoetics, the passage is arguably one that draws attention to the materials and techniques of writing itself. The term *dïafáno* is defined by Covarrubias's 1611 Spanish dictionary as having the meaning of the Latin *translucere* or *pellucidus*, and the English 'pellucid' originates in the seventeenth century according to the *OED*. The 'pellucid paper of the sky', prefiguring Stéphane Mallarmé's cosmic throw of the dice by three hundred years, is the surface on which the cranes form letters with their quill feathers. The word *pluma*, feather, has a marked presence in the poetic and non-poetic writings of Góngora and others discussed in this book. It refers to the bird feathers used as a tool of writing and by extension to everything that can be understood to emanate from them (one example states that 'there is no copy of me but my feather'). The cosmic flight of the cranes is then again brought back to the realm of the earth through the imagery of the cultural technique of writing with quill feathers on paper. Understanding the sky as a 'pellucid paper' also points to the cultural technique of navigation that is already present through the association of sails and wings, turning the night sky into an enormous map. Pellucid paper seems to be exactly what defines the natural coalition of poetry and bureaucracy in the kingdom of secretaries.

Media, Cultural Techniques and Technographies

In the 1980s, a number of German scholars started to draw attention to the 'materiality of communication', the title of a foundational conference and an anthology edited by Gumbrecht. As a reaction to what they saw as the exclusive focus on hermeneutic interpretation as the core practice of the humanities, these scholars wanted to overcome the 'everyday Cartesianism' of this method, and to focus on the technologies and material objects that permeate culture (Gumbrecht 1988: 389). The struggle to overcome everyday Cartesianism has continued and gained momentum in the twenty-first century, not least in the wake of new technology and environmental crisis. In a description of the dawn of 'German media theory' written some twenty-five years later with the advantage of hindsight, Siegert writes:

> German media theory shifted the focus from the representation of meaning to the conditions of representation, from semantics to the exterior and material conditions that constitute semantics. Media therefore was not only an alternative frame of reference for philosophy and literature but also an attempt to overcome French theory's fixation on discourse by turning it from its philosophical or archeological head on to its historical and technological feet. [...] The focus on the materiality and technicality of meaning constitution prompted German media theorists to turn Foucault's concept of the 'historical apriori' into a 'technical apriori' by referring the Foucauldian 'archive' to media technologies. (Siegert 2013: 50)

In his contribution to the *Materialities of Communication*, Gumbrecht seeks to clear the field for alternative concepts in the humanities, and to establish a space for less anthropocentric and more concrete and physical forms. In a discussion of the premise of hermeneutics and the possible alternatives or complements to this practice, Gumbrecht describes a shift that goes 'from interpretation as identification of given meaning-structures to the reconstruction of those processes through which structures of articulated meaning can at all emerge' (Gumbrecht 1994: 389). This shift has since gained influence in humanities and social sciences, where the subsequent digitisation of culture has itself pointed towards the impact of technological materiality on the constitution of culture in contemporary society, and thus opened new avenues for understanding the past in its material underpinnings as well.

At that early point in the 1980s, 'media' denoted less a new set of objects to study than a change in the frame of reference for the analysis of phenomena studied by the humanities. As Friedrich Kittler put it in a famous essay collection of 1980, the project was then about 'expelling the spirit from the humanities', a play on the German term *Geisteswissenschaft* as 'science of the spirit' (Kittler 1980). This redirection in the humanities seems to have been particularly important in Germany, with its long tradition of such inquiries. Kittler assumed a pivotal position for this change of perspective during the last few decades, and since his death in 2011 a great deal of work has been put into negotiating his legacy. As Geoffrey Winthrop-Young puts it: 'one of the more peculiar qualities of Kittler's media-theoretical work is the uneasy juxtaposition of a wealth of detailed case studies and the ongoing insistence on the impact of historically changing 'discourse networks' on the one hand, and a reluctance to define medium and/or media on the other' (Winthrop-Young 2013: 13). In this sense, 'media' becomes a tool for defamiliarization of cultural objects and raises the possibility of investigating their material construction.

Perhaps Kittler's most influential work was the book *Aufschreibesysteme 1800/1900*, translated into English as *Discourse Networks*, which he defines in the broadest sense as 'technologies and institutions that allow a given culture to select, store, and process relevant data' (Kittler 1990: 369). The concept is thus useful for anyone interested in understanding how culture constitutes itself through its materiality, allowing Kittler to perform a detailed analysis of the inherent power structures of such systems, and at the same time to raise historical awareness by insisting on the changing nature of such discourse networks, i.e., they are always *historically specific*.

Gumbrecht situates Kittler's work in the tradition of Heidegger's history of Being, and understands Kittler's media history as a response to an increasingly technological and digitised world, which the late Heidegger in his thinking through technology could only suspect. 'Kittler, in contrast, is concerned with thinking the world of objects – a conception I am calling "ontological" – wherein the world of things becomes present and tangible ("ready to hand") to one's own body to the extent that the body experiences itself as part of this world' (Kittler 2014: 368). (Other media scholars who could be labelled 'Heideggerian' include John Durham Peters and Siegert himself.) This approach to thinking the past through its material objects is also a central part of the present book, in which the current wave of digitisation operates as a lens for the writing of cultural history. This perspective also allows for a non-linear conception of history, where certain media technological concepts of contemporary culture can be used to better understand aspects of the past. Siegert has, for instance, discussed early modern ships in terms of 'cybernetic machines', as a means of excavating the historical calculation practices that permeate digital culture (Siegert 2003: 75). The last poem discussed in this book is a *cento* composed of lines from Góngora's poetry that constructs a verbal printed memory of him with his own words. While it may seem natural to trace this tradition back to antiquity, it can also be illuminating to try to understand it in relation to contemporary concepts of the movement of information.

Gumbrecht's *Production of Presence* is a further cornerstone for my theoretical approach in subsequent discussions. In his insistence that cultural objects reveal themselves not only through their abstract meaning but also through their physical presence, he has pointed out important ways of thinking about the past (and the present):

> What is present (very much in the sense of the Latin form *prae-esse*) is in front of us, in reach of and tangible for our bodies [...] If *producere* means, literally, 'to bring forth', 'to pull forth', then the phrase 'production of presence' would emphasize that the effect of tangibility that comes from the materialities of communication is also an effect in constant movement. (Gumbrecht 2004: 17)

This focus on the production of presence is also an attempt at overcoming Cartesian dualism and its dismissal of the human body as *res extensa* in order to clear the ground for an integrated understanding of the 'presence effects' and 'meaning effects' which arise from any given cultural object. Gumbrecht points out poetry as the most striking example of the simultaneity of presence effects and meaning effects, noting that these phenomena often find themselves in tension or in oscillation. Of the empirical material discussed in this book, this observation can perhaps best be illustrated by the striking historical account from Córdoba in 1612 of an enormous catafalque to which were attached pieces of paper with written poetry describing the catafalque and its effects on the human body in hyperbolic and mythological terms. According to contemporary sources, the spectators of this event were drawn to the poetry hung on the monument while being sensually immersed in the effects of illumination, odour, and reflected light to which the poetry with its deictic gesture referred. This event and the poetry produced for it are discussed at length in Chapter Four.

It bears repeating that an ontology of presence is not meant to replace the practice of interpretation, but rather to complement it. As we have no direct access to the physical presence of the past (which is always contingent and lost in time), we have to reconstruct it from the sources available, such as *descripciones*, *relaciones*, and poetry. The concept of presence is used in this book in accordance with Gumbrecht's interpretation of Heidegger's 'unconcealment of being' to uncover aspects of culture that fall outside of pure meaning and to unfold relations between objects in a network. Gumbrecht gives the example of the Catholic Eucharist's use of particular materials (bread and wine) to make something absent in time and space (the body and blood of Christ) present (Gumbrecht 2003: 29). As John Durham Peters points out, the cultural technique of writing 'is a means of using the hand and the eye to speak across distances, of processing complex and massive arrays of data, of transforming space into time and time into space, and of giving us access to a realm beyond time's irreversible flow' (Peters 2015: 304). A good deal of the material discussed in this book shares the feature of using different cultural techniques to produce presence effects for something absent. It also allows the defamiliarization of objects like books, monuments, or portraits that can then be described through the historically specific conception of them in Spain around 1600.

As Gumbrecht notes, early modern culture is richly endowed with examples of the divergence between a dominant cultural self-reference and our historical retrospective on that culture. Early modern culture finds itself with an inheritance from medieval self-reference, where man understood himself as intrinsic to and surrounded by a world created by God. But it is also the dawn of a secularization of culture, which can easily result in misunderstandings when approaching objects from a time when secularization has extended itself fully over human self-reference in the West.

The dichotomisation of body and spirit that later took place, starting with Descartes's 'discovery' of the *cogito*, gave rise to an epistemological structure in which thinking relied on a 'subject/object paradigm'. In such a frame of self-reference, humans are eccentric to the world, which presents itself as a surface to be interpreted. As Gumbrecht puts it:

> It also becomes more and more conventional to think of the world of objects and of the human body as surfaces that 'express' deeper meanings. Indeed, the paradigm of expression (chronologically) emerges with and (systematically) belongs to the same epistemological context as the paradigm of interpretation. World-interpretation begins to be understood as an active production of knowledge about the world: it is mainly seen as 'extracting inherent meanings' from the objects of the world – and in this aspect lies the decisive step toward modernity. (Gumbrecht 2003: 27)

This worldview in which the subject is an eccentric disembodied observer of the world slowly emerges with modernity and finds its consolidation in the nineteenth-century practice of hermeneutic interpretation. The empirical material investigated in this book – produced after the strict theological worldview of the middle ages but before the dominance of what we have come to associate with 'modernity' – presents a challenge to that framework.

Further critique of the epistemological subject/object split of modernity has in recent years come from philosophy, where the new approaches of Speculative Realism, New Materialism and Object-oriented Ontology have criticised the Kantian paradigm of 'correlationalism' which holds that the objects of the world are only accessible through the human mind (Morton 2013; van der Tuin 2012; Meillassoux 2008; Harman 2010; Shaviro 2014). These scholars have pushed the struggle against everyday Cartesianism lamented by Gumbrecht further, and form part of a twenty-first-century new metaphysics.

Since the early 1990s, Bruno Latour has also presented a substantial critique of the anthropocentrism of scholarly practices and argued for attention to objects and other non-human agents. Latour's consistent attention to the object and his urge to avoid givens like 'the social' when trying to explain a phenomenon, has been foundational to this 'post-human' or 'post-anthropocentric' turn. As Latour puts it in his introduction to actor-network theory, 'objects are suddenly highlighted not only as being full-blown actors, but also as what explains the contrasted landscape we started with, the overarching powers of society, the huge asymmetries, the crushing exercise of power' (Latour 2007: 72). An object like the Chacon manuscript consists of a number of relations between human and non-human actors that permeate different domains traditionally held to be separate ('political', 'literary', 'art historical', for example). A political actor like Olivares placed it in his library, which in turn puts it in relation to a number of non-human actors; a portrait is attached to the manuscript, under which lines of poetry insist on its agency as an object. The network consists in a series of associations between different actors. The dispersed empirical material in this book repeatedly stresses the agency of objects, their history, production and effects on human beings.

The concept of 'media' in this book is not meant to function as a universal category that explains everything attached to it, but rather to construct a specific focus on the interaction between humans and non-humans. Furthermore, as a term often used to describe a later phase of 'modernity', and often associated with contemporary culture, it produces an important historical dislocation when applied to early modern culture and insists that it too was dependent on certain material and technological tools for its existence. Peters, who understands media as 'infrastructures of being, the habitats and materials through which we act and are', has recently stressed the importance of not forgetting that media are older than the twentieth century: 'Like new media, ancient media such as registers, indexes, the census, calendars, and catalogs have always been in the business of recording, transmitting, and processing culture; of managing subjects, objects, and data; of organizing time, space, and power' (Peters 2015: 19).

In recent years, the concept of 'cultural techniques' (*Kulturtechnik*) has gained significant influence as a development of German media theory, aimed at overcoming media theory's single-minded focus on the 'hardware' of media in order to consider how culture is constituted through operational sequences in the first place. Drawing on the etymological roots of the Latin word *colere*, the notoriously slippery notion of 'culture' is then understood from its roots to be technologically constituted in the broadest sense. *Colere* and *cultura* refer to cultivation of the soil, so cultural techniques focus on the processing of materials into different practices (*techne*), or, as Siegert puts it:

> As a historically given micro-network of technologies and techniques, cultural techniques are the exteriority and/or materiality of the signifier. When we speak of cultural techniques, therefore, we envisage a more or less complex actor network that comprises technological objects as well as the operative chains they are part of and that configure or constitute them (Siegert 2015: 11)

Winthrop-Young further points toward the ambition to avoid given concepts and try to understand what constitutes them in the first place: 'the study of cultural techniques aims at revealing the ontic operations that underlie and give rise to ontological distinctions which are then liable to take over thought' (Winthrop-Young 2013: 10). In this way, cultural techniques can be seen as a further development of so-called German media theory, which aims at investigating the relation between the discursive/symbolic and the material/technical in a less restricted sense than that originally advocated by Kittler. It has been described as a move from an 'anti-hermeneutic' stance in the 1980s and 1990s – which may have been necessary to clear ground in the German academic milieu but was also limiting in scope – to a post-hermeneutic approach in the last decade. This post-hermeneutic stance is less polemical than the sometimes one-sided focus on the 'hardware' of culture, which at worst led to the dichotomisation of culture and media. The theoretical concept of cultural techniques therefore seeks to overcome such dualism and understand the interrelatedness of what we term media, culture and technology by focussing on the operations that historically and logically precede the concepts that come from them. The actor-network theory of Bruno Latour is here incorporated into a historical and material approach to culture:

> Cultural techniques inevitably comprise a more or less complex actor-network that includes technical objects and chains of operations (including gestures) in equal measure. The 'human touch', the power of agency typically ascribed to humans, is not a given but is constituted by and dependent on cultural techniques. (Siegert 2015: 193)

In an often-quoted passage, Thomas Macho gives an illuminating example to explain how epistemological concepts exist as practices long before they become institutionalised (or epistemologised), and so can be traced back to avoid the 'taken-for-grantedness' of culture:

> Cultural techniques – such as writing, reading, painting, counting, making music – are always older than the concepts that are generated from them. People wrote long before they conceptualized writing or alphabets; millennia passed before pictures and statues gave rise to the concept of the image; and still today, people sing or make music without knowing anything about tones or musical notation systems. Counting, too, is older than the notion of numbers. To be sure, most cultures counted or performed certain mathematical operations, but they did not necessarily derive from this a concept of number (Macho 2003: 179).

Thus the impulse of cultural techniques is about uncovering the operational sequences, involving actors, things and practices, which are only later understood as the established foundation of 'culture'. Actors are assigned agency and become subjects, and the objects they produced are understood as 'natural', although they could not exist without these operations. As Siegert points out, the idea behind cultural techniques as a research tool is to avoid taking universal categories for granted and instead to investigate the underlying ontic operations that produce what we understand as *culture*:

> The concept of cultural techniques, therefore, is vehemently opposed to any ontological usage of philosophical terms: *Man* does not exist independently of cultural techniques of hominization, *time* does not exist independently of cultural techniques for calculating and measuring time; *space* does not exist independently of cultural techniques for surveying and administering space; and so on. (Siegert 2007: 30)

In this sense, poetry, an epistemological object too often taken as a universal transhistorical phenomenon, does not exist independently of cultural techniques of processing, storage and transmission, be they material objects (such as manuscripts or computers) or cognitive and corporeal ones (human memory and voice). The point of departure for this book is the observation that the majority of the poets of early modern Spain did not publish their poetry (in the sense of producing a printed book available for the market) during their lifetimes. The questions then are, where and how did the conceptual object of these cultural techniques physically exist? Which were the basic ontic operations necessary for its existence? In which physical and material contexts was it inscribed? What was the relation between the symbolic work it produced and the material context to which it often, in a deictic gesture, referred? What is the relation between material storage and temporality in the context of an era obsessed, as this one was, with the written word?

Vismann has further underlined how cultural techniques also work towards overcoming the anthropocentric restrictions of the subject/object paradigm of modernity. Human subjecthood is then understood as an act of assignation, an act that is in itself a technique:

> The study of cultural techniques raises questions about how things and media operate. Thereby, it traces the fiction of sovereign subjectivity, the myth of the subject as legislator, instigator or perpetrator, back to the techniques that make it possible in the first place. (Vismann 2013: 88)

The cultural techniques associated with the Paper King, with his extensive use of writing, acts, files, surveys, and registers, can be understood as an origin of modern bureaucracy. In this context, writing and documents assume a pivotal position for the constitution of 'society' and 'culture'. As will become clear in the subsequent discussion, a legal concept like 'authorship' can be understood as an act of assignation dependent on certain cultural techniques, a fact that can be illustrated by all the symbolic work put in to establish it (portraits, taxation, authorization, laudatory verses and so on). A quality that is all too often understood as inherent to literature itself can thus be seen as the outcome of ontic operations that precede it. 'Ontic operations' are the factual processes that preced concepts. Frequently employed in the field of cultural techniques, it has an important place in the work of Martin Heidegger. 'Ontological difference, is between the ontical and the ontological, where the former is concerned with facts about entities and the latter is concerned with the meaning of Being, with how entities are intelligible as entities' (Wheeler 2017).

Parallel to this development from media to cultural techniques in Germany, the concept of 'technography' has been developed in a similar direction in Anglophone scholarship (Pryor & Trotter 2016: 7-17). James Purdon derives his notion of the concept from 'a union of the material and the symbolic [which] is ingrained within the concept of technology itself from the earliest times' (2018: 6). Like cultural techniques, technography posits a continuity between the technics of culture and its symbolic operations. In the case of the texts we have *a posteriori* agreed to call literature – such as those pieces of writing circulated in the network investigated in this book – technography can be used to highlight, in Steven Connor's words, 'writing about any technology that implicates or is attuned to the technological condition of its own writing' (Connor 2016: 18). As the following chapters aim to show, this was often the case with the writing understood as poetry in the kingdom of secretaries. Poems directed toward portraits are a case in point. But of equal importance is the writing produced as manuals for secretaries and for writing, technographic to its very core, and indiscriminately produced and circulated by those same actors we like to call poets. The most important common ground of technography and cultural techniques might be what Purdon describes as the ambition to 'seek a more radical conception of the symbiosis of the technical and the symbolic that is written into the idea of technology from the beginning' (2018: 7). Indeed, technography and cultural techniques are used in this book as a critical resistance to the givenness of supposedly transhistorical abstract concepts and as an insistence on a non-discriminating understandning of the dialectics of materiality and discourse.

Another important concept investigated in this book is memory. While permeating to some extent all three chapters, memory is highlighted as a point to which the investigation leads in the final chapter. The concept of 'cultural memory' as developed by Jan and Aleida Assmann is useful as a tool for this discussion. Cultural memory is constituted by the materially stored remembrances of the more or less distant past by which a 'society' forms its 'identity'. Its distribution is controlled through institutions and actors, and in the case of early modern Spain the task of poetry seems to be precisely one of storage and transmission. This culture was very attentive to the nature of death and the brevity of human life, a tendency that found its vital expression in concepts like *memento mori* and *vanitas*. At the same time, the sovereign established his power precisely through cultural techniques of storage and transmission. Storing the ephemeral in the material thus became a possible solution to the imminent threat of death and forgetting. 'The original task of the poet was to preserve group memory', writes Jan Assmann about early civilization, and indeed this task was very much present in early modern Spain, although perhaps reconfigured (Assmann, 2011: 39). If the materially recorded cultural memory of ancient times preserved the group memory of a heroic past, the infrastructure of media around 1600 allowed the sovereign to construct cultural memory in the present, thus making the present, too, 'heroic'. Assmann further points to the 'three functions that must be performed in order to fulfill the necessary tasks of creating unity and guiding action: storage, retrieval, and communication – or poetic form, ritual performance, and collective participation. It is generally accepted that the poetic form has the mnemotechnical aim of capturing the unifying knowledge in a manner that will preserve it' (41-42). Materially stored poetic knowledge as cultural memory permeated virtually all spheres of this empire. But its clearest expression is perhaps memory of the dead. As Assmann puts it, 'memories of the dead are the primal form of cultural memory', occupying an intermediary position between cultural and communicative memory. Such memory is 'communicative in so far as it represents a universally human form, and it is cultural to the degree in which it produces its particular carriers, rituals, and institutions'. Thus the movement from manuscript culture as a technique of storage, through the portrait as a 'magical' means of overcoming death and absence, to inscriptions on tombs and funerary monuments forms one major trajectory of this book.

Ontology of the Book: Lettered Culture

Giueseppe Arcimboldo's *The Librarian* is a still-life allegory of the lettered culture of the early modern era (see Figure 3). Painted some ten years after the Paper King's ascension to the throne, it is an ambiguous image, which seem to cut through many of the tensions related to issues of literacy and knowledge. At first, it may look (at least to a twenty-first-century viewer) like a celebration of bookish culture, a joke, or an ingenious portrait. But the image can also be understood as a critique of the tendency to celebrate erudition to the point where life seemed to vanish from the human being. As one scholar has recently put it, 'the metaphorical idea of calling a man bookish becomes visual reality' (Dacosta Kaufmann 2009: 96). On the other hand, it also presents the object of the book as a living entity, pointing towards the early modern era's animistic conception of material things. The book has taken over the body; the quiet object, which is supposed to serve the human subject, has rebelled and now looks back with a cold gaze. The enigmatic paintings of Arcimboldo present a problem to modern scholars because of the impossibility of reaching a final interpretation of their supposed meaning. Yet, regardless of the interpretation one chooses to assign to the image above, it testifies to the central place accorded to the object of the book in this discursive order. On the one hand an instrument of knowledge and power, the book was also perceived as a

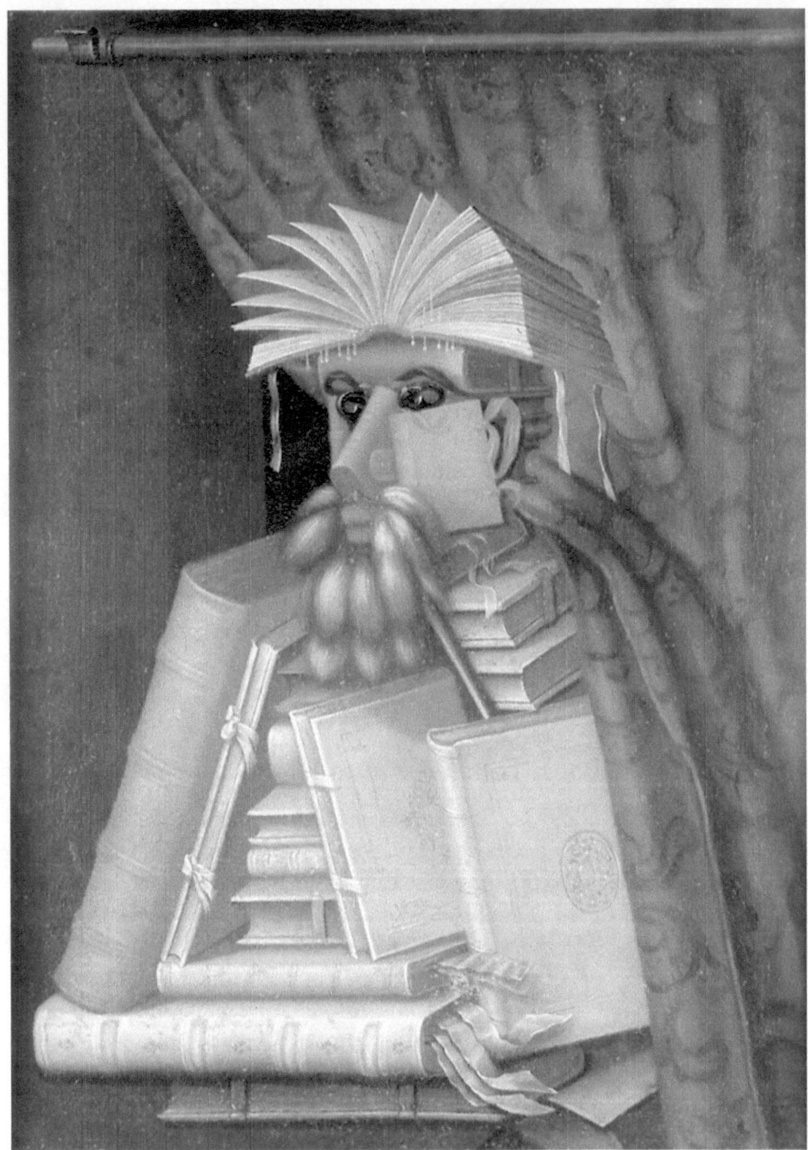

Figure 3. Giuseppe Arcimboldo, *The Librarian* (1566). Source: Wikimedia Commons.

threat to a harmonious order, and was often connected to the finitude of the human being in *vanitas* paintings. The book was also a medium of storage for the voice of the absent or dead human being, and this spooky aspect of the object contributed to its ambiguity. As Quevedo put it in a famous sonnet on reading practice, through a few carefully selected books one could 'listen to the dead with one's eyes', lines that John Durham Peters describes as defining 'the heart of media theory' (Peters 2015: 304).

To turn from symbolic work to ontic operations, the printed book was a heavily regulated object in early modern Spain. Although no legal copyright existed to protect authorship, anyone who wished to produce and disseminate such media objects first needed to obtain approval from the theological and legal authorities. The Inquisition could still intervene if the subject matter was considered heretical in any way, but approval was necessary even to be able to produce the book in the first place. It was also mandatory to identify the author of a book on its cover, not to protect the intellectual property contained in it, but so that someone could be held responsible if the work was considered unlawful. As Roger Chartier puts it:

> The Spanish authors of the Golden Age were aware of the processes that are the object of any history of written culture. Three of these are essential. The first is created by the plurality of operations used in the publication of texts. Authors do not write books, not even their own books. Books, be they manuscript or printed, are always the result of multiple operations that suppose a broad variety of decisions, techniques, and skills. (Chartier 2013: 17)

The legal document of the *privilegio* authorised by the King was a way of protecting the printed book from being copied by others. Quite different from the later copyright that protected the intellectual property of the work, this privilege only protected one material edition of a book during a limited period of ten years in a limited geographical territory (Moll 2009).

During the era of Philip II, the printed book started to be considered a powerful medium capable of spreading heretical ideas and 'vain matters, dishonest and of bad example' (Simón Díaz 1983: 8). The rise of Protestantism in Europe and the Counter-Reformation were driving forces in this new conception of the book as an object that needed to be controlled. The effectiveness of the printing press invented by Gutenberg in the mid-fifteenth century had by then created a situation in which books and other printed matter were increasingly seen as a threat. In 1558, the Spanish Royal Council began to regulate the printing and circulation of books. The existence of Lutheran cells in Seville and Valladolid was one justification for the new law, as was Philip's own experience of 'laxity' in religious beliefs in the Netherlands (Dadson 2013: 22). Henceforth, every book had to be examined before publication, pages had to be counted and clearly numbered, and a copy and its original had to be submitted so that no changes could thereafter be made. Every book had to open with the licence, taxation statement, name of the author and printer, and the place and year of publication. Anyone who did not submit to this regulation would be permanently exiled and forfeit his merchandise. Furthermore, the Inquisition established a long list of prohibited books the possession of which was punishable by death:

> We command that no bookshop owner, nor book salesman, nor any other person, of whatever status and whatever condition, shall carry, offer or sell any book, or work printed or to be printed, of those that are banned and prohibited by the Holy Office of the Inquisition, in whatever language, of whatever quality and matter of such a book, or work, under penalty of death, and loss of all goods, and that such books be publicly burned. (Dadson 2013: 9)

Prohibited books were thus to be publicly burned – perhaps along with their human possessors – to set an example, as happened in the case of Giordano Bruno, who was publicly burned alive along with his books in Rome on February 17 1600. This order lasted for almost two centuries, and is thus an important context to bear in mind when considering the lettered culture of early modern Spain.

Any book printed during this time will generally contain an abundance of such information, which is useful when trying to understand the book on an ontological level. To take a well-known example, Cervantes' *Segunda Parte de Don Quijote*, printed in 1615, has all of these features, which are often omitted in modern editions. Besides the name of author, printer, place and year, the book carries a taxation notice, which establishes the number of pages and its price accordingly (seventy-three *pliegos* at four *maravedis* for each paper fold). The books of early modern Spain were thus not officially valued according to 'quality' but according to the price of paper (García Aguilar 2009: 31). After the taxation, there follow no fewer than three approbations. The first one, written by Gutiere de Cetina at the order of the Council, states that the book 'does not contain anything against the faith or morals, rather it is a book of lawful entertainment, mixed with much moral philosophy' (Cervantes 1613: 3). The second approbation further testifies to the morality of the novel in stating that it 'does not contain anything against our Holy Catholic faith or morals, rather much honest recreation and gentle entertainment' (4). The third approbation is several pages long and was commissioned by de Cetina, the first censor, which establishes an interesting chain whereby the state commissions a scholar who in turn commissions a *licenciado* to approve the book. This approbation repeats that the book contains no heretical or immoral features, and praises its high erudition, which is used to 'exterminate the vain and deceitful novels of knights'. The author further testifies that when the Archbishop of Toledo, Bernardo Sandoval de Rojas, received the French ambassador on the 25th of February the same year to discuss future marriages between royals of each kingdom, many of those who accompanied the ambassador had asked 'which ingenious books were currently considered the best'. The author then recounts that when he mentioned Cervantes the assembled company were all very excited, expressed the high esteem that he held in their country, and asked to meet him in person. The presence of this anecdote in the paratext of *Don Quijote* testifies to the need to justify the printing of a novel of 'entertainment'. After the approbation, a lengthy licence, signed by the King and written by his secretary, asserts that the book can be printed for twenty years (instead of the usual ten-year period). However, ten years later that would not have been possible. In 1625, the new régime of Philip IV and the Count-Duke of Olivares prohibited the printing of all 'books of comedies, novels and others of this genre', because their harmful nature had been recognised (Moll 1974: 98). A further justification of these legal measures taken against the printed book was that there were already too many of them:

> We strictly order there to be particular attention paid to prohibiting the printing of books which are not necessary or convenient, nor dealing with matters which should or could be excused, or in whatever way they are read, because they are already abounding. (Simón Díaz 1983: 12)

In these circumstances, it is perhaps not surprising that manuscript culture remained influential throughout the seventeenth century, two hundred years after the invention of the printing press. There are a number of factors that explain the co-existence of the old medium of the manuscript and the new medium of print. One is the strictly regulated bureaucratic operations involved in the printing of books, which meant that anyone who wanted to limit the number of readers and actors involved in the dissemination of a written work might prefer manuscript to print. Another is the association of the printed book with commercial interests, which in a society based on heraldic status and inherited fortunes was frowned upon as pertaining to the *vulgo*. The *vulgo* was also the supposed consumer of the printed books of 'entertainment', whereas the manuscript required connections through an actor network based on the movement of objects and humans.

Excavating Góngora: Philology and Interpretation

Luis de Góngora y Aragote was born in 1561 in Córdoba. In his younger years he studied in Salamanca and became a *racionero* – a junior-ranking prebendary – at the Cathedral of Córdoba. At a young age he acquired a certain reputation in the Court of Madrid with his romance 'Hermana Marica'; sent by letter and disseminated in manuscript, it had the ladies at court asking about the Andalusian poet as early as 1581. From age twenty-four to age fifty he served as Canon in the Cathedral of Córdoba, a post that involved carrying out administrative and ecclesiastical tasks. A man of the Church, his professional life evolved around the practices of the Cathedral, in which he took part continuously. At the same time, he wrote and disseminated poetry. This writing practice was neither integral nor opposed to his status in the clergy (Paz 2012: 36). Indeed, many poets of this era served within the Church, if not as clergymen then as secretaries, librarians, or some other administrative function within the expanding beauracratic apparatus of the Kingdom of Spain. Many of them had also, like Góngora, studied and graduated from one of the universities in the country's expanding academic establishment. According to Richard Kagan, the number of universities increased from six in the fifteenth century to thirty-three around 1600, each of which educated between 4000 and 7000 students a year (Kagan 1974: 63). No other country in Europe had such a large proportion of its population enrolled in universities. This education taught students classical languages and texts, preparing them for positions within the expanding bureaucracy of Spain, elsewhere in Europe, and overseas.

Around the turn of the century the reputation of Góngora's poems increased, and they were regularly included in anthologies with titles like *Flores Ilustres*. In 1611 he left his duties at the Cathedral of Córdoba and passed on the prebend to one of his nephews (Paz 2012: 39). Between this year and 1617, when he installed himself at the Court of Madrid, not much is known about Góngora's life. From his poetic production it is possible to deduce his presence in various events of historical significance: at the memorial service of the death of Queen Margaret in 1612 in Córdoba, in Toledo in 1617 at the celebration of Cardinal Sandoval de Rojas, and so on. During this time he also composed his major and most influential poems, the *Soledades* and *Fábula de Polifemo y Galatea*, both of which were first disseminated in Madrid around 1613. This led to the biggest literary debate in Golden Age Spain, which revolved around the supposed 'obscurity' of the learned poetry associated with Góngora, known as *culteranismo*.

In 1618 he became Royal Chaplain at the Court of Philip III, a post he probably gained because of his poetic reputation as well as his connection to the ministers the Duke of Lerma and Rodrigo Calderón (Paz 2012: 41). These two ministers who supported Góngora soon fell out of grace, and after the death of Philip III Calderón was executed in 1622. Góngora's protector and fellow poet, the Conde de Villamediana, was assassinated on the open street the following year, and several of his other friends and protectors died. His ambitions at Court, which consisted in gaining positions and influence, were generally frustrated and in vain. With the accession of Philip IV, the Count-Duke of Olivares rose to power, and he seemed more inclined to recognise the poet, granting him two habits of the Order of Santiago that he conferred upon relatives. In his correspondence of these years, Góngora appears as a sad and disillusioned man, (a *desengañado* as the contemporary terminology would have it), who wishes to spend his old age in Córdoba, but is constrained by financial obligations to his family and forced to stay in Madrid. He finally left the capital in 1626, by which time he had become mortally ill. He wrote two testaments and died in Córdoba in 1627. The last contemporary printing of his works was produced in Lisbon in 1667; not until the advent of modernism at the turn of the twentieth century was his poetry rediscovered.

The elaborate and ingenious poetry – so influential and debated during the seventeenth century that it could be argued that Góngora was the most important poet of the Spanish Golden Age, and even one of the most significant in Europe – seems to have been regarded as almost unreadable during the following centuries. In the early 1900s, following the discovery of Góngora manuscripts, a group of poets including Federico Garcia Lorca started reading him again and found in him a precursor to their modernist projects. In 1927 they gathered to celebrate the tercentenary of Góngora's death and formed the group *Generación del 27*, perhaps the most important Spanish poetic movement of the last century. One of the poets, Dámaso Alonso, was also a productive scholar and philologist who dedicated considerable work to excavating Góngora from the manuscripts and documents in dusty archives. In 1927 he published his first extensive monograph, *La Lengua Poética de Góngora*, which aimed precisely at doing the early modern poet justice after centuries of misconception (Alonso 1927). Along with philologists Miguel Artigas, Juan Millé Gimenez, and, before them, Foulché-Delbosc, Alonso thus literally made Góngora available again for the twentieth century. One of Alonso's main achievements was to debunk the long-lived myth of the 'two Góngoras': the 'prince of light' and the 'prince of darkness', generally chronologically divided around 1613, the period of his major poems. Alonso's method was an intensive linguistic analysis of Góngora's poetry, which showed that the 'difficult features' – hyperbaton, syntactical and lexical obscurities, repetitive formulas, and the like – were present in the earliest, most popular romances as well as in those later poems deemed obscure, and that the difference was one of degree. Another of Alonso's major contributions was his philological study of the abundance of dispersed manuscripts and prints in order to produce a critical edition of Góngora's poetry, a task that has since been continued by, among others, Robert Jammes and Antonio Carreira with important results.

Such editorial work is generally based on achieving one consistent and 'critical' text out of the many manuscripts that attributes a poem to a certain author, and it has been decisive in making a poet like Góngora available today. In the past century, however, this practice has to some extent been rooted in modernist conceptions of an ideal and original work held together by the pivotal position of the human subject as independent and original creator. It is no wonder that a poet like Alonso, to whose group Góngora's poetry was so important, should work with such conceptions. The result though, is that 'Góngora' can appear as a singular and unified intentional poetical subject whose work fits well in a modernist canon. The interpretation of his poetry is often based on this appearance, whereupon the main task of the scholar is to explain the linguistic/semiotic system and present a plausible interpretation based on the attribution of meaning.

The bibliography of Góngora studies is immense and hard to account for in a limited space and it has experienced something of a boom in recent years. There exists a difference between the more philologically-oriented Spanish scholarship and the Anglo-American, which has been described as being more informed by 'theory'. The 'theoretical' basis of the Anglo-American interest in Góngora, however, has generally drawn from various incarnations that could be placed within the 'linguistic turn', hence the attention to the historical and material conditions of existence of Góngora's poetry has not been its main focus. Spanish studies, on the other hand, have been attentive to these aspects while not being particularly open to theory and new modes of understanding the past. Amelia de Paz, perhaps rightly, has recently argued against the (in her view) excessive documentary value ascribed to the Chacon manuscript. Quoting Leopold von Ranke's classical maxim of 'wie es eigeintlich gewesen', she concludes that 'our idea of Góngora is only a critical construction, which can be erroneous. Without the basis of the facts, all of our figurations are a beam of light in the water' (Paz 2011: 81). This classical historicism can, of course, be necessary when establishing critical editions and biographies, but it differs significantly in emphasis from more recent ways of approaching the past and its material traces, like the study of new materialism or cultural techniques.

This book, informed as it is by media theory, has an affinity with the philological endeavour of returning to particular manuscripts but seeks to conduct the research through more speculative and philosophical modes of understanding the past. Chrystal Chemris has recently summed up what she calls 'a new wave of critical attention to Góngora', and perceives 'ongoing methodological conflicts between philology and theoretically oriented literary criticism' (Chemris 2014: 419). These conflicts seem to be based on the fact that the 'theoretically oriented literary criticism' is generally informed by theories of the linguistic turn, while more recent theoretical developments interested in objects and materiality of the past may in fact share several interests with philology.

However, some of the more recent continental scholarship has widened the scope through novel approaches. Mercedes Blanco's rethinking of the concept of the 'Baroque' as 'a system of ideas and values, as thought and aesthetics, but also as an assemblage of practices and techniques' emerging around 'writers, printers, buyers of books and collectors of manuscripts, academies, patrons, commentators and critics of poetry', which *a posteriori* is understood as 'baroque literature', seems to have certain affinities with current media theoretical approaches (Blanco 2012a: 16). Another contribution is the volume *Poder y Saber: Biblioteca y bibliofilia en la época del conde-duque de Olivares*, edited by British scholars and introduced by John Elliott (Lawrence et al. 2011). This book gathers different attempts at reconstructing the complex network and practices around the Count-Duke of Olivares, to reveal the relations between power and knowledge so emphatically stressed by Michel Foucault.

The material sources of Golden Age poetry are generally quite difficult to handle, as the operations involved in its production, dissemination and reading were generally not ordered or centralised in the way they would later be. The recognition of the importance of the autograph manuscript, for instance, came about a hundred years later, with important implications for the concept of such a thing as 'literature' and the installment of intellectual property protected by copyright, as recently demonstrated by Roger Chartier (Chartier 2015). Carreira writes that 'the contemporary fetish of the autograph was infrequent, as poets rarely spent time amending their drafts, when there were people who made a living of doing it and did not charge much for it' (Carreira 2004). Poems were written, copied, attributed, read aloud, sent in letters, given as tokens of exchange, and used to establish relations within a network of actors; it was usually only after the author's death that they were unified in a single printed copy, which in the case of Góngora was considered by many to be faulty and inconclusive. The modern idea of originality as an absolute aesthetic criterion would have been completely alien to the actors within the early modern network. Dámaso Alonso's article on a manuscript containing writings by the hand of Góngora may serve as an example of this epistemological difference. However curious and interesting it may be to a reader of the twentieth century to see the handwriting of the poet, it obviously did not mean as much to his contemporaries. Rather, the writing by the poet himself was termed *borrones*: 'blottings' (Alonso 1978: 463-72). Notwithstanding, the philological work of scholars like Alonso, Rodriguez-Moñino, Jammes and Carreira is related to the approach presented in this book, as it aims at returning to the manuscripts and associated media to reconstruct the ontic operations involved in the conceptual object of poetry. The work these philologists have done in locating, describing, and dating different manuscripts is also a precondition for the existence of this study, as it often follows data assembled by them but investigates it from a different theoretical perspective and returns to the archival sources of manuscripts and prints.

The most important philological impulse for this book comes from Antonio Rodriguez-Moñino's essay 'Construcción crítica y realidad histórica en la poesia española de los siglos XVI y XVII' (Rodriguez- Moñino 1965). Even though his concept of a 'historical reality' is foreign to contemporary historiography, the problem of 'critical construction' is not. The main issues raised by Rodriguez-Moñino, which is still relevant today, are, first, the supposition that the people of early modern Spain had access to the same Golden Age literature as is accessible through modern editions, and, second, the tendency to disregard the vast documentation in archives and libraries, as well as the abundance of manuscripts and printed books which are preserved (17). In brief, there is a lack of awareness of the material aspect of historical literature and a tendency in modern scholarship toward anachronism in supposing that the physical existence of texts followed the same media-technological rules as today. As Rodriguez-Moñino puts it, 'the dissemination of lyric poetry was conditioned by its material possibilities of access and these were minimal' (19). He then names forty-five of the most influential poets from the end of the reign of Philip II and the defeat of his invincible Armada in 1588 to the death of his son Philip III in 1621. Among them are Góngora, Cervantes, Quevedo, San Juan de la Cruz, Lope de Vega and Calderón de la Barca. Of these forty-five poets, only a dozen had printed a book of poetry during their lifetimes. From this fact Rodriguez-Moñino draws the conclusion that the printed book of poems was an exception among the great poets of the Golden Age. Even though Rodriguez-Moñino's thesis has been widely accepted during the fifty years that has passed since its publication, scholarly attention has seldom taken it fully into account, with the exception of philologists.

Trevor Dadson has in recent years attempted to nuance Rodriguez-Moñino's view by pointing to the existence of collective printed books, *romanceros* and *cancioneros*. Dadson admits, however, that what complicates the comprehension of this process is the lack of originals which clearly show the author's intervention in the correction and development of the work (Dadson 2012: 77). The problem thus once again comes down to an issue of the conception of authorship and originality, which evidently differed in the early modern era and leaves modern philologists longing for reliable autographs. Rodriguez-Moñino further affirms that even the existence of single-author manuscripts was relatively rare due to the high cost of production and the direct connection to specific persons and places they implied. In the case of a sought-after poet like Góngora, there exist about thirty manuscripts *integri*, which are exclusively devoted to his poetry, and hundreds that are *mutili*, that is, mixed with other poets (Carreira 2004: 610). While this number is relatively high, the possessors of these manuscripts always belonged to the aristocracy in some sense, and dissemination beyond that sphere (where they had a crucial function) was not common. The way for 'the people' to know popular poetry, apart from the oral transmission which it supplemented and sustained, was primarily through 'loose papers' (*pliegos sueltos*), which were small, short and cheaply printed notebooks often distributed by blind salesmen traversing the kingdom on foot (Rodriguez-Moñino 1965: 50).

As Gumbrecht writes in *The Powers of Philology*:

> The identification and restoration of texts from the past establishes a distance vis-á-vis the intellectual space of hermeneutics and of interpretation as the textual practice that hermeneutics informs. Rather than rely on the inspiration and momentary intuitions of great interpreters, as, for example, New Criticism did, philology has cultivated its self-image as a patient craft whose key values are sobriety, objectivity, and rationality (Gumbrecht 2003: 4).

In this sense, this book has a philological agenda in trying to return to the specific documents and understand poetry on material terms. It is also based on archival work with manuscripts, both in the National Library of Spain in Madrid and in digital copies. The key difference may be that instead of viewing the multiplicity of material objects as problematic and needing to be cleaned and presented in an objective and critical way, the approach presented here consists in embracing the historically-specific material multiplicity of texts to try to reconstruct the basic ontic operations that make the phenomenon of poetry possible in the first place. Such an endeavour is close to the intrinsic 'power' that Gumbrecht sees in the philological practice as a longing for presence: 'in different ways, all philological practices generate desires for presence, desires for a physical and space-mediated relationship to the things of the world (including texts), and that such desire for presence is indeed the ground on which philology can produce effects of tangibility (and sometimes even the reality thereof)' (7).

History, Epistemology and Modernity

Bruno Latour's critique of the concept of modernity has shed light on the way epistemological shifts change our view of the past. As he points out in *We Have Never Been Modern*, the modern constitution as a split between nature and culture, humans and non-humans, the things of the world and the transcendental subject, is grounded in the works of Kant:

> It is with Kantianism that our Constitution receives its truly canonical formulation. What was a mere distinction is sharpened into a total separation, a Copernican Revolution. Things-in-themselves become inaccessible while, symmetrically, the transcendental subject becomes infinitely remote from the world (Latour 1993: 56).

The perceived distance between the human subject and the things-of-the-world may also explain the relative lack of critical attention to objects and things in twentieth-century philosophy, with notable exceptions such as Heidegger, Walter Benjamin and Gilbert Simondon. Drawing a very blunt line through western metaphysics, it could be said that this process starts with Descartes's formulation of the *cogito*, is reinforced through Kantian correlationalism and finally grounded in hermeneutics as an art of interpretation in a chronological outline that starts in the late seventeenth century, just after the period in focus throughout this book, and ends around the turn of the twentieth century. The emergence of an increasingly technological and digital world in the past few decades may then be related to the longing for a material and physical understanding of that world, and the need to overcome certain restraints of older epistemologies which no longer seem to do justice, for example, to human self-reference and its relation to non-humans, or the relation between nature and culture. Thus the critique of Cartesianism and hermeneutics as presented by Gumbrecht adds to this re-evaluation of modern western metaphysics and along with Latour and other scholars of recent years forms an attempt to rethink the relationship between the human being and the world it inhabits over time.

Consequently, an understanding of the historical specificity of culture becomes important as a point of access to the physical and material dimensions of the past. Approaching Spanish Golden Age poetry from this perspective allows one to grasp the coexistence of subjects and objects, of nature and culture, just before their modern reconfiguration makes it difficult. But in order to gain access to such a world, it is first necessary to overcome the split set up by 'modernity'. In Latour's description of the 'Moderns', one finds a double split with regard to the human subject that articulates itself through space and time. In space, the human being is detached from the physical world, nature from culture, subjects from objects and so on. This spatial dimension is further developed in Latour's recent book *Facing Gaia*, where the Anthropocene acts as a point of departure to reopen modern notions of nature and redistribute their contents (Latour 2017). In time, the 'Moderns' are articulated as those who leave the archaic past behind and progress toward the future. In his recent follow-up, *An Inquiry Into Modes of Existence*, Latour describes the temporal dimension of the 'Moderns' in the following way:

> The modern ideal type is the one who is heading – who was heading – from that past to that future by way of a 'modernization front' whose advance could not be stopped. It was thanks to such a pioneering front, such a Frontier, that one could allow oneself to qualify as 'irrational' everything that had to be torn away, and as 'rational' everything toward which it was necessary to move in order to progress. Thus the Moderns were those who were freeing themselves of attachments to the past in order to advance toward freedom. In short, who were heading from darkness into light – into enlightenment. (Latour 2013: 9)

The time/space dimension of modernity has also been the subject of a critique presented by Gumbrecht in recent years. He sees the 'historicist' viewpoint of time articulated in the nineteenth and twentieth centuries as the decisive foundation of a worldview that may now be coming to an end. In that 'chronotope', as he calls it, the past was always left behind in the progress towards a future, and man found himself in the present as an imperceptibly short moment of transition between past and future. Today, as an effect of various physical and material processes, among them the digitisation of culture and ecological crisis, Gumbrecht describes how a time conception of the 'ever-broadening present of simultaneity' becomes the product of a closed future and an ever-available past (Gumbrecht 2014: 73. In Latour's depiction of this same process – as the closure of a 'parenthesis of modernity' in the Anthropocene epoch, in which the fundamental distinction between nature and society seems to collapse – the relationship to the past similarly becomes different. 'From this point on, the past has an altered form, since it is no more archaic than what lies ahead' (2014: 10). The spatial dimension of Gumbrecht's critique is his recurring and persistent insistence on the often-overlooked presence of cultural objects and phenomena, the notion 'that things inevitably stand at a distance from or in proximity to our bodies; whether they 'touch' us directly or not, they have substance' (2014: xi).

Thus the work of Gumbrecht and Latour in defining these changing forms of self-reference contribute to the intellectual framework of this book, which is naturally very different in scope. Returning to the historically specific material studied in it, a temporal bracketing of modernity and its coordinates is necessary to arrive at a different conception of early modern phenomena such as Spanish Golden Age poetry. The term 'early modern' is used in this book for lack of a better term for chronological designation. The term 'Baroque', often associated with cultural objects of this time, is avoided throughout, in an attempt to avoid preconceived ideas of the past fostered by modernity. The fact that 'Baroque' is a more recent term, unheard-of in the time it is meant to designate, makes it less useful for the present discussion, although many interesting attempts to appropriate the term have been made over the years (Deleuze 1991; Hills 2011). Furthermore, the fact that the term is loaded with different meanings in different academic disciplines makes it hard to handle in an overtly interdisciplinary study.

The 'modern' of the term 'early modern' should be understood in line with the critique presented by Latour, as a threshold to that modernity which would soon constitute itself, but in which the splits and separations are not yet fully established, allowing for the discernment of different relations between subjects and objects. The present study tracks the ontic operations of certain cultural phenomena such as poetry, follows these phenomena through a network of actors (human and non-human), focusses on the materiality and presence which constitute them, and tries to come as close as possible to these lost physical and temporal dimensions of culture.

The Network and the Nodes

This book is divided into three main chapters which follow each other logically and constitute an attempt to investigate the materiality and operative sequences of Spanish Golden Age poetry from different angles. The analysis starts with the material objects of manuscripts and prints that make up the ontic part of poetic ontology. The argument then follows the investigative directions found in this material, rather than subsuming it to a given order. Certain important features of these objects, such as the portrait and conceptions of memory, are then investigated in subsequent chapters. There is no *a priori* of the poetry itself; all documents and objects are read on the same terms, in an attempt to produce a 'flat ontology' of humans and material objects. Poems sometimes inform historical events in undocumented ways, while other documents and objects inform certain poetic writings. The aim is thus not to 'explain' the poetry through its 'context', nor to use the poetry to explain historical events, but to avoid such divisions and show the relations and techniques of the actor network itself, to uncover the operations which produce the conceptual object of poetry.

The first chapter investigates the ontic operations and materiality of Góngora's poetry through the different actors and material objects that existed in a system of relations to produce the concept of a 'poetic work' and their various entanglements. The circulation of manuscripts is highlighted to discuss the implications of this cultural technique. Thereafter, the different material objects produced after Góngora's death for the perpetual storage of his poetry are analyzed in detail. The relational ties between different actors, and the function of certain objects as mediators, play an important role in this network. Thus the chapter shows how a conceptual object such as 'the works' of a poet like Góngora involved a vast number of operations and relations in their material existence and symbolic work. Such conceptual objects tend to be confused with the ontic operations that always precede them, and the aim of the investigation is therefore to reverse the order and study the poetry through its materiality and the relations of the actor network in which Góngora is a node.

The second chapter follows a recurring feature of the media objects from the preceding chapter: the visual author portrait in a codex. The presence of the human image in the codex and its relation to poetic writing is thoroughly investigated to reveal the construction of authorship. Furthermore, the relationship between poetic writing and portraiture as cultural techniques of subject constituition is discussed through poems dedicated to specific portraits. The relationship between storage and memory is further analyzed through a book of portraits, which functions as a memorial archive of human beings deemed worthy of remembrance. The conception of images and objects as living entities with agency is then analyzed and related to physical spaces (sacred as well as profane) of exhibition and presence.

The third and final chapter focusses on poetry as a memory practice. The double nature of storing ephemeral poetic discourse and of storing ephemeral life through cultural memory is analyzed through poems directed to, or conceived of, as inscriptions on tombs (funerary epitaphs). The chapter opens with a discussion of the library of the Count-Duke of Olivares, the destination of the Chacon manuscript, an object that is analyzed in different ways throughout the book. Monuments and containers in historically specific events to which poetic writing refers in a deictic gesture are then discussed with attention to emblematic materials such as ashes and stone to uncover the conception and construction of cultural memory and its temporality in this order. Certain deaths were conceived of as public spectacles due to their symbolic value and violent nature. Such were the cases of Villamediana and Calderón who both became part of cultural memory through the concepts of *vanitas* and *memento mori*, which were of major significance in early modern Spain. Finally, a *cento* poem of Góngora's own poetry is analyzed as a funerary monument.

Historico-Philosophical Interlude 1

In the late middle ages lyric poetry was often collected in multi-author anonymous manuscript songbooks, bound together in a codex of parchment or in chapbooks (Galvez 2012). A 'work' of poetry was thus often contained in a unique material object with its own specific history of compilation, production, transmission and reception. According to Marisa Galvez, 'the remembering of medieval lyrics, that is to say songs, through the physical and conceptual book undergirded the transformation of ephemeral, anonymous lyrics into modern conceptions of poetry and the poet' (3). These songbooks were often called *cancioneros* in the Iberian peninsula, and were still in the early modern era a frequent medium for the transmission, dissemination, and storage of poetry. The transformation from anonymous and fluid oral lyrics to written texts associated with a single named author was a slow process, and it was not until the eighteenth century, with the formation of literary archives and the invention of legal copyright that 'modern' authorship was established (Chartier 2013). The notion of authorship was slowly emerging, which meant that poems in the seventeenth century could still be anonymous, attributed to different authors, and rewritten in variations. In the late middle ages, poetry was often composed by networks of poets and readers, as opposed to the modern expectation of a single intentional subject; what we today consider to be 'medieval poetry' is built on the material traces contained in artifacts such as manuscript songbooks. Lyrics were usually transmitted orally and received communally, and the books from which we can today philologically construct those texts were secondary storage media. Poems were thus not written through individual, subjective introspection directly translated into a book but in communal spaces where the technique of annotation formed a solution to the 'problem' of their ephemeral quality by offering a means of more or less permanent storage. From the thirteenth century onwards the songbook establishes itself as a genre through poets, compilers, and readers, although it continues to be a medium of disparate texts and variations due to all the actors involved, and so does not adhere to clear distinctions between author and compiler (Galvez 2012: 8).

The traditional linear historical narrative offers a teleological perspective on poetry as moving from song to book, and from multi-authored lyric anthologies to single-authored books. This process of 'modernization' is reinforced by the idea of the printing press as doing away with older media due to its efficiency. However, from the late middle ages onwards, single-authored books of poetry (such as Petrarch's *Rime*) coexist with anonymous multi-authored books (which are still in a majority in the seventeenth century), just as printed books of poems coexist with a vast dissemination of manuscripts, both single-author and multi-author. Even though the effect of the newer medium of print seems to have been quite limited in Spain in the first century after its introduction, it did have a major impact on the conception of the book as an object (Gumbrecht 1990: 180). According to Gumbrecht, a major effect of the introduction of the printing press was the differentiation of communicative forms that in oral practice had remained undifferentiated. These differentiations between, for instance, singing a text, speaking a metrically bound text and speaking a prose text gave rise to lyric poetry and novels in the 'modern' sense (181). The printed songbooks of the sixteenth century often focussed on the compiler and official recipient (to whom the book was dedicated), rather than on the authors of individual poems. The observed pragmatics of compilation also tended toward practical use and divided the texts accordingly. The printed book may also be conceived, in Latour's term, as an 'immutable mobile', that is, an object capable of being widely disseminated yet remaining the same, as opposed to the manuscript, which is always singular and in a process of alteration (Latour 1986).

The cultural technique of constructing authorship through material objects in early modern Spain can be understood as a continuation of an older practice found in the manuscripts of Italian chansonniers of Occitan lyric, which existed from the mid-thirteenth century on and are among the earliest known anthologies of lyric poetry in any European vernacular. Like many of the manuscript and printed poetry books of the seventeenth century, these objects memorialised individual poets through *vidas* (biographies) and portraits preceding the lyric corpus. But the naming of authors in medieval chansonniers may be misleading to the modern reader, as 'rather than creating stable identities as metonymic headings of lyric corpuses, these names reveal a particular troubadour as a multiauthored, fluid assemblage arising from the hermeneutic position of the songbook reader' (Galvez 2012: 58). By organizing texts in a way that to some extent followed a sacred tradition of indexing corpuses under proper names, providing them with *vidas*, and including prose comments and illuminated portraits, the compilers created prestigious cultural objects for their aristocratic patrons. The use of portraits in books and the association of poetry with sovereignty can further be seen in the medieval songbooks, for example in the portrait of of Alfonso X in the *Cantigas de Santa Maria* (c.1270-1290).

This cultural technique was still used in seventeenth-century poetical manuscripts and printed books, where the author may not be anonymous any more, but instead requires explanation and justification through portraits, *vidas*, and commentaries. Furthermore, the objects themselves tend to work as mediators in the social-textual network, establishing relations of power within it. On the one hand, the sovereign justifies sovereignty through the inclusion of the proper name in the object; on the other hand, the compiler, the poet, and other actors are associated and granted access to this sovereignty ('protection' is the word most frequently employed in this connection).

I

The Materiality of Golden Age Poetry: Between Manuscript and Print

Before he died in 1627 Góngora left a manuscript of his collected poetry with detailed facts about dates and circumstances for each poem. Antonio Chacon writes in the introduction of this manuscript that he and Góngora together gathered his complete poetic works. After Góngora died Chacon produced the manuscript in three volumes on calfskin parchment, exquisitely crafted by one of the best calligraphers in Spain. The rarity of this collaboration – the fact that Góngora himself dated and gave details of his collected poetry – cannot be stressed too strongly (Carreira 1991). The production and fate of the manuscript and other media of poetry will be discussed in detail in this chapter.

The lyrical poetry of Góngora was never printed during his lifetime; it was only accessible in manuscript form. Yet he came to be the most celebrated and discussed of all Golden Age poets. As Manuel Sanchez Mariana puts it in his history of the manuscript, 'perhaps no other lyrical poet, of the extensive number that have written in Spanish, has achieved the fame, without having printed anything significant, of Don Luis de Góngora' (Sanchez Mariana 1991: ix). How was this possible? One might think that Góngora, in avoiding the printing of his poetry was an elitist exception in a time when the printing press was well established and provided a larger number of people than ever before with written texts, but that was not the case. As mentioned above, Rodriguez-Moñino has shown that of the forty-five most celebrated of the Spanish Golden Age poets, including Góngora, Cervantes, Calderón, Quevedo, Villamediana, and Paravicino, only a dozen saw their poetry in print during their lifetime (Rodriguez-Moñino 1965: 23). The number of manuscripts of these poets that has survived to our days is generally not high. But one of the exceptions is Góngora, who seems to have been the only poet of the time whose manuscripts were exploited on the book market by professional sellers (34). There exist today, primarily in the Biblioteca Nacional de Madrid, but also dispersed in Spain and the rest of the world, a large number of almost identical manuscripts of Góngora, which could indicate the existence of a workshop in Córdoba dedicated to manually copying his poetry (35). As is the case with almost all poets of the time, none of the preserved manuscripts of

Góngora are autographs, but rather are the product of professional copyists or friends of the poet.

It goes without saying that the contemporary readers of Golden Age Spain did not have access to the vast number of editions that we have today. When we think about poetry, we generally think about those printed editions that have been established as the correct ones. The general reader finds a set of poems in a book attached to a name and the experience of reading poetry may begin. That was not the case for the reader in the early seventeenth century, who had to be savvy and knowledgeable in order to come across the desired poetry. In addition, by contrast with the literary market today, poetry was also publicly available during spectacles and other events where it would have an unquestionable place. This historical difference, obvious as it may seem to some philologists, is rarely taken fully into account when discussing Spanish Golden Age poetry. The effect is often that a contemporary media situation is anachronistically projected onto the past, as if our view of poetry was eternal and not historically specific. There are a number of implications of the practice of producing and experiencing poetry in an early modern setting that concern the properties of manuscript and print, involving far more actors than just the poet. These implications are often overlooked, and it is the aim of this chapter to give a detailed analysis of some of them. Góngora is particularly interesting, as he is somewhat caught between media formats and demands, with implications for the poetry itself and its historically specific conditions of production and dissemination.

As a starting point, it may be illuminating to consider the time and energy it takes to produce just one manuscript copy of a collection of poetry. While one printing press around 1600 in one day could produce about 3600 impressions, a copyist would need several weeks or even months to produce just one manuscript copy of a few hundred pages (Wolf 1975: 67). To even produce a manuscript copy of a collection of poetry it was necessary to have access to some sort of 'original' from which a copy could be made, which in turn presupposed having contact with someone who at some stage would have gotten the poems from the poet. This might have happened by taking notes at a public event where the poetry was read, or by acquiring a manuscript from the poet. Most poets, however, never bothered to keep any material original of their poems. The few surviving autograph codices, i.e. those written by the hand of the poet, generally consist of loose papers that have been patched and bound together (Carreira 2004: 605). Most contemporary codices that gather poems by one author are the work of copyists and friends or aficionados who collected whatever they could acquire from notebooks containing poetry that had been attributed to a certain author. Several poets, like Francisco de Figueroa and Doctor Juan de Salinas, are said to have succeeded in burning the remaining papers with their poetry on their deathbeds.

The Argensola brothers, Lupercio and Bartolomé, whose poems circulated in manuscripts until their death, are an interesting example. When

Lupercio Leonardo de Argensola died in 1613, he ordered that all his poems should be burned. His brother Bartolomé Leonardo de Argensola, however, wrote in a will addressed to his nephew, Gabriel Leonardo de Albión, that 'all the other papers of letters that I have, and that I for my own pleasure and curiosity have produced' should be looked after 'for themselves and their withholding, without being dispersed or coming into foreign hands [...] In faith of this, I do not demand them all to be burned' (Pérez 2009: 29).

Bartolomé Leonardo de Argensola's words show how only with an explicit demand to care for the 'papers' with 'letters' that he had composed, and only under the promise to not let them be dispersed or fall into foreign hands, could he refrain from the demand to have them burned. This is to say that rather than letting them turn into an uncontrolled immutable mobile he prefered his poems to become a pile of ashes. The posthumous faith in the public memory of a poet, who, like the vast majority, had not published his works, was thus rather complicated and related directly to their material storage on paper. In the prologue to the 1634 edition of the Argensola brothers' *Rimas*, Gabriel Leonardo as editor writes the following:

> I hope to receive gratitude from those who have wished to have these papers united and to enjoy them restored to their true original state, so little cared for by their authors, that it has been equally difficult for me as it would have been for a stranger to gather them; because as they never sought recognition, they did not conserve their papers much longer than it took to write down with the quill what they had conceived within their minds. (Argensola 1950: 26)

The difficulty of editing the book was thus due to the carelessness with which the authors treated their 'papers'. As many did not preserve them long after the poems had been written down, the editor was often left with manuscript copies made by other collectors, in which each poem might differ from the other due to a number of factors.

In *Viaje del Parnaso*, a long poem about the lyrical poets of the Spanish Golden Age, Miguel de Cervantes writes, 'I have written countless romances, and the one about Jealousy I hold highest, while others I dislike' (1614: 28v). Of these countless romances that Cervantes claims to have composed there have survived no more than twenty, all of which had happened to be included in printed editions or manuscript collections of poetry. Thus the material existence of the lyrical poetry of Golden Age Spain was far from uncomplicated. Generally, when an author was done with his poem, the first possessor of it would make a copy in which he might or might not bother to mention the name of the poet, since he himself knew who had written it (Carreira 2004: 10). From such a copy would follow several more or less faithful manual reproductions, thereby turning every reader into a collector who gathered the papers with poetry he happened to come across, in this way creating his own collection of poetry. Once the reader/collector had gathered a sufficient number of poems, he could have them copied and bound together with parchment. That is, if he could afford it. If the reader/collector was less well-off, he might just have bound the notebooks with poems together and written 'POESIAS VARIAS' or 'RIMAS DE VARIOS INGENIOS' on the cover. The vast majority of manuscripts that have survived until today are of this kind, creating a particularly complicated philological situation. The task of the editor is to compare as many versions as possible in order to establish one correct and 'critical' edition, thereby making the poetry accessible to a contemporary public. But with regard to the reader/collector of Golden Age Spain, no such editions ever existed; each reader had to navigate a multiplicity of manuscripts and prints with different variants of the poetry. It could be argued that the idea of the critical edition, useful as it is today, is to a large extent the product of a nineteenth- and twentieth-century view of literature in general and poetry in particular, and not of the historically-specific presence of the poetry that confronted its initial readers (Cerquiglini 1999).

The fact that Góngora was the only poet whose manuscripts were commercially exploited on the book market, as well as the many volumes dedicated to his work that have survived until today, testifies to the enormous interest in reading and owning his poetry that existed in Spain around 1600. At the end of his life, he was extremely well known. He was celebrated for his romances as well as for the complexity of his longer poems, while others saw it as their task to publish letters and treatises' explaining how terrible they thought his poetry was (Romanos 2012). All of this attention was directed towards Góngora without his ever having printed an edition of his poems. These circumstances make Góngora a particularly interesting case, as he seems to have been caught between old and new media formats.

On the one hand the economic value of a Góngora manuscript was extremely high; on the other hand, those who sold many copies of their printed work could make a substantial amount from that. Writing for economic profit seems to have been thought dishonourable by most lyric poets, while writing for patronage and having the poems read at court was not. Part of the explanation for this fact is that the financial rewards of a position at court achieved through poetic production could be far higher than those of a printed book, while writing for print could also be understood as an indication of the poet's (lesser) social status. As Harry Sieber puts it:

> The relationship between writer and patron was based on an exchange of benefits: the author and his work profited from the prestige of a wealthy and powerful arbiter of good taste, and the patron enjoyed the propagation of his image as patron of the arts. [...] With certain frequency, courtiers, officials and writers served as go-betweens or brokers, arranging patronage

> transactions as well as pensions, court positions and honorific titles. (Sieber 1998: 88)

Rather than earning a limited income, patronage was about gaining a position that allowed the writer to earn a living by becoming associated with the sovereign power structure.

The elaborate manuscript, which was the medium of Góngora's poetry, was associated with ingenuity and had an almost auratic quality, whereas the newer medium of print was associated with speed and (relative) mass production. In his discussion of the body and the printing press, Gumbrecht contends that the introduction of the new technology in the Iberian world produced a shift from body to book as the vehicle for the constitution of meaning (1985: 212). It may be precisely this general tendency to locate meaning in the immutable mobile of the printed book that Góngora and other poets opposed in circulating their poetry exclusively in manuscripts. By doing so, they obstructed the arbitrary attribution of meaning on the reader's side and could hardly be held accountable for any problematic content, which, as will be shown, often happened to those who disseminated printed materials in early modern Spain.

Technography: Instructions for the Execution of a Cultural Technique

Pedro Diaz de Morante, who served as a secretary to Philip II, composed and published four volumes on the art of writing between 1616 and 1631. According to Morante himself, he used all the money he had earned during his forty-year career as a writing teacher to produce these books for the common good. Morante was one of the leading propagators of a unified and 'scientific' manner of writing, which furthermore had the advantage of increased speed. Throughout the front matter of his books, he laments the lack of rigour in the common writing practice at the Court of Madrid, and in 1625 he even appealed to the Council of Castile for a specific regulation concerning who could teach the skill of writing (Cotareli y Mori 1916: 53). This need to control the art of writing is on a par with the prohibition to publish books of entertainment issued in the same year by the Council. John Elliott has insisted that the true motif of that legislation was the propaganda program of the Count-Duke of Olivares, and the tendency to control writing and related media is apparent in these legislative operations (Elliott 1986). Morante insists on the 'science of writing' as a tried and tested practice following specific rules to achieve a clearly defined goal. Today, when writing is so self-evident that it is often taken for granted, it can be hard to imagine the importance conferred upon this cultural technique, which had hitherto been less widespread and more limited (Bouza 1992). The political implications of this process in Spain have been described by Siegert as the end of the 'travel kingdom' – in which the physical presence of the sovereign legitimised power in local places – and the beginning, with the paper king Philip II, of a 'bureaucratic kingdom', which instead relied on written documents such as *cédulas reales*, *relaciones* and *descripciones* as the anonymous nodes of power (Siegert 2003: 70). The correct composition of such documents is one of the aims of Morante's books, and, since secretaries and other bureaucratic actors who produced them also produced poetry, we can see how the power of the quill came to be formed around different scenes of writing.

In the second part of *Arte de Escribir*, Morante proposes that the Council establish an academy of the 'Art of Writing' to ensure the science of the practice. Elementary techniques such as writing with quill and ink on paper were thus a heavily regulated affair, and Morante was convinced of the importance of establishing 'the truth of the science of writing' (Morante 1624: 22). This proposition is evidently far from later developments like graphology, where the form of the letters was perceived as revealing personality. Writing with quill and ink on paper was thus not an *ad hoc* practice, but like every cultural technique dependent on the correct execution of a set of rules.

Morante's invention of a writing technique was focussed on speed and efficiency. The Italian manner of connecting the letters in fine lines was deemed too illegible to be useful; he therefore tried to make the lines thicker while increasing the relative speed of their production by omitting the lifting of the quill. As Morante himself puts it:

> The teaching of this book and art of writing is the following: Primarily the quickest and most efficient ever seen, which is of a Hispanicised Italian kind, with more form, fullness and elegant manner than the Italian fine letter of Italy, because it has more body and form; the Italian letter that the Italians write, is a letter without body, form, or Art (Morante 1631: 25).

The speed of the technical writing practice was mirrored by the teacher's efficiency: Morante claimed to be able to teach anyone to write in just three months. Arguably, relative velocity was also a major factor in the development of an efficient media bureaucracy. As an early modern technography, this is the programme for a writing machine.

The second volume of the *Arte de Escribir* is explicitly directed towards princes, who are said to be in dire need of properly mastering this art. This insight was probably based on Morante's experience of working as a secretary of the Paper King, and teaching his grandson, Don Fernando de Austria, the art of writing. Towards the end of his book, Morante explains the importance of correctly holding the quill in a manner he calls 'Spanish'. This grip, he writes, can be seen in the self-portrait he has included in the book (see Figure 4). He then claims that the 'Spanish' grip he has invented is superior to the Italian, Flemish and French grips. In inventing a new grip and a new writing

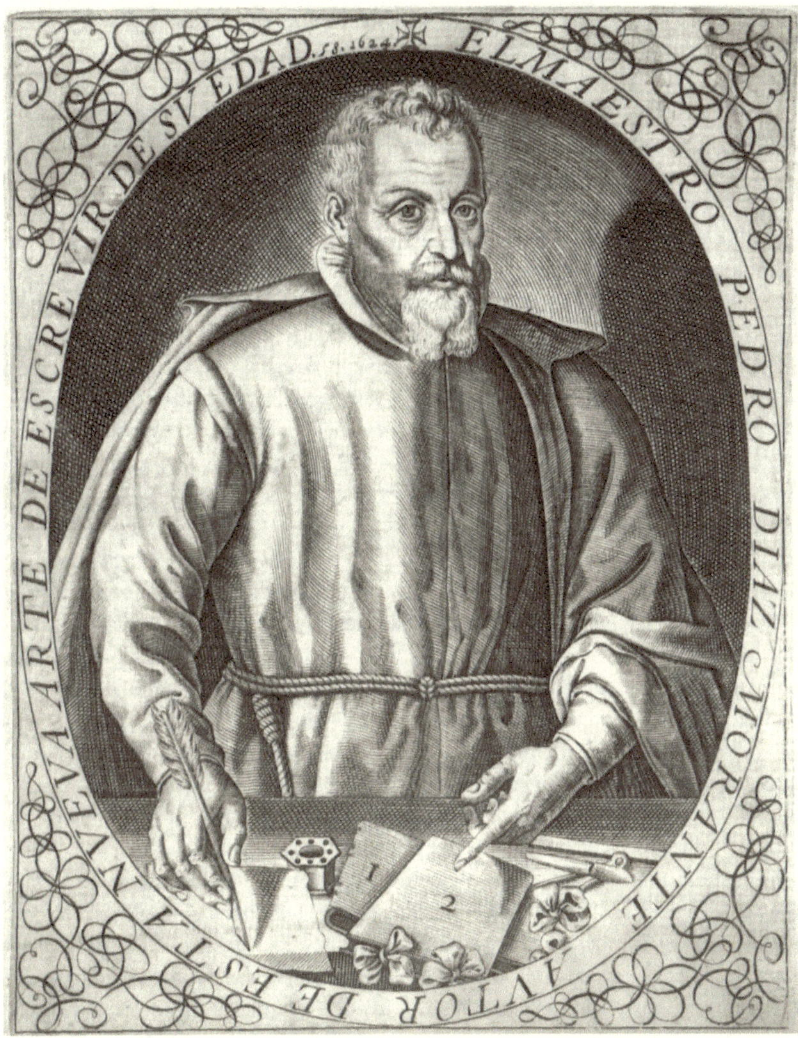

Figure 4. Pedro Díaz Morante, Portrait of Pedro Díaz Morante. *Segunda parte del Arte de escribir* (1624). Source: Hathi Trust.

technique conceived of as an improvement on the Italian, Morante seems to be doing with that technique what many poets were doing with poetic forms: developing a national renaissance designed to be internationally superior; this in turn connects the technography of writing to the political project of world domination.

> The Italian letter, which is written in Italy, has neither form nor body, and all of it is spirit without body, while my letter is a corporeal letter, with form, bastarda in Griffo's style, which is

> not to be written with two fingers in the Italian manner but with three in the Spanish manner. (23)

Morante's recurring insistence on the body of his letter expresses his desire to give the immaterial a material body through a technical practice. Indeed, he considers the Italian manner of writing inferior due to its lack of the necessary body to house the spirit of meaning. Discussing writing as a cultural technique, Sybille Krämer emphasises that, 'through embodiment, the immaterial, such as meaning, but also knowledge and information, becomes not only visible and audible, but also becomes, in the most literal sense, *tangible*' (Krämer 2003: 529).

The cultural technique of writing with quill and ink on paper is described in meticulous detail throughout Morante's work. Here, the art of writing well proves to be dependent on a number of technical operations and the correct usage of tools. As Vismann points out with regard to execution and procedural rules, 'reproducibility and learnability are among the key features of cultural techniques'. The historically specific practice thus connects the object and the subject: 'Whenever rules are implicitly stored in a machine or explicitly contained in the form of written instructions, they establish a connection between certain operations and their performers: that is to say, the agents commonly known as subjects and objects' (Vismann, 2013: 88). It is in this sense that Morante´s book can be understood as technography, in that it is both a case of technical operations coming into being through writing and of those technological operations being inscribed into political and cultural spheres.

With regard to the tools of writing, Morante explains that one should buy a hundred feathers of the best quality, always from the right wing of the bird, and find the ten best-shaped and clearest of them. Without such perfection of the tool, one would not be able to write correctly. The regional origin of the bird is also of importance; Morante favours French feathers in general and, for specific purposes, those brought back from America. This exemplifies how the human-nature relation established through the media bureaucracy of the expanding empire fed into the techniques of power. The sharpening of the feather is a further point of importance, which depends on the style of writing one wishes to accomplish:

> The cutting and sharpening of the quill for thicker and thinner letters is in the following way: Cut a little of the back of the shaft, where the tip will be, or the top of the quill with which one writes, and then turn it up by the channel of the shaft and cut a larger piece; throw away this piece, turn it over on its back and cut open a bit of the shaft in the middle, where the first cut was made, and cut off small pieces on both sides of the crack until it becomes thin or thick depending on the letter one wishes to write; and before

> cutting the edge of the quill, take a little of the rear part above the tip, not too much, but so that it is a third of the full thickness of the shaft, and then cut the thickness or thinness corresponding to the letter that is to be written. (Morante 1623: 25)

Besides the selection, sharpening and handling of the quill, Morante also gives advice on the type of paper that is to be used:

> One should write on the famous paper from Genoa, or on the heavier paper that usually comes from Venice; and if it is a bit uneven, pound it just a little, and when one writes in Italian letters on such paper, the hand has to be very easy and careful, and the point of the quill very thin and long, and a little more open than what is appropriate for gross letters. (Morante 1623: 26)

Morante's four volumes on the art of writing had a major impact on the growth and spread of this cultural technique in early seventeenth-century Spain. An indication of the importance of Morante's teachings of the cultural technique of calligraphic writing are the numerous eulogising verses and other words of praise that various poets devoted to his books (Egido 1995: 82). His third volume, for instance, opens with verses by Lope de Vega:

> Phoenix, for the third time may the quill of your wings commence its flight, [...] Your life rises from your quill to your sun, Your immortal lines from your hand, which on heavenly paper, a second Apollo, May you only admit astounding impressions from letters with such beauty, So that you can live immortal through them. [...] You, have finally given with your quill (brush of your memory) of yourself a copy, Eternity for you, and glory for Spain, [...] An indivisible point of the circumference of your quill. So that in the books of Fame you will remain written on eternal plates, may the quill that you govern with such rare skill, just as the sun does not stop among the golden rays of the heavens, write your name in parallel lines, whereby the one and only Morante's, letters will be gold, and his paper diamond. (Morante 1629: 4)

Lope employs the influential trope of the Phoenix and its feathers as an image of the cultural technique of writing with quills on paper. Just like the bird, which is reborn from the ashes of heavenly fire, the human being, through the use of the feather as a tool, can live on past his own death in material memory. Lope´s feathers, writing on diamond paper, echoes Góngora´s pellucid paper, but perhaps lacks the elegant ingenuity of the latter's concept. The trope of the cosmic potential of the feather-turned-instrument of cultural technique played an important role at the time. The quill takes on more-than-human qualities of flight and immortality through its association with the sky and its ability to overcome the dimensions of time and space. More than anything, poets, painters, and writers seem to have striven to abolish the passing of time and to overcome the inevitable death of the body through material traces understood as communication beyond death. While this conception of writing and monuments can be traced back to ancient Egypt (Assmann 2011), the historically-specific configuration that it took around 1600 is made evident through the recurring insistence on the actual tools of the cultural technique as the producers of this effect. In this sense, the ontic operations of sharpening a quill in the correct manner, mixing the ink, and finding the right paper, precede the ontological effect of perpetuation of memory that was so important to the actors in this network, and was notably expressed through the trope of the Phoenix.

The use of the Phoenix in association with the cultural technique of writing may at first seem to operate as a metaphor. But through this vivid association of mythological and actual feathers, the conception of the tool and technique increasingly assumes the ability to produce perpetual storage. We might compare it to the way the concept of 'clouds' is used today. As John Durham Peters has shown, the 'data clouds' of the present are deeply intertwined with the meteorological clouds from which they get their name (Peters 2015). Successively, cloud services become a material part of data storage and virtual networks. The 'cloud' is no longer just a metaphor but an integral part of how we understand and build a networked society, and increasingly so, since the data overload of digital 'clouds' produces a carbon overload visible both in the sky and as a dark horizon of the future of the Anthropocene. In a similar way, the writing quill in Spain around 1600 is increasingly configured as the feather of the Phoenix, as more and more people learned how to make the past present through the cultural technique of writing in an expanding bureaucratic empire. The ontic operations thus give rise to a symbolic order in which this function, the artful embodiment of presence, becomes crucial to how people understand concepts like death, memory and futurity.

The fourth volume of Morante's *Art of Writing* contains another poem by Lope, which follows the concept developed in the poems discussed above: 'May eternity offer your *ingenio* paper, and Phoenix feathers, in great abundance' (Morante 1631: 10). The medium of paper, so omnipresent and sought after in this time, is thus offered to Morante by eternity, while he is given quills from the Phoenix. Lope further praises the images of animals and birds, drawn with the feather, which Morante included in all of his volumes.

Fray Hortensio Félix Paravicino also praises this fusion of writing and painting, or rather painting with the feather, in a manner reminiscent of writing as an exercise for the hand:

> Whoever notices that a lion painted in one stroke by Albert Dürer […] is now displayed in San Lorenzo el Real as a marvel

> of art, and that Pedro Díaz Morante forms the features of not only a lion, but a whole gamut of beasts and birds, and not in the manner of feathers, as those who draw, but with great force, like those who write freely. And I have seen that, and anyone who whishes can see it, his portrait of H.M. (God save him) on horseback, with lance and shield, in only one stroke, with more durable spirit of the quill in his hand than ink and quill, and so he is sure to recognise a rarity never before seen in any nation or time. (Morante 1631: 5)

Paravicino compares Morante's images with those of Dürer and insists on their status as art through the former's specific technique of painting with the quill in a single stroke (see Figures 5 & 6). As a prime example of this technique, Paravicino mentions the portrait Morante made of Philip IV, grandson of the Paper King, to whom he used to serve as a secretary. The particular bird portrayed in this plate is the Phoenix, which creates an interesting visual thematisation of the cosmic and immortalising potential of the cultural technique of writing.

In 1650, Joseph Casanova published his writing manual, *Primera Parte del Arte de Escribir Todas Formas de Letras*, which aimed to show all the types of writing used in Spain at the time. Like Morante, Casanova seeks to perfect this art through efficiency, but above all his work is another testimony to the historically-specific conception of the cultural technique of writing with quill and ink. To Casanova, who relies on St. Augustine, writing is a divine practice invented by God himself and genealogically preserved through generations from Adam down to the seventeenth century: 'But the most certain and truthful thing is that the first inventor and teacher was our great God, who through our first father Adam, communicated this through infused science, along with the other Sciences, arts and practices' (Casanova 1650: 10).

In the preface to the reader, Casanova describes the difficulty of writing well, and the even greater difficulty of materially producing correct manuals, since the engraver who made the plates was not usually trained in calligraphy and therefore might distort the form of the letters. Both Morante and Casanova were engravers and calligraphists, and so made all their engravings themselves. The time-consuming process of producing these important books was not rewarded with the esteem it deserved, according to Casanova, who learnt the technique of engraving so as to be able to produce books himself. To engrave just one line of letters would take him more than a full day's work. The perfection of the letters is of such importance that Casanova explains in detail the process of engraving a plate, just to show the reader that he has correctly mastered the technique, even if his originals made with ink and quill are always superior. According to Casanova, a common complaint was that a printed manual was inferior because the author himself did not make

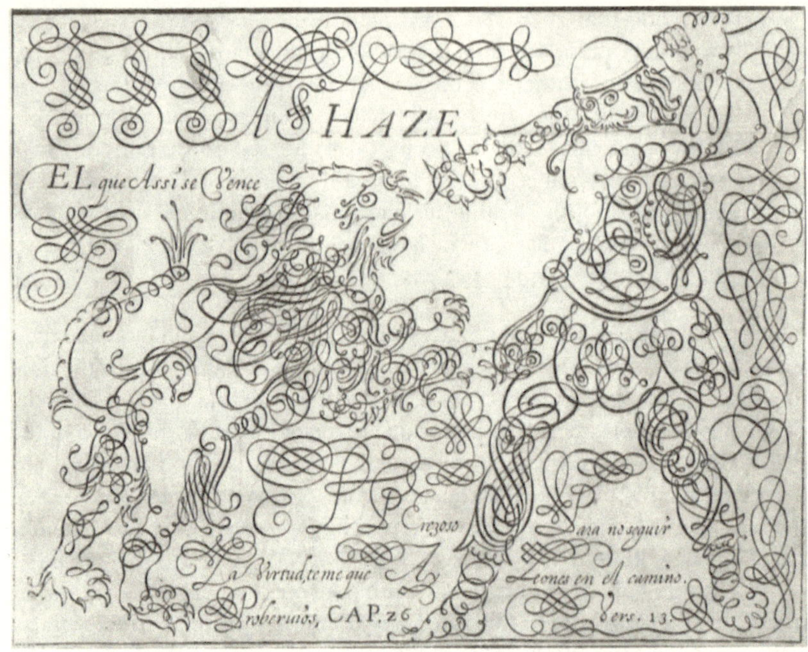

Figure 5. Pedro Díaz Morante, 'Lámina Caligráfica no. 27'.
Segunda Parte del Arte de escribir, 2nd edition (1657). Source: Hathi Trust

the plates. The complicated process of transferring the cultural technique of writing from one medium to another is thus made evident.

Casanova's first chapter is dedicated to defining the subject matter and describing its history. He refers to Pliny, who claims that the technique of writing is eternal, which leads Casanova to conclude that it started with the world itself. In Casanova's conception, writing, through its ability to conserve ephemeral speech, makes man almost immortal. The presence of this statement in a manual of writing shows how the poetic tropes of the Phoenix and the recurring insistence on a material afterlife were widespread during this period.

Casanova's first two chapters form a history of writing as a cultural technique, recounting the various materials and techniques employed since antiquity, information that could be found in the so-called *Polianteas*, the miscellanies of classical learning which were published throughout sixteenth- and seventeenth-century Europe. Pliny and St. Augustine are used by Casanova as sources without differentiation, merging religious history with the available information on the ancient world. Reaching the present, Casanova praises Gutenberg's invention of the printing press which, he writes, has been the decisive factor in making an abundance of forgotten and lost books available again, so increasing mankind's general knowledge. But even if

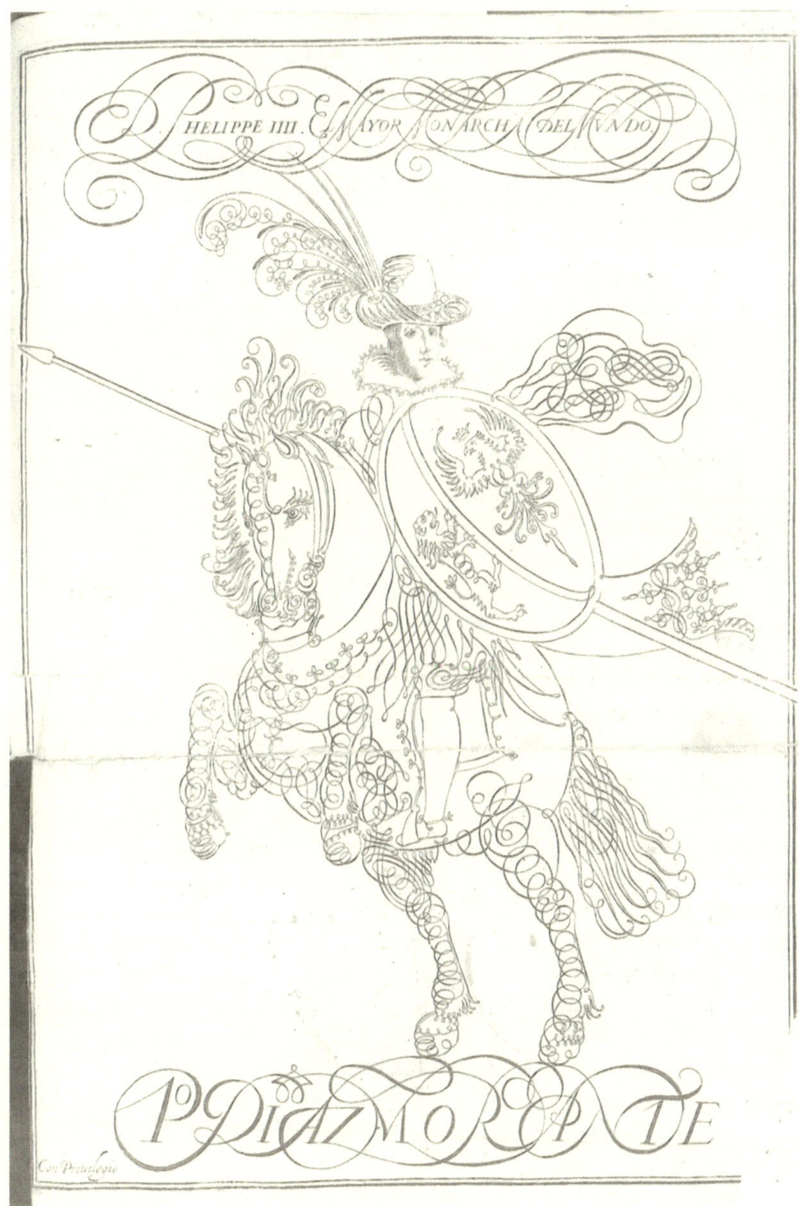

Fig. 6. Pedro Díaz Morante, *Portrait of Philip IV*. 'Lámina independente 1'. Source: Internet Archive

this mechanical invention has many advantages, handwriting and manuscripts are still superior: 'If, however, we seek general perfection, there are such distinguished Masters and Writers that they easily exceed with their quill the best Prints of Plantino or Moreto' (Casanova 1650: 10). This insistence on the advantages and power of the quill is found throughout the poetry of the time, revealing the significance attributed to this cultural technique. As in the case of Morante's *Arte de Escribir*, Casanova's book opens with a large number of technographic poems, praising the cultural techniques of inscription, in which the word *pluma* abounds. The first of them is by Calderón, who praises the ability of the quill to make the past present and give voice to the mute:

> In learned letters it could
> make the past present,
> the mute speak and perceive the absent,
> all those who died not to die in Print. […]
> Duration not consumed by time,
> so that its author is granted a second being.
>
> [Pues en doctos caracteres pudieron
> Hacer de lo pretérito presente,
> Hablar lo mudo, y percibir lo ausente,
> Los que en la Estampa a no morir morieron. […]
> Duraciones que el tiempo no consuma,
> Por quien su Autor segundo ser recibe.]
> (Casanova 1650: 7)

Aurora Egido sees the abundance of poems like this one by Calderón in the front matter of Casanova's work as an expression of the fraternity between writing and poetry (Aurora 1995: 84). Beyond a connection of sister arts, however, the cultural technique of writing with quill and ink is the material precondition for storing the information of ephemeral poetic discourse. The oral and ephemeral aspect of poetry is precisely what makes the durable storing of it on paper such an important practice for these actors. The notion of proper information storage through the employment of the correct instruments (*pluma*, *buril*, *pincel*, *papel*), was thus a recurrent and important theme. Thus writing about writing and its material basis is an action that reveals the historically specific conception of this cultural technique around 1600 in Spain. Furthermore, the insistence on temporality reveals the urge to let the past live in the present and to preserve the present for the future, 'as if it never stopped being':

> Making its memory eternal, because things that happened a thousand years ago become present. […] The events that once took place are shown and represented, so that it seems they never ceased to exist. […] Everything would be lost and without being, if there were no letters (Casanova 1650: 5).

Casanova further points to the quill as an instrument of power: 'the secretaries of the Popes, Emperors, Kings, Monarchs, Princes, Bishops and Lords of the world, [...] could they attain these positions, if not through their good quill? Of course not'. The kingdom of secretaries was thus perceived as such while being constructed. The power of the quill, according to Casanova, is immense, and it is notable that he does not talk about literacy in general, but about a specific and regulated use of the *pluma*, this magic instrument that assumes a privileged position and can animate dead material or overcome the laws of space and time.

In 1648 Baltasar Gracián published the first version of his *Agudeza y Arte del Ingenio*, a book that has been aptly described by Mercedes Blanco as an 'archive of the Baroque practice'. Although the term 'Baroque' is not operative in this book, Blanco's reading of Gracián and Góngora is very convincing in that she does not presuppose a 'Baroque' culture, which then is ascribed to a certain work but rather locates historically specific practices in these key texts that are pivotal expressions of the time, in a gesture reminiscent of Bruno Latour's 'moderns'. Gracián's work can be understood as a manual or instruction book for the techniques of *agudeza* and *ingenio*, the latter being a frequent term in the poetry and treatises of this time. To Gracián, the writings produced by the *ingenio* are 'living bodies, with a conceptual soul; the others are cadavers which rests in tombs of dust, eaten by worms' (Gracián 1648: 2). The notion that the processed inanimate material of paper or parchment can acquire life and soul through the correct employment of a technique is also recurrent in the poetry of Góngora and others. The contrast between life and death expressed through words like 'dust', 'tomb', and 'living bodies' is an important part of the conception of this cultural technique. Gracián's work constitutes the symbolic order of that which is produced materially and described by Morante and Casanova, and, as Blanco points out, Gracián's art of *ingenio* is far from sporadic or instinctive but rather based on clearly defined rules of operation (Blanco 2012a: 23). These treatises provide a set of material and intellectual rules for what would later be understood as 'Baroque poetry'. The hallmarks of this poetry, which according to the contemporary conception assume the power of storing the ephemeral, are *pluma* and *ingenio*.

Around 1611 Góngora wrote a poem for Luis de Babia's book on the history of the Popes, *Cuarta parte de la Historia Pontifical* (1613). The dating of this sonnet is difficult, as it was written for a book that was printed in 1613 (in which it is not included), while the Chacon manuscript ascribes it to the year 1611. Thus it could have been written before the publication of the book for which it was intended, which Góngora could well have known in its manuscript version. Due to its use of tropes such as paronomasia, this poem has been intensively discussed since the seventeenth century. As its appearance coincides with the *Soledades* and *Fabula de Polifemo y Galatea*, it has also been considered a key text in the change Góngora's poetics supposedly underwent during this time. The great Hispanist Marcelino Menéndez Pelayo, for instance, wrote that Góngora proceeded from being the 'prince of light' to being the 'prince of darkness'. Góngora's contemporary commentator Salcedo Coronel devotes no less than six pages of his book on Góngora to explain why calling a book of history a poem, as Góngora does here, is correct and acceptable, though other commentators had thought it scandalous (Salcedo Coronel 1644: 148-59). Gracián cites the poem in his *Arte y Agudeza del Ingenio* as a perfect example of paronomasia, yet a hundred years later, Ignacio Luzán quotes it as a horrible example of 'cold paronomasia' and the metaphor of the quill as a key to time lost as 'excesses of a deliric fantasy without reason' (Gracian 1648: 192; Beltrán 2004: 45).

Critics have discussed the poem in the twentieth century with regard to the year and the nature of its composition (Paz 2009: 63). Here, the last two tercets are quoted as a primary example of the conception of the cultural technique of writing with quill and ink as a practice that was able to overcome the passing of time and store information perpetually for future memory.

> Quill, that makes celestial cloves
> eternal in the bronzes of its history,
> is a key to time and not a quill.
>
> To their names it opens immortal gates,
> not of transient memory, no,
> which shadows seal in tombs of foam.
>
> [Pluma, pues, que claveros celestiales
> Eterniza en los bronces de su historia,
> Llave es ya de los tiempos, y no pluma.
>
> Ella a sus nombres puertas inmortales
> Abre, no de caduca, no, memoria,
> Que sombras sella en túmulos de espuma]
> (Góngora 1981: 183)

The quill is depicted as a key to time, which opens the gates of immortality and so is able to create a perpetual memory of the *claveros celestiales* (the popes), in the (durable) bronze of its history. The negation of the word *pluma* is produced through the celebration of its almost magical abilities, as it works as a key through material memory. The last line is particularly difficult; long before the French poet Stéphane Mallarmé, Luzán interpreted it in 1737 as a metaphor for the whiteness of the paper page. This interpretation was contested by his contemporary Iriarte, who preferred to understand the last line as an allusion to the myth of Icarus. Javier Nuñez Caceres reads the last two lines as referring to the fragile memory from which the popes are redeemed through the exceptional *pluma* of Bavia (Caceres 1974: 544). As the poem plays with durability by opposing immortality and bronze with fragile memory and the ephemeral quality of foam, it seems reasonable to conclude that the last tercet expresses the ability of the *pluma* to redeem lives lost to oblivion through their inscription on a material surface. This conception of the cultural technique of writing is present throughout a good many contemporary texts, and in Góngora in particular the focus is often on the ability of the instrument itself, rather than the human subject, to effect such redemption.

The Circulation of Góngora Manuscripts in Madrid

Góngora's fame began as early as 1580 when one of his first poems, 'Hermana Marica', caught the attention of the Court of Madrid and people started asking about the poet (Carreira 2004: 608). By 1613, when he published the longer poems of *Las Soledades*, he was already both celebrated and despised according to taste. The complexity of his poems gave rise to a vast number of commentaries by 'erudite' persons explaining the many learned references, as well as some rather vicious attacks on their 'shallowness'. Juan de Jáuregui published the *Antidote Against the Pestilent Poetry of the Solitudes* (1614) in which he asked God to condemn the law that Góngora had followed in composing the poems. Ironically, some of the attacks on the poems were published in printed editions, while the poem itself was only accessible in manuscripts. Francisco Cascales wrote that, 'this poetry is useless, as I can prove. It is of no use as a heroic poem, nor as a lyric poem, nor as a tragic or comic poem; so it is useless' (Cascales 1634). Cascales's words here resonate with the legislation prohibiting printed books in the reign of Philip IV in judging the criterion of usefulness to be important with regard to any written document. Other commentators were more impressed, writing in praise of the density of the *Solitudes*. This kind of attention and scrutiny would usually be paid only to classical authors, with whom Góngora was constantly compared. Even when trying to prove the uselessness of his work, Cascales compares Góngora with Virgil and Horace.

Soledades seems to have been well known at court already by the summer of 1613 (Osuna Cabezas 2008: 76). Lope de Vega, who worked as a secretary for the Duke of Sessa at this time, came across a copy of the poem, which seems to have provoked the first criticism. An anonymous letter that circulated in Madrid in September of the same year has been attributed to Lope. In it, the author ironically writes as a friend of the poet, alerting him of the existence of the *Solitudes*, which he doubts can really have been written by Góngora. The letter starts with a reference to the circulation of the manuscript itself: 'A notebook with uneven verses and erratic harmonies has appeared in this court under the name of Solitudes, composed by your grace. And Andrés de Mendoza has taken to disseminating copies of it' (Arrancón 1978: 40). The author thus testifies to the way the poems were circulated at court. He then proceeds to talk about how useless the poem is with references to the tower of Babel and the obscurity of the language. Later he writes: 'please do what you can to gather these papers, just like your aficionados are doing'. Again, the author of the letter insists that Góngora take action on the material existence of the poetry by gathering these papers and taking them out of circulation.

Góngora responded to the attacks with a letter by sarcastially lamenting that he had to respond to an anonymous writer, but promises to do so without vituperation, and adds that 'as the letter came cloaked in warning and friendship, I do not cut my quill in a satirical style'. This metaphorical reference to the preparation of the instrument of writing can be understood as underscoring the embodiment of this cultural technique:

> For an action to be considered good you say in your letter that it has to be useful, honourable and delightful. I then ask: is the poetry, and even the prophecy (since poets and prophets are called *vates*) useful? It would be an error to deny it; aside from anything else, its first utility consists in the education of any student today; and if the obscurity and intricate style of Ovid – which in *Ex Ponto* and *Tristia* was apparently so clear, and so obscure in *Metamorphoses* – causes the understanding to vacillate as it works through the discourse (as it grows with any strong act), and hence reaches what could not be understood from a superficial reading of the verses, you have to admit that poetry is useful in sparking the *ingenio* because of the obscurity of the poet. You will find the same quality in my *Soledades* if you have the capacity to go beyond their surface and discover the mysteries contained therein. (Arrancón 1978: 43)

Here Góngora takes on the issue of the usefulness of his poetry that was attacked by the anonymous author; and as the above quotation from Cascales illustrates, this was a common topic in the attacks against him. Just like his commentators, Góngora found support in classical poetry. If Ovid could be obscure in *Metamorphoses*, then it must be acceptable for a contemporary poet as well. Classical poetry appears as a kind of frame against which every poetic expression must be tested. This idea of invention is thus quite different from the modern one, and instead relies, at least in part, on the ancient and medieval concept of *inventio* (Noble-Wood 2014). Although, with the *Soledades*, Góngora came to be hailed as the inventor of a new poetry, his work is constantly compared with the classical sources to which it frequently alludes. The major break with past traditions that constitutes the poems rather lies in the fact that they refuse to belong to a genre, being both lyric and epic at the same time (Blanco 2012b). The argument put forward by Góngora that poetry serves as an intellectual exercise gives the contemporary reader an idea of what poetry could be. Rather than a mirror of the soul of the subject who produced it, the poem is understood to be a means of intellectual contemplation, which relates to how one reads Biblical and other sacred texts, as well as to the conception of knowledge as intrinsic to the practice of sovereignty.

In 1613, when *Soledades* was circulating in Madrid, Góngora wrote a sonnet on the physical movement of the poems in the city:

> Against those who spoke ill of *Soledades*
> With little light and less discipline,
> according to someone very critical and ignorant
> the Solitude emerged in Madrid and then
> walked slowly towards the Palace.
>
> The gates of Latin were shut to her
> by one who sleeps in Spanish and dreams in Greek
> pretentious ignorant, who, in blind passion,
> recites his own stuff, and silences the divine.
>
> To the wind the banner is a light pomp,
> there is no passage granted to greater glory,
> nor any voice not accusing her of foreignness.
>
> For the time being, then, wasting memory,
> alien envy, rather than her proper wax,
> leads her through Carmen to Victoria.
>
> [Con poca luz y menos disciplina,
> Al voto de un muy crítico y muy lego,
> Salió en Madrid la Soledad, y luego
> A palacio con lento pie camina.
>
> Las puertas le cerró de la Latina
> Quien duerme en español y sueña en griego,
> Pedante gofo, que, de pasión ciego,
> La suya reza, y calla la divina.
>
> Del viento es pendón pompa ligera,
> No hay paso concedido a mayor gloria,
> Ni voz que no la acusen de extranjera.
>
> Gastando, pues, en tanto, la memoria,
> Ajena invidia, más que propria cera,
> Por el Carmen la lleva la Victoria.]
> (Góngora 2000: 641)

In this sonnet, the manuscript of the *Solitudes* is equated with a procession called the Virgin of Solitude that had marched through Madrid on the preceding Good Friday. Processions of this kind were, and still are, common in Spain during Easter. Generally, many people would gather with candles to follow the procession, which would consist of idols of saints or virgins accompanied by religious chants and incense. The Virgen de la Soledad however, had few followers that year and therefore few lights, which Góngora here transfers to his own poem and the few 'lights', i.e. supporters, surrounding it (Salcedo Coronel 1644: 516). This is also a reference to the accusations of obscurity that recurred in the criticism against his work; Francisco Cascales, as we have seen, called Góngora 'the prince of darkness'. The poem, like the procession, walks slowly to the Palace to be received at Court. The procession would start at the church of La Latina, which is also a neighborhood of Madrid, march through a street called Carmen and end up at the church of La Victoria. The doors were shut at La Latina: a reference to Quevedo who said that the poem lacked the grace of the Latin it was imitating. He is the one who sleeps in Spanish but dreams in Greek, a recurring satire on Quevedo by Góngora, alluding to his translation of *Anacreon* (Paz 1999: 34). Finally the end of the poem uses the path of the procession to allude to the path of the poems of *Soledades*, which has Latin syntax and which by Carmen (poetry in Latin) leads to Victoria (Victory). The last tercet describes how the poem overcomes incomprehension and jealousy, reaching victory in Madrid, just as the processional *Soledad* arrived at the convent of Victoria (Salcedo Coronel 1644: 521). The constant equation of the poem with the procession throughout the sonnet creates an image of the way the manuscript itself moves from hand to hand in Madrid. It can be understood as an animation of the object itself, which is ascribed agency. Thus the sonnet produces an allegorical image of the physical circulation and presence of the manuscript poem.

The circulation of *Soledades* started as a rather intimate affair; manuscript copies were passed among Góngora's closest friends and admirers. This dissemination grew progressively, copy by copy, in virtually all the poetic circles in Spain; in Córdoba, Sevilla, Madrid and other cities the poem attracted more and more attention. Commentary started circulating in the same manner, in manuscripts and from hand to hand (Góngora 1994: 21). A general idea of how the circulation of the manuscripts worked can be glimpsed in a letter from Góngora's friend Pedro de Valencia, who would subsequently write a *censura* in which he advised Góngora on how to improve the poem:

> But with great pleasure and attention I have read the *Soledades* and the *Polifemo*. Of this I heard one night Don Enrique Pimentel read a part in the presence of Father Hortensio; the contador Morales has also recited it, and both have promised me a copy but they have not given me one. (Gongora 1994: 84)

The poems were read in small groups and, after having heard them, listeners could request – but were not always awarded – a copy. Father Hortensio, who Valencia says was present at the recitations, is the royal preacher Paravicino who would later play a decisive role in caring for Góngora's poetry after his death, having been appointed executor of his will. Valencia finally got a copy of the poem from Pedro de Cárdenas y Angulo, who seems to have stored a number of Góngora manuscripts. This example illustrates what Robert Jammes refers to as the early and extremely private dissemination of manuscripts. Later, as the number of holders of a copy grew, this would give way to wider dissemination, in which each manuscript might differ from the others, as when Andres de Mendoza disseminated a large number of copies along with a short commentary in intellectual circles around Madrid in 1613 (Góngora 1994: 86).

The Problems of Print

During Góngora's lifetime his poetry and most of the commentaries were exclusively circulated in manuscript form and copied intensively by writers and readers. Upon his death in 1627, printed editions of his collected poetry started to appear in the bookshops. During the 1620s, when Góngora was widely read and famous for his poetry, various actors initiated parallel projects of perpetual material storage. One of them was the poet himself, who with diminishing funds and growing debts started to consider having his poetry printed to save him from the most acute financial trouble. Góngora had been courting favour with the Count-Duke of Olivares in the 1620s, as his former protectors had died after the change of régime in 1621 from Philip III to Philip IV. The execution of the Count of Oliva, Rodrigo Calderón, for witchcraft and murder in 1621 was followed by the murder of Conde de Villamediana in 1622 and the death of the exiled Count of Lemos later that same year. In the 1620s the Count-Duke of Olivares had become known as a protector of letters and thus one to whom the poet turned when seeking support. In 1623 Góngora wrote a sonnet to gain the favour of the Count-Duke, and its sentiment quite clearly shows the situation from which the poet is seeking protection:

> In the funeral chapel I stand condemned
> with no recourse but to leave this life;
> I lament the cause more than my departure,
> besieged and expelled as I am by hunger.
>
> Guilt without doubt is being unfortunate
> even worse, the condition of being inhibited;
> of these I accuse myself in this farewell,
> and at least I will part confessed.
>
> May the sharp iron examine my luck,
> since it promises me, despite its cutting edge,
> high pity from your excellent hand.

Since inhibition has been mute,
the verses, my lord, of this sonnet,
shall be tongues, and tears not in vain.

[En la capilla estoy y condenado
A partir sin remedio de esta vida;
Siento la causa aun más que la partida,
Por hambre expulso como sitïado.

Culpa sin duda es ser desdichado,
Mayor, de condición ser encogida;
De ellas me acuso en esta despedida,
Y partiré a lo menos confesado.

Examine mi suerte el hierro agudo,
Que a pesar de sus filos me prometo
Alta piedad de vuestra excelsa mano.

Ya que el encogimiento ha sido mudo,
Los números, señor, de este soneto
Lenguas sean, y lágrimas no en vano.]
(Góngora 2000: 585).

The first quatrain plays on the word *capilla*, which refers both to the chapel in which those condemned to death wait and to the Royal Chapel where Góngora was Chaplain. The second line contains another ambiguity as it talks of 'leaving this life', meaning both going back to Córdoba and committing suicide. The following quatrain laments the inhibition of the poet, as he has been unable to achieve protection, and perhaps also indirectly has refrained from publishing his works (which could be a financial remedy). In asking for the help of the Count-Duke, in the last quatrain the poem turns in on itself in hoping that the written verses will act as the physical effects of a speaking tongue and shed tears. The written document, like the *cédulas reales* of the Paper King, is thus meant to act as a substitute for the physical presence of a body. The situation in which the poet finds himself as he starts to consider a printed edition is one of extreme desperation.

Achieving the favour of influential actors in the Court was far from a simple matter. In the same year Góngora wrote the following to his friend Cristobal Heredia, who helped him with his financial state and was based in his native Córdoba:

> Now, my lord, I take the quill so as not to take a rope and get it all over with and let you rest from my nightmares [...] I have prepared my drafts for edition, and they will be printed by Christmas, because, sir, I admit I should condemn, and I do

> condemn, my silence, being in such great need of money, and I will ignore the shame it will cost me to send these childish verses to the printer (Góngora 2000b: 434).

This quotation illustrates Góngora's attitude with regard to the medium of print; he understands it is a childish and shameful act that only serves to make a quick profit in the most desperate situation (in this case to avoid suicide). Printing the poetry became a possibility only after all other attempts to solve the desperate situation had failed. Góngora's reluctance to print his poetry seems to have been motivated by the shame with which print was associated. In his satires on Lope this is also a recurring topic. Several of his satirical sonnets directed against Lope are motivated by the publication of a printed book of poetry, and the recurring theme in all of them is the 'vulgar quill' of Lope, which belongs only in the theatre (habitually associated with financial profit), and by Lope's lack of noble status. The main verb – frequently put in the imperative mood in these sonnets – is *borrar*, to erase, just as Lope's anonymous letter against Góngora's poetical manuscripts of the *Soledades* asked him to gather and get rid of them. Thus poetry, to the Golden Age poet, is not to be associated with financial gain through vast dissemination, but rather an intimate practice for a specific environment.

The printed edition that Góngora mentions in his letter was, however, never produced, and two years later he writes to Heredia once again concerning the manuscripts of his poetry: 'I ask that you search for the manuscript and buy it, if they do not say that it is not produced in Córdoba' (Góngora 2000b: 444). Góngora is asking his friend to buy him a manuscript copy of his own poetry, which he has heard is being produced in Córdoba. This producer of manuscripts is probably the origin of the several identical copies that have survived until today and were exploited commercially at the time. The purpose of this acquisition for Góngora was to gather his poetry for an edition. It is noteworthy that he himself does not possess a copy of his own poetry but is obliged to ask his friend many miles away in southern Spain to get one for him. These manuscripts were widely sought after and thus extremely expensive, as Góngora himself expresses in another letter on the matter later the same month: I ask that you buy the manuscript for me even if you have to pay with an arm and a leg, so that I can get from it whatever can get me out of here free from debt' (Góngora 2000b: 445). The poet who did not have access to what he himself had written had to worry about the high price of a manuscript of his own poetry. This points to the operative sequence of the medium in question; the material storage of words on paper is an object not necessarily in the power of its supposed producer, but rather that of the writer who copied it.

A week later Góngora writes to his friend again to tell him that the desired manuscript has arrived: 'The manuscript arrived in time; and I kiss your hands for having helped me. Now it is up to me to correct and add what

I have done since, aiming to print it in September, in the hope that it will give me at least half the money that they assure me I would gain' (Góngora 2000b: 448).

After only a week Góngora had acquired the expensive manuscript and was convinced that he would be able to print an edition during the coming autumn. He also offers his friend Heredia to be part of the business of printing his poetry. There is reason to believe that the manuscript that Góngora refers to is the 'Alba Manuscript' (see Figure 7) stored today at the Biblioteca Nacional in Madrid, since this manuscript contains a page with the text 'These works are the originals of Góngora who gave them to His Highness the Duke of Alba, and which His Excellency in turn donated to the bookstores'.

The dates of the letters show that Góngora has the manuscript acquired and sent to him in June, and at that point he is convinced he will have them printed by September. But in the next preserved letter, dated 14 October, Góngora tells of further problems associated with his project. In searching for patronage, Góngora has been offered the service of two influential actors, both of whom want his collected poetry to be dedicated to them. One was the Count-Duke of Olivares, Gaspar de Guzmán, first minister of King Philip IV. The other one was probably the Count-Duke of Alba, to whom the surviving manuscript was dedicated.

> I did not write to you with the last courier since it was on the eve before his Majesty's departure, hence I was occupied until ten in the evening in the quarters of the Count-Duke without being able to negotiate anything [...] Yesterday morning with his foot in the stirrup he said to me 'You do not want to print, Sir'. I answered him: 'The pension could mitigate the effects'. He answered me: 'I have told you that they have been working for you since the 19th of February; when he gets back he will take care of everything, do not worry'. With this I was left in tension, because I see that he surely wants the service [habit of the order of Santiago] to be met by the dedication of my drafts, and I am therefore impeded from printing, since the two who want to participate in it are more than is good for me, thus I am like the magpie, neither flying nor walking (Góngora 2000b: 449).

The progress of Góngora's business in the Court of Madrid was slow, as he was trying to convince the Count-Duke of Olivares to grant a position for his nephew in the prestigious religious order of Santiago, as well as a pension to solve his own financial trouble and allow him to return to Córdoba. Above all, the letter reflects Góngora's resistance to printing his works. As the conversation between him and the Count-Duke reveals, it was only to resolve his financial state that he was willing to change his mind. The year before, in 1624, a large number of editions of poetical works had been published.

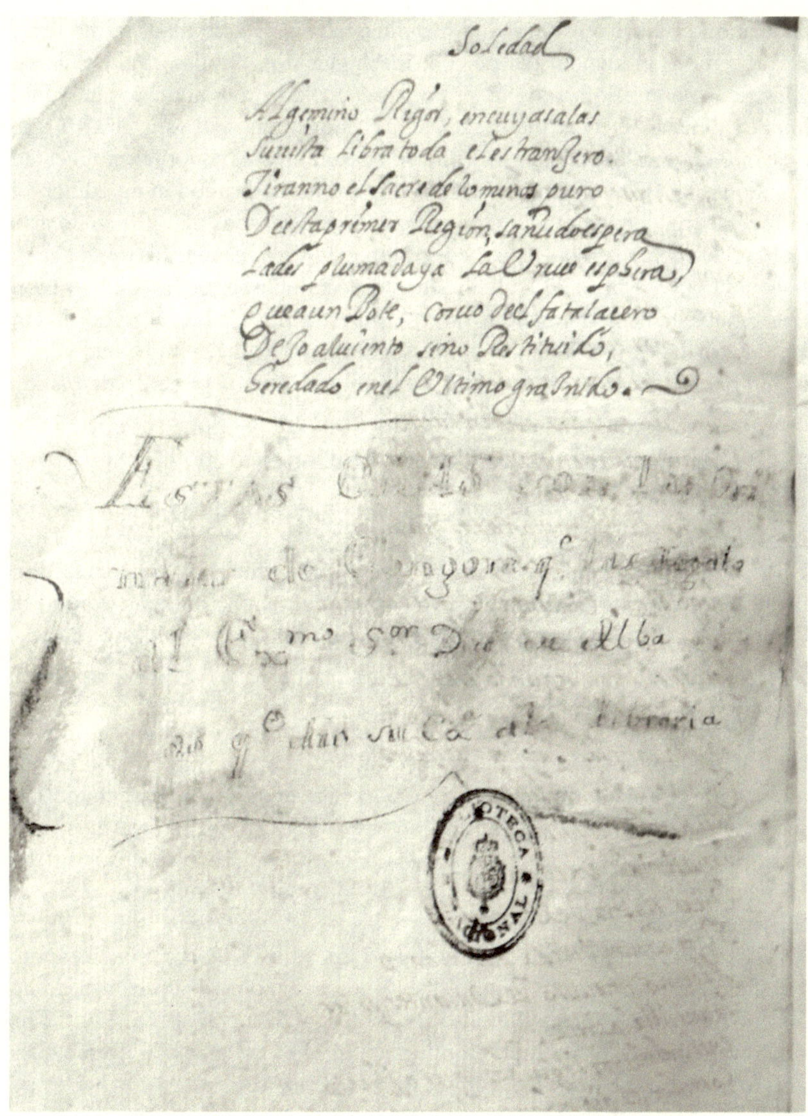

Figure 7. The Alba Manuscript. Source: Biblioteca Nacional de España

Of the ten first editions of poetry printed that year in Madrid, three were dedicated to the Count-Duke (Moll 1984: 926). One of these dedications was reproduced in Lope de Vega's *La Circe con otras Rimas y Prosas*, published by the same Alonso Pérez who would later publish the first printed edition of Góngora a few months after his death in 1627. The editors of poetry did not care for the literary oppositions between authors like Lope and Góngora; they seem to have been focussed strictly on publishing profitable books. The dedication of a printed book to a specific person was customary at the time, and the more influential the person, the higher the prestige of the edition. This dedication also served to protect the book, as any attack on it would implicitly be directed at the holder of the dedication, and as is clear in the case of Góngora, the dedication entailed certain favours. But the complicated situation with two influential Dukes asking for his dedication in an edition of his poetry may be the reason that this printing never took place. It could also be that Góngora's resistance to the medium led him to change his mind again. It would not have been difficult for him to find a publisher, so his final decision not to publish likely stemmed from his own reluctance. Soon after this letter, Heredia died. Without the help of his Andalusian friend, whom he had hoped would participate in the business of publication, Góngora began to despair.

Marginal Materiality: the Vicuña Edition of 1627

Soon after this unsuccessful attempt at an edition Góngora was approached by Antonio Chacon to prepare a manuscript of his collected poetry. While Chacon was producing this exquisite manuscript, which will be discussed in detail below, someone else had already prepared and printed an edition of Góngora's collected poetry, just three months after the poet's death in 1627. Shortly after Góngora's death in May, there appeared in the bookstores in Madrid a printed codex with the title *Obras en Verso del Homero Español* (see Figure 8), containing the collected poetry of Luis de Góngora. The cover of the book had no information about the author, and the reference to Homer was a cause for debate among some contemporary readers and commentators. As Joseph Pellicer would state in an edition of Góngora's poetry a few years later, if the poet was to be compared to any of the Classical authors, it should not be Homer, who was an epic poet, but rather Pindar, and 'Pindaro Andaluz' was the subtitle used by Pellicer in the title of his *Lecciones Solemnes*.

The *Obras en Verso* was edited by Juan Lopez de Vicuña and dedicated to Cardinal Antonio Zapata, who besides being a bishop, a counselor of Philip III and Viceroy of Naples, was also the Inquisitor General of the realm. The book was printed in the royal printing house of the widow of Luis Sanchez and financed by the book merchant Alonso Pérez (the same Pérez who had published Lope in 1624 and would publish the second complete edition of Góngora's works in 1633) (Góngora 1963: xix). The book was finished by the end of 1627, and was available in the bookshops of Madrid in early 1628, only months after the death of Góngora. The dedication states that the humility of Góngora, who did not print his poetry, was so great that it caused desperation among the erudite in Spain, who had difficulty in acquiring his poetry. In the prologue, the author further describes the difficulty of finding physical copies of Góngora's poetry:

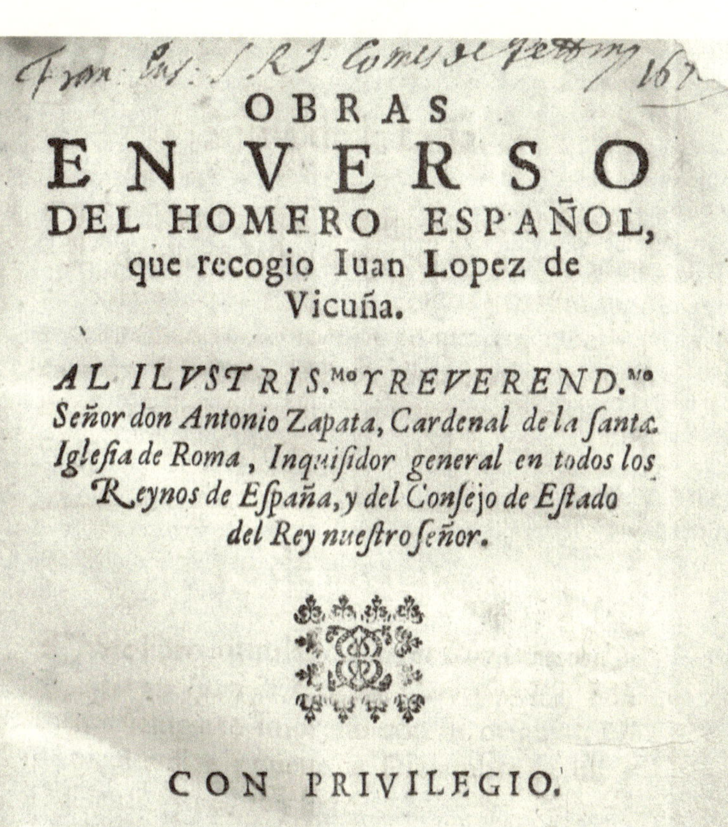

OBRAS
EN VERSO
DEL HOMERO ESPAÑOL,
que recogio Iuan Lopez de
Vicuña.

*AL ILVSTRIS.[mo] Y REVEREND.[mo]
Señor don Antonio Zapata, Cardenal de la ſanta
Igleſia de Roma, Inquiſidor general en todos los
Reynos de Eſpaña, y del Conſejo de Eſtado
del Rey nueſtro ſeñor.*

CON PRIVILEGIO.

En Madrid, Por la viuda de Luis Sanchez,
Impreſſora del Reyno.

Año M. DC. XXVII.

A coſta de Alonſo Perez, mercader de libros.

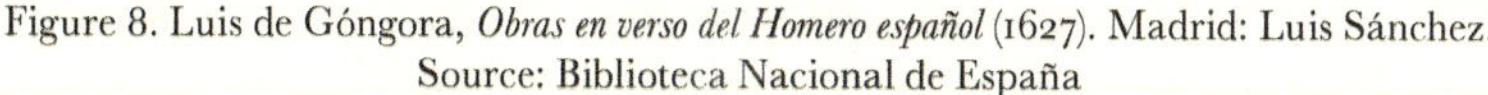

Figure 8. Luis de Góngora, *Obras en verso del Homero español* (1627). Madrid: Luis Sánchez. Source: Biblioteca Nacional de España

Twenty years have passed since I started gathering the works of our poet, as the first one in the world. He never kept originals of them: care was required to find them and present them to him, who set out to work them over again; because when we put them in his hands, he could hardly recognise them, in such state were they after having run through many copies. (Góngora 1627: 9)

This quote clearly testifies to the unstable material existence of Góngora's poetry. It is said to have 'run' through many copies, a term used to describe the physical movement of manuscripts but also the movement between manuscripts. This movement can be related to the concept of *mouvance* proposed by Paul Zumthor to describe the oral and anonymous aspect of medieval poetry (Zumthor 1972). There are certainly differences between the materiality of medieval poetry and that of the early modern era, but a certain sense of movement, of escaping the fixity of the medium of print, seems to persist.

Vicuña was the first to publish the collected works of Góngora, although, as the prologue states, the book includes only the poetry written up to 1620. The licence, taxation notice and approbations are all from 1620. Vicuña had thus managed to obtain the licence necessary to print a book, valid for ten years, without the participation of the poet himself while he was alive and in Madrid. When the book was published in 1627, one of the authors of the two approbations had been dead for four years. But the licence to print was valid for ten years, so Vicuña was legally entitled to print the book. The former ruler Philip III had signed the licence towards the end of his life, and when in 1625 the Count-Duke of Olivares was asking Góngora to dedicate an edition to him, he might have been unaware that there existed a legal document from the former government which gave another the right to print this book. The legal document is in itself an actor in this network, exercising a certain power even after the human subject associated with it was no longer present (Vismann 2008). With this certificate, Vicuña could print and disseminate Góngora's poetry without his involvement, a right that was granted by the document that regulated access within the bureaucratic apparatus.

In the above quote from the prologue, Vicuña talks about putting the works in the hands of the poet, as if he had contact with him. Soon after Vicuña's edition became available in Madrid in early January 1628, the Inquisition prohibited it. In 1625 the Reformation Junta had banned the printing of 'books of entertainment' such as comedies and novels. Poetry was not explicitly mentioned in the legislation, but the only poetry book withdrawn during the prohibition (which lasted until 1634) was in fact Vicuña's *Obras en verso del Homero Español* (Cayuela 2011: 373). In 1627 the ban on printing had been widened to include more types of written text; the official reason being simply that 'there were too many' (Lawrence 2011: 170).

On 11 January 1628, Fray Hortensio Felix de Paravicino, who was one of the executors of Góngora's will, wrote a memorandum to King Philip IV and his Royal Council. This autograph letter was the first in a series of reactions to the existence of the Vicuña edition, and was published by Fernando Bouza in 2011:

> Master Fray Hortensio Félix Paravicino as executor of Don Luis de Góngora along with the illustrious Cardinal Guzmán who

> may rejoice in glory, and Don Alonso de Cabrera and Don Francisco Manuel, says that while he was alive, someone tried to print the works of Luis de Góngora and the Council awarded him the honour to ask him of his will, and understanding that he did not want to print them, they suspended the licence which had been awarded through a third party. And now that the said Don Luis has left many debts and considerable obligations, among other services he asked his executors to dispose of these works for the said satisfaction and now it has come to their attention, after having lost a manuscript of his poetry produced willingly for Diego de Contreras, that some works have been printed without the consent of his executors, I ask your Excellency that these books are withdrawn and that no one will be allowed to sell them without an order from the executors. Fr. Hortensio Félix Paravicino. Madrid, Eleventh of January 1628. (Bouza 2011: 361)

This memorandum to the King clearly testifies to Góngora's reluctance to print his poetry, and the fact that the Royal Council on its own initiative had informed itself of his will further shows how the printing of poetry was understood to be problematic. This incident also relates to Vicuña's words in the prologue, where he states that having understood that Góngora did not want to have his poetry printed, he refrained from doing so, when in fact the Council had withdrawn the licence. The memorandum also casts light on the way in which Vicuña went about producing the book. After having had the licence to print withdrawn, he waited until the death of the poet and then had it printed without the mandatory name of the author on the cover and the licences in the hope that it would not be discovered that the licence to print had in fact been suspended. As the direction of this memorandum to the King shows, however, the business of printing Góngora's poetry was a major event that concerned various actors in this network. Paravicino also testifies to Góngora's attitude to the medium of print as a last resort; reporting that he died with many debts and considerable obligations, being obliged to ask the executors of his will to have an edition printed to resolve these financial matters. Another point of interest in this memorandum is the mention of a lost copy of Góngora's complete poems, which was to be produced on the responsibility of Diego de Contreras in accordance with Góngora's will.

Seemingly unrelated to the presentation of the memorandum to the King, a letter of accusation against the Vicuña edition was signed by el Padre Horio and sent to the Inquisition only two weeks later on 26 January 1628:

> In a book of various poetry that they call the Spanish Homer gathered by Juan López de Vicuña, dedicated to the illustrious Don Antonio Zapata, Cardinal of the Holy Roman Church, General Inquisitor, there are many propositions that are

> completely against our morals, obscene and dishonest, unworthy to be dedicated to such a grand Prince, and unworthy of his dignity as General Inquisitor; others are offenses against prominent persons, others scandalous (Góngora 1963: xxiv).

This letter of several pages proceeds to give examples from the book, deeming them heretical and against the religious laws in Spain, specifically, the seventh rule in the Roman and Spanish law that prohibits and condemns books that treat, tell, or show heretical things. Among other things, Góngora is accused of being a Lutheran, which in a country that had taken the lead in the Counter-Reformation was obviously a serious crime.

Another, even more extensive letter of accusation was written, including further examples of heretical instances in the book. This letter clearly goes beyond the realm of the Inquisition, insisting on the lack of literary value in the poetry of Góngora. The letter starts with the appeal 'that it should be withdrawn for being without author and with a false dedication' (Góngora 1963: xxx). Thus the book was to be stopped because of the lack of an author's name on the cover, as well as for being dedicated to the Inquisitor without his permission. The peculiar status of the book was thus connected to various instances in the bureaucratic network, including the regulation of the patronage, which connected different actors through a hierarchical system, and the legislation on printing books, which required that every such object could be easily traced to a human subject.

The author of this letter, the Jesuit priest Padre Pineda, starts his letter of accusation by listing what he perceives as Góngora's reasons for not having printed his poetry:

> Because the said book is against the honour and reputation of the author, and having it printed and published makes manifest an aggravation; because the author, caring prudently for his honour, did not want to, nor did he permit in his life, that his works be printed, since they blatantly spoke against the dignity and decency of his status as priest, appointed by such a principal and Holy Church of Spain, as the one at Córdoba, and Chaplain of his Majesty, the titles of which are in serious conflict with the indecent compositions and works full of every sort of shamelessness, from jokes and vulgarities (and even these says S. Bernard, are blasphemies coming from a priest), ending up in pure lasciviousness and intolerable decadence, and even naughtiness, for which the very author censored them, when he called his Muse *picaresque*. These are so common and frequent in the said book that they are offered at every step. And it is clear that the author did not want or permit that they be printed or published, since the compiler tells the reader on page 6, *that the*

> *modesty of the author did not permit them to be public*, and on page 4, in the dedication, *that the modesty of the author was so great, that while alive, he caused loathing and desperation among the truly studious: because persistently he withheld the easy and agreeable communication of his works, which they would have enjoyed hade he permitted them to be printed.* And so the compiler himself confesses that he had proceeded immodestly in having them printed and published, against the modesty and sense of shame of the author (Góngora 1963 xxx).

According to Padre Pineda the fact that Góngora never printed his poetry had to do with his shame regarding the improper content of the poems. Góngora was a priest in the Church of Córdoba and Royal Chaplain, and this is further taken as a reason for the undignified verses never to be printed. The accusations of Padre Pineda have rarely, if ever, been taken seriously, since Damaso Alonso has shown that he had personal reasons for objecting to the poetry in question (Góngora 1963: xxxix).

In 1610 Góngora participated in a poetry contest (*justa poética*) in Seville that was held in connection with the canonization of Ignatius of Loyola, the founder of the Society of Jesus. Góngora's contribution, 'En tenebrosa noche, en mar airado', was placed second after the winner, Juan de Jáuregui. This twenty-seven year-old poet (Góngora was forty-nine at the time) who would later compose the *Antidote Against the Pestilent Poetry of the Solitudes* had both his uncle and his patron in the jury of the contest. Upset about these circumstances, Góngora composed a satire about the event, ridiculing the Jesuit priest and former professor of philosophy Fray Padre de Pineda, who also formed part of the jury: 'So in this unjust joust am I to be judged by an intransigent ginger Jesuit? Patience, Job – if you have any left after the prolix scribbling of His Boringness' (Góngora 2007: xiii).

This poem is one of many examples of Golden Age poetry being contingent to a historically specific event. In his sonnet Góngora ridicules Pineda's red hair as well as his book on Job. That Pineda would have remembered this insult eighteen years later when he was asked to scrutinise the edition of Góngora's poetry published by Vicuña is not unlikely. But the fact that in his letter to the Inquisition Pineda insists on the shame associated with the printing of Góngora's poetry should not be overlooked, since it actually echoes the words Góngora himself used in his letter to Heredia. This is not to say, as Pineda does, that Góngora would have refrained from printing (because he considered any heretical qualities in his poetry to be indecent) due to his connections with the Church, but it does show that the dissemination of printed matters was considered to be potentially harmful. Vicuña, on the other hand, insists on the 'easy and pleasant communication' offered by the printing press (Góngora 1963: 13). In Pineda's accusation, Vicuña confesses in his own words to having had the immodesty to print the poetry against the modesty of the poet himself. The official reasons for actually withdrawing the book were the lack of the author's name on the cover and the 'false' dedication. However, Pineda's whole argument is based on the fact that this poetry should not be printed. Whatever personal reasons he may have had for disliking Góngora's poetry, a clear boundary is marked between manuscript and print in his letter of accusation.

The first letter of accusation, by Padre Horio, is registered at the Council on 27 January 1628, the same month that the book could at the earliest have been available, as the taxation notice establishing the price of the book at 4 maravedis per sheet was signed on 24 December 1627. But the Inquisition did not act on this first letter, which is probably the reason Pineda's more extensive letter was sent in June 1628. Subsequently, the Inquisition did order that the book should be withdrawn, and Vicuña was taken in for interrogation. The following is an excerpt from the Inquisition's minutes, transcribed by the bibliographer Jaime Moll:

> Asked to state and declare what motives he had for having dedicated the book of the works of the Spanish Homer to Cardinal Zapata, the General Inquisitor, he said that seven or eight years ago, a Don Juan de Salierne, resident in this area, now deceased, had gathered all the works of Don Luis de Góngora in a manuscript book and tried to print them, for which reason he obtained a privilege in the name of the declarant, who was his close friend, and that he also gave him three hundred and fifty reales, handing it [the manuscript] over to this witness with all the necessary censorships and precautions, but at that point he did not try to print, having understood that the said Don Luis de Góngora did not approve of having his works printed in his lifetime, and then five or six months ago, when the said Don Luis de Góngora had died, the declarant worked with Alonzo Pérez, merchant of books, to have the book printed, which they did in virtue of the said privilege, and as it is customary to dedicate every book to a great man, after having discussed finding a good dedicatee with different persons, and particularly having taken notice of the opinions of the aforesaid Convent of our Lady of Constantinople, where some of the nuns told him there was no one better than the Illustrious Cardinal Zapata, General Inquisitor, and to the declarant this seemed sounded like a good idea. (Moll 1997: 32)

In the first lines of these minutes, the person interrogated is said to call himself Juan de Carasquilla Vicuña and to be aged twenty-five. Thus Vicuña had used a false name, or at least changed his real name from Carasquilla to Lopez, when publishing the *Obras en Verso*, probably because of the associated risks. The fact that Vicuña was twenty-five years old in 1628 also means that he can hardly have been collecting Góngora's poetry for twenty years as is stated in the prologue. In the interrogation it becomes clear that his 'friend' Juan de Salierne, dead at the time of publication, was the one who possessed the manuscript and took the initiative of printing the book, giving him three hundred and fifty *reales* to play a part in it: in short, by allowing him to publish the book in Vicuña's name. As the name Juan Lopez de Vicuña already appears in the approbations from 1620, we can assume that Salierne, who was head of the business, changed the name to avoid trouble with either the authorities or the poet, as Vicuña at that time was a seventeen-year-old newcomer to the publishing world of Madrid.

The interrogation also shows that Salierne became aware that Góngora did not want his poetry to be published while he was alive. It is therefore probable that Salierne had direct or indirect contact with Góngora, which would explain the phrase, 'when we put the manuscripts in his hands, he hardly recognised them'. It would also give resonance to the sentence, 'Twenty years have passed since I started gathering the works of our poet, first in the world', which cannot be attributed to Vicuña because of his young age. The most probable explanation is that Vicuña reused an older document written by Salierne and adjusted it as he thought necessary, and then signed it with his own (false) name. As this investigation reveals, a large number of actors were involved in a single printing of a book of poetry, and anonymity and changes of names abounded.

How it was possible to get a privilege without the involvement of the author in the first place is something that no one has been able to explain; however, the Royal Council subsequently informed itself of Góngora's position and suspended the licence in accordance with his will. Knowing that the printing of the book would not be possible, Salierne handed over the manuscript with the *privilegio*, censures, and other legal documents to Vicuña, who at that time must have been about seventeen years old. As Jaime Moll has shown, he was the younger brother of Andrés de Carrasquilla, who had a short but intensive career in the book world of Madrid, publishing seventeen books between 1619 and 1623. After his brother stopped publishing in 1624, Juan de Vicuña published three books, one just a few months before the *Obras en Verso*, using his brother's mark (Moll 1997: 35).

The book itself bears traces of this affair, as there are two copies of it in the Hispanic Society of New York with small but significant variations. In one of the copies, the sonnet 'To Isabel de la Paz', which tells of the life of a young prostitute, ends with the lines 'this is, dear reader, the life and miracles of Isabel de la Paz, be my sonnet Staff to the blind, Guiding-star to wanderers'. This version of the Sonnet is found in most of the manuscripts, but in the other copy of the book, the penultimate line has been changed to 'Of such endeavours, shall my sonnet be' (Góngora 1963: xxxv). Vicuña, or someone else, must have intervened during the printing of the book and changed the name Isabel de la Paz, as it was too blatant to be published in a printed book.

On page 20 of the same copy there is another variant. The original of this poem, as it was entitled in the manuscripts, is 'To Don Francisco de Quevedo who wanted to translate a book in Greek that he did not understand', and reads as follows:

> Spanish Anacreon, no one who meets you,
> would not say with courtesy,
> that even if your verses [feet] are elegiac,
> your smoothness tastes of cooked must.
>
> Don't you imitate the Terencian Lope,
> who upon Belerophon each day
> over clogs of comic poetry,
> puts on spurs, and takes a ride?
>
> With special care your whimsy glasses
> say they want to translate Greek,
> while your eyes have never seen such words.
>
> Lend them to my blind eye for a while,
> so I may bring forth some lazy verses,
> and you will understand any gibberish.
>
> Anacreonte español, no hay quien os tope,
> que no diga con mucha cortesía.
> qua ya que vuestros pies son de lejía,
> que vuestras suavidades son de arrope.
>
> ¿No imitaréis al terenciano Lope,
> que al de Belerofonte cada día
> sobre zuecos de cómica poesía
> se calza espuelas, y le da un galope?
>
> Con cuidado especial vuestros antojos
> dicen que quieren traducir al griego,
> no habiéndolo mirado vuestros ojos.
>
> Prestádselos un rato a mi ojo ciego,
> porque a luz saque ciertos versos flojos,
> y entenderéis cualquier gregüesco lugeo.
> Góngora 2000a: 634)

In the second copy of the edition, the title has been changed to 'To a gentleman who wanted to translate a Greek book he did not understand'. In both cases, the name of a person has been replaced with a general denominator. The fold containing these changes has been inserted after the original printing, showing that Vicuña may have been warned about the reactions to the book. Satires with personal names circulated freely in manuscript form, but in a printed book they could be considered too explicit and get the publisher into trouble. This was another reason for a poet of the time to be careful about the medium of print.

After the interrogation by the Inquisition in 1628, no further traces of Vicuña have been found (Moll 1997: 34). Ironically, the dedication, for which Góngora had two candidates when considering printing, the Duke of Alba and the Duke of Olivares, and which may have been one of the reasons why in the end he did not print, was in fact the main problem with the edition published by Vicuña. A dedication was not only customary in any printed book but also had important implications for relations between the actors in the publishing network. A fake dedication, as in the case of *Obras en Verso*, could mean serious trouble, while the right dedication at the right time could be a salvation. The object of the book is thus an assemblage of material and symbolic that constructs sovereignty and power through its regulated association with influential human subjects.

Parchment is Forever: the Chacon Manuscript

On the 12 December 1628 Don Antonio Chacon signed his dedication to the Count-Duke of Olivares that opens their three-volume manuscript edition of Góngora's poetry (see Figure 9). This manuscript was exquisitely prepared with the finest calligraphy (probably by Pedro Díaz Morante, author of the *Arte de Escribir*) on expensive calfskin parchment. In it, Chacon asked Góngora to date and give the circumstances of each of his poems. This is the primary and most authoritative source for Góngora's poetry, and a point of reference for any modern edition. As Góngora's poetry had been circulating in manuscripts from hand to hand, allowing aficionados like Chacon to gather only what they could come across, the need for a stable edition was great. As Chacon himself writes in the dedication, it was the defects of the existing manuscripts, the loss of many poems that had been attributed to others, and the faulty underground edition by Vicuña, that motivated him to prepare a better edition with the aid of Góngora himself. Having collected the poetry for eight years, he started in the same year that Salierne and Vicuña got their licence to print. Chacon was not the only person collecting Góngora's poetry, but somehow he got the confidence of the poet and convinced him to help prepare the edition.

However, Chacon is never mentioned in any of Góngora's letters. The only traces of contact between the two consists of two *décimas* dedicated to Chacon, and the manuscript itself, which indicates that they spent time together in Madrid during Góngora's last years. That period of time, the 1620s, would also coincide with Góngora's frustrated attempts to prepare an

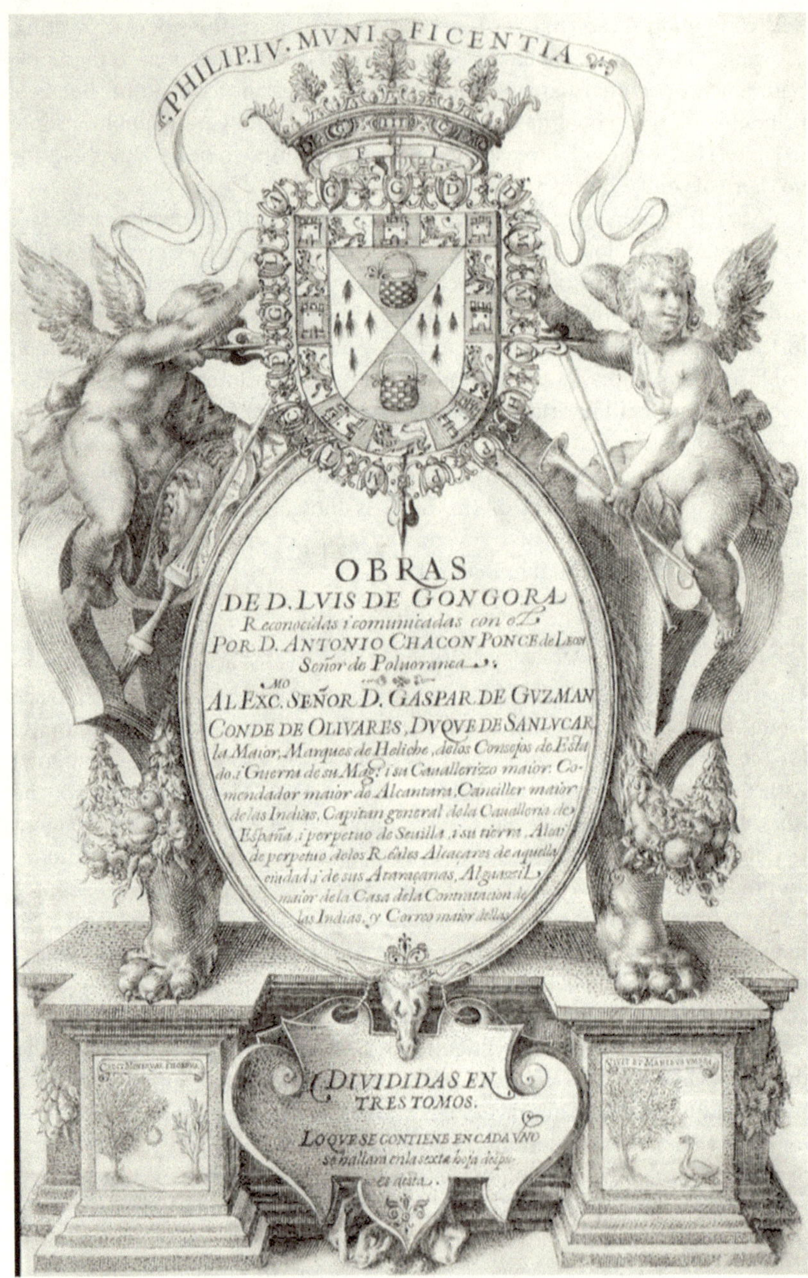

Figure 9. Frontispiece of the Chacon Manuscript.
Source: Biblioteca Nacional de España

edition for print around 1625. This has led some critics to believe that Chacon helped Góngora to prepare the edition that he himself was considering, as is shown in the letters (Mariana 1991: x). But that speculation does not conform with what Góngora writes in the letters to his friend Heredia in which he offers him part of the enterprise and asks him to buy a manuscript in Córdoba so that he can prepare it for the edition.

As Góngora did not seem to have any other interest in printing than getting quick money to resolve his financial problems in a desperate situation, we can only speculate about his real reason for preparing this edition with Chacon just before his death. Miguel Artigas thought it plausible to assume that the Chacon manuscript was meant for print, but that the medium had to change when the Vicuña edition came out soon after Góngora's death. The book was then withdrawn by the Inquisition, making it impossible to print a Góngora edition without going through extensive legal proceedings (Artigas 1925: 213). The idea that the Chacon manuscript was meant for print is repeated in more recent scholarship, such as Jeremy Lawrence's otherwise convincing article (Lawrence 2011: 165). Lawrence is certain that the peculiarities of the manuscript could not make any other sense then to serve as the basis for a printed edition. Antonio Carreira also favours Artigas' argument of a printed Chacon edition, supporting it with the fact that the personal satires were excluded from the manuscript (Carreira 1998: 83). But this can also be explained by the mention in the front matter of the manuscript that Olivares could publish a printed edition, if and when he saw fit. There is not necessarily any conflict between the object being destined as a singular gift to Olivares and this gift later having been assigned multiple purposes.

Around 1600, the medium of print and its particular relation to authorship and subsequently to copyright was not yet fully established. For a poet who refrained from printing, despite increasing demand, until he found himself in a most desperate situation, the manuscript produced by Chacon and Paravicino could rather have been understood as the perfection of the old medium of the manuscript. Certainly, it could serve as a base for a printed edition, but its primary destination, as it explicitly states, was the library of the Count-Duke, considered both more prestigious and more reliable than any printed edition made for profit.

However, Góngora was reluctant about printing, and what was far more important seems to have been the dedication, which would give him the aid he needed. Furthermore, a printed edition dedicated to the Count-Duke could, of course, have been allowed if he had wanted to print. The Count-Duke had royal permission to do more or less what he wanted with the flow of information. The privilege for the Vicuña edition was also, as was any privilege, awarded for that specific material edition, from which the Chacon manuscript differs considerably.

The basis for the Chacon manuscript was prepared towards the end of Góngora's time in Madrid, probably before he suffered a stroke in March

1626, certainly before he left Madrid for Córdoba in September the same year. Given these facts, it seems reasonable to assume that he may well have been involved in the project to produce a parchment manuscript for the Count-Duke of Olivares, as this medium would fit well with the attitude he held throughout his life with regard to the editing of his poetry. The fact that parchment can last for thousands of years while paper has a significantly shorter life span shows that the choice of medium had to do with technical means of material storage. As my introduction made clear, the parallel use of paper and parchment in medieval Europe had to do with the different status of the documents. As we have seen, printing was to Góngora only a last resort, even though his poetry was in high demand and the printing of *Rimas* of living poets was becoming increasingly popular in the 1620s, perhaps also fuelled by the 1625 prohibition on the printing of comedies and novels. Nevertheless, the effect of printing was not always favourable even in terms of the market, as the poet Manuel de Faria y Sousa noted: 'Something like this happened to Góngora and Villamediana; since they had been printed, there were those who did not want them [in print] for eight reales, having been prepared to pay two hundred for the manuscripts' (Faria y Sousa 1646: 5). Neither of those poets printed their poetry while alive, and de Faria y Sousa's later comment from 1646 shows how their value radically decreased as soon as they were available in print.

The calligraphy of the Chacon manuscript is one of its most striking features. It is generally considered a masterpiece of this cultural technique, and it has been suggested that Pedro Diaz de Morante, or someone from his school, was responsible for its exquisite italic script (Mariana 1991: xii). The four volumes of Morante's *Art of Writing* were published between 1616 and 1631 in Madrid, thus coinciding in time and place with the production of the Chacon manuscript. Paravicino, who wrote the biography of Góngora for the manuscript and was further involved in the project, also wrote the lengthy approbation for Diaz Morante's fourth and final volume published in 1631 and quoted above. It is thus not improbable that Diaz Morante himself may have crafted the italic letters of the manuscript. The similarities between the manuscript and Morante's books consist not only in the craft of the italic letters, but also in the adornments and *mise-en-page*.

The Chacon Manuscript opens with the following dedication to the Count-Duke of Olivares, Gaspar de Guzman:

> With the recognition I owe for the favour your Excellency has given, allowing me to take pleasure in matters in which I have been able to serve you, and whereby I simultaneously meet the obligation of my friend for having granted me this happiness, I offer to your Excellency the Works of D. Luis de Góngora, with whom I enjoyed friendship in the last years of his life: he is now dead; and his memory (which lives on in them) is more in need

> than ever of the protection of your Excellency: not so much for the censorships of his rivals, being unknown to most of his *afficionados*, due to the defects with which they have circulated even in the best manuscripts, many of them having been lost, and quite a few of them having been unfairly adopted, but for an underground printed edition having given these insults to vast publicity in a volume which in the name of D. Luis renewed them; and withdrawn (if only for lack of his name), now there has come another, so much worse that it can only be dispelled by the rays of a favour stemming from I do not know what, if of your grandeur, or of your Excellency's erudition now when you have desired these works for your Library. When I gathered all the materials that I and D. Luis' diligence could acquire in eight years, and when I examined them with him, he amended them in my presence with more attention than he usually mobilised, and when I asked him to inform me of the circumstances of some whose interpretation depended on his instruction, notifying me of the subjects of all of them, and of the years in which he composed each one, I was only prompted by the interest stemming from my affection for these works. But for D. Luis the gift of prophecy that turns out to be the illustrious honour of the Muses may have dictated to him internally the proper usefulness of distinguished glory by conceding me in writing what none of his other friends had been granted. And if D. Luis' ultimate yearning to entrust his works to me was behind this satisfaction of my desire, thereby satisfying it, I now fulfill his wishes just as eagerly: and even exceeding them; since he died anxious to dedicate his Works to the name of your Excellency, which would grant them a safe haven in your grandeur, he did certainly not dare to hope for the honour and eternity which they now assume, by your favour of accommodating them under your shadow and protection. May our Lord protect your Excellency in the many years I wish for the well-being of these kingdoms. Polvaranca, December 12th 1628 (Góngora 1628: 4).

The first thing that Chacon expresses in this dedication is that he satisfies the wishes of his friend Góngora in offering these works to the Count-Duke. At the end of the text he returns to this idea, when describing how Góngora died wanting to dedicate his works to the Count-Duke. There is no reason to distrust Chacon's words; unlike Vicuña, he seems to have been a close friend of the poet. In addition, Chacon states that now Góngora is dead, his memory is more in need of the protection of the Count-Duke than ever before. According to Chacon, this need for protection is based on the fact that Góngora's works are constantly mistreated, and he refers to the underground edition of Vicuña, 'given vast publicity' by the medium of print, as evidence of the problem. The Count-Duke, on the other hand, had desired these works for his private library, where they would be in safe storage. Chacon then states that his only motive in collecting all the poems that he and the poet could provide over eight years, as well as Góngora's notes on the dates and circumstances of composition, was his own affection for the work of his friend. Góngora, on the other hand, in the strain of 'ilustre honor de las musas' wanted them to be dedicated to the name of the Count-Duke, as this would guarantee the 'honour and eternity' that the protection of this influential actor could offer. The insistence in this dedication on memory and eternity follows the choice of medium: the finest parchment, associated with the eternal storage of important documents.

The dedication by Chacon is followed by a short biography, 'Life and writing of Don Luis de Góngora' ['Vida i escritos de Don Luis de Góngora'] signed with the initials 'A.A.L.S.M.P.' an acronym that stands for Anonymus Amicus Lubens Scripsit, Moerens Posuit, meaning 'An anonymous friend wrote this willingly, put it here sadly'. The author of this biography, known as the 'Vida Menor', was long believed to be Joseph Pellicer, since he wrote the biography of Góngora known as the 'Vida Mayor'. However, Luis Iglesias Feijoo (1983: 164) discovered a letter that proves that the author of the biography included in the Chacon manuscript was in fact the Royal Preacher Fray Hortensio Felix de Paravicino, a close associate of Góngora and an aficionado of his poetry, famous for his learned and intellectual sermons.

In his first testament, Góngora appointed Paravicino as one of its executors, entrusting him with the power to care for parts of his works. Paravicino, in turn, was connected to the young Joseph Pellicer, one of the collectors of Góngora's work eager to prove his erudition to the world. When Pellicer wanted to publish his *Lecciones Solemnes* it was Paravicino who awarded him the legal right to do so. On 1st October 1629, Paravicino writes a letter to Pellicer, in which he mentions a 'Vida de Don Luis', which Pellicer wanted to use for his edition:

> The Vida of Don Luis is locked up in a drawer, I brought the keys and I will be back within fifteen days from the date of this letter, God willing. If your Grace would be willing to leave me out of a business so foreign to my profession, I would be very grateful, and if not, listen to this: If comedians slander the Polyphemo to be printed, those dogs to whom envy spurs their anger, what will they say of the author of his Life? Surely they will say that I deserve the offense, if I caused it among verses, since I was not even excused by the pulpit (Iglesias Feijoo 1983: 164).

Pellicer was preparing his *Lecciones Solemnes a Las Obras de Don Luis de Góngora* for publication, and wanted to include the biography referred to as 'Vida de Don

Luis' in his new book. But Paravicino was not so inclined; there was a reason that it was signed 'Anonymus Amicus' in the first place, and was intended for a manuscript destined solely for the library of the Count-Duke and his associates. Paravicino, like Góngora, was avoiding the wider publicity of print in order to protect his status as a Royal Preacher. The strong inclination to the poetic language of 'cultismo' in his orations was already attracting criticism, of the same type that had been directed against Góngora, and so he had the biography locked up in a drawer. As Iglesias Feijoo demonstrates, this shows that Paravicino was the anonymous friend who wrote this biography (Pellicer also alludes to these circumstances in his version of the biography without mentioning Paravicino's name). As Mercedes Blanco has noted, Paravicino writes poetry but does not allow it to be disseminated in print because of the vital anonymity and protection offered by the medium of manuscript (Blanco 2012c: 45).

The biography recounts that at the end of his life Góngora fell ill, and had to return to his native Córdoba to die, since only the place of his birth was worthy to host his tomb:

> He fell very ill; and in a pause from his sufferings (which attacked his head) he returned to Córdoba: Because the only place worthy of his tomb was the place that honoured him in being his fatherland. The damage in his head did not harm his judgement: it was in his memory that his disease caught on: maybe because in dying Don Luis had to distribute his memory to all of us (Góngora 1628: 7).

This description of Góngora's disease suggests that he suffered some kind of stroke or some form of dementia, causing him to lose his memory at the end of his life, and the author proposes that because Góngora died bereft of his memory, it had to be distributed 'to all of us'. The greatest store of this memory was to be the manuscript in which the biography itself is included, the need for which is repeated with reference to the malicious edition of Vicuña:

> Even if Don Luis was free from new accidents of this world, his works have suffered: and whether of greed or curiosity, they were printed hastily: with such errors, not repaired and all deceitful, that it has been necessary to recollect them, now with love, now with authority. (Pellicer 1630: 7)

Thus it was with love and authority that this parchment manuscript was to store the memory of the poet in those verses, which during his lifetime were kept in his own memory.

Chacon writes in an explanatory note to the manuscript that, 'as much as he wrote they were rarely written in his hand. And he never conserved any of his own writings' (Góngora 1628: 11). Chacon's words show that even in his own lifetime, autograph poems by Góngora were extremely rare, which makes the desire for them for philological reasons in the twentieth century all the more peculiar. Another interesting feature among these notes is the statement that satirical verses are omitted from the manuscript, 'which have offended certain persons, whether they are of good or bad quality, so as not to renew in the memory of Don Luis the just discontent he had with regard to the publicity in which they have been kept until now' (11). This note resonates with the censorship of the Inquisition, though in a different tone. The censored poems in Vicuña's edition were all satirical, and those that mentioned recognizable persons (Quevedo and Isabel de la Paz) were changed in some copies. The operations involved in disseminating poetry were delicate since the written word in perpetual storage had to conform to morality regulations.

The biography in the Chacon manuscript, presumably written while Góngora was still alive (lubens scripsit) and finished after his death (moerens posuit), ends with a paragraph on the significance of the manuscript itself:

> He found friendship (which did not seem to be of love for himself or fear of the foreign) in D. Antonio Chacon of Polvaranca. The ashes of D. Luis lit a fire in his truth, when among his friends so many had seen it burn out. He gathered them in the lifetime of D. Luis with fondness and care: he communicated them to him with liberty and doctrine: and upon his death he copied them in beautiful calfskin parchment, in wonderful letters and consecrated them the generosity and esteem of the COUNT-DUKE of SANLUCAR in the learned and eternal monument of his Library. The same generosity and esteem of the COUNT-DUKE, and his glorious ambition to illuminate the letters of Spain, and honour the *ingenios* of it, will permit, when appropriate, to produce a second printed copy, to secure the credit of Don Luis, treated badly in this tumultuous and abusive printing, for the luster of this nation with the public fame of the quill of Don Luis. (9)

Paravicino testifies to the way in which Chacon collected the works of Góngora during his lifetime with affection and care, communicating them with him and after he died having them copied in beautiful calfskin parchment and even more beautiful letters so that they could be dedicated to the Count-Duke and stored in the 'learned and eternal monument of his library'. Here, the connection between the medium of the parchment manuscript and its destination is highlighted by means of their mutual association with eternal storage. The library of the Count-Duke is considered to be a 'monument', which can be understood as the library having a significance of honour and prestige beyond the purely textual material contained in it. The energy with which various actors collected the poetry, and the wish of the Count-Duke to have it dedicated to him to store in his library, show that the mere possession of precious manuscripts played an important role at the time. Thus the interest was not only in reading the poem but also in owning the artifact, and the better the manuscript, the higher the prestige of the object. The object is thus invested with a particular agency in this network, as a solution to the problem of overcoming death and oblivion, and acquiring posthumous *fama*.

When the Count-Duke saw fit, he could use this eternal medium to make a second copy, to be disseminated through the medium of print. Such a copy would be directed at securing his credit after the tumultuous printing of the Vicuña edition. The tension between the older and more reliable medium of manuscript or parchment and that of unreliable print is pushed to the fore. Thus a significant historical difference can be identified: something written by the human hand was understood to be more reliable than that which is produced mechanically.

Interestingly, the Count-Duke never prepared such an edition; he seems to have been content to store the manuscript in his library. Thus the one edition that had been thoroughly overseen by the poet himself never reached the hands of the public, at least not until the twentieth century, when it was discovered by the French Hispanist Foulché-Delbosc after having been lost for two hundred and fifty years. In this respect, for the contemporaries of Góngora there never existed an authoritative edition of Góngora's poetry, but only different versions of manuscripts and, after his death, printed editions. This tempted the most erudite commentators to expose their *ingenio* by explaining the references of the poems. As Paravicino writes in the biography on Góngora, 'writing about the credit, and the slander, and everything apologetic on the one hand, and other such things requires more time, and more notes of erudition, than these lines permit: and there are many *ingenios* out there fighting in full turmoil' (7).

Soon after the manuscript was handed over to the Count-Duke, Chacon received a position in the military order of Santiago, the same type of favour with which Góngora had been rewarded for the benefit of his nephews. These influential positions, awarded by the Count-Duke who was the first minister of King Philip IV, suggests a rather different view of the matter than the idea of an edition printed to turn a quick profit, and instead associates the medium of manuscript with a different and more rarefied and influential sphere. The exchange of the object produces sovereignty in the human subject, and the object itself works to secure this status for all the actors involved.

Stabilising the Unstable

José Pellicer (see Figure 10) published his *Lecciones Solemnes a Las Obras de Don Luis de Góngora* in 1630, dedicating it to Cardinal-Infante Ferdinand of Austria, King Philip IV's younger brother, who served as Governor of the Spanish Netherlands and Cardinal of the Holy Roman Church. But the *censura* of the

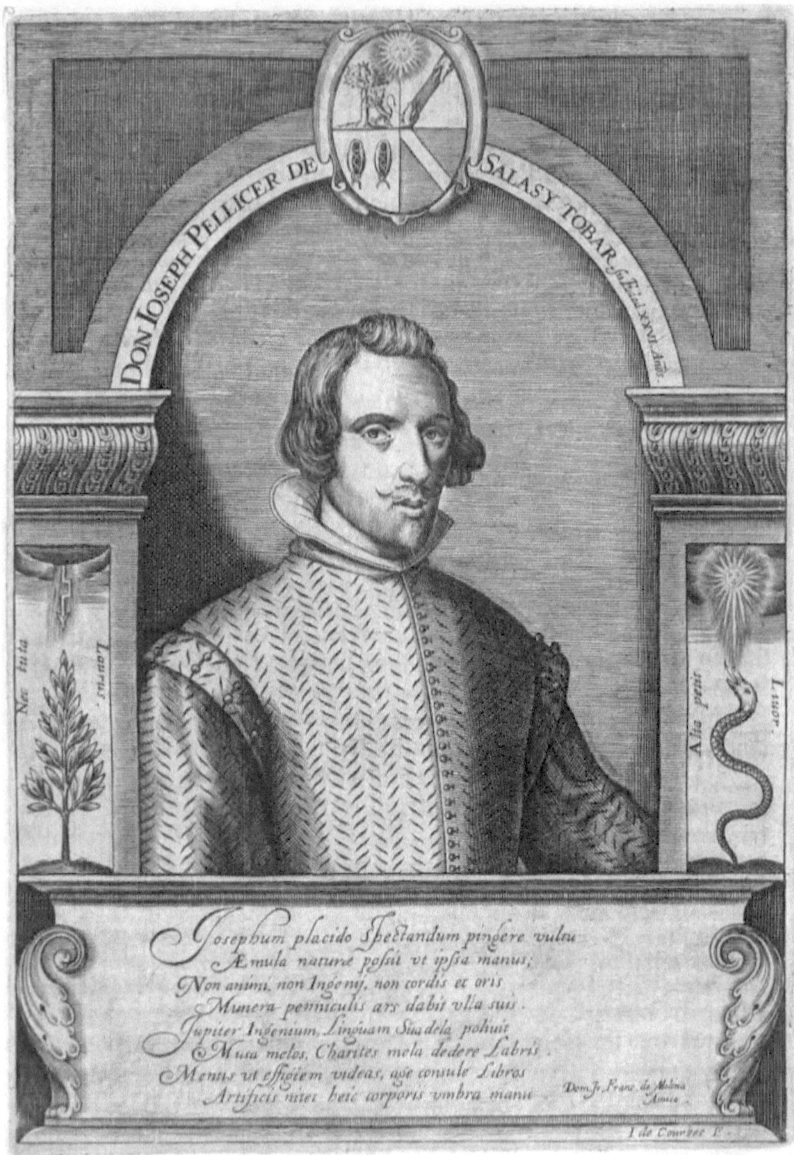

Figure 10. *Portrait of Joseph Pellicer.* Source: Biblioteca Nacional de España

book is actually dated 4 June 1628, thereby coinciding with the withdrawal of the Vicuña edition by the Inquisition in that same month. This led Miguel Artigas to speculate that Pellicer may have been behind the withdrawal of Vicuña's edition, fuelled by jealousy over not being the first to print Góngora's poetry (Artigas 1925: 211). Further support for that idea is found in the legal document, dated 6 June the same year, in which Paravicino gives Pellicer the right to print the book and at the same time demands the prohibition of any other printing of the works of Góngora (Sliwa 2004: 911).

The fact that the volume's censorship, licence and taxation notices are all dated to the summer of 1628 indicates that Pellicer was preparing his edition soon after Góngora's death. That Vicuña's edition was already published surely annoyed him, as well as the fact that another erudite aficionado, Garcia Salcedo Coronel, managed to publish his commentary on Góngora's poem 'El Polifemo' in 1629. Thus all of these projects of editing and publishing the poetry need to be seen as synchronic; in fact, from 1620 until the end of the 1630s, the materialization of Góngora's poetry was an ongoing process. The ontic operations involved in creating perpetual storage for the object of poetry involves a number of interconnected human and non-human actors. The poetry itself has no stable existence, but only exists through linked actors (human and non-human) and the cultural techniques involved in its production.

Pellicer has become famous for including a vast stock of references (too vast, according to many twentieth-century critics) in his commentaries, for competing with others and attacking them, and for being a person who 'steals' material from others and signs it with his own name. Dámaso Alonso, generally considered the most important Góngora scholar of the past century, has been instrumental in creating this image of Pellicer (Iglesias Feijoo 1983: 145). When critics judge seventeenth-century writers through a modernist epistemology, they presuppose, among other things, a singular and original creator of a final and authorial work. That Pellicer and his contemporaries may have had other conceptions of 'stealing' and commenting on learned poetry should be taken into account when discussing these issues.

In his dedication, Pellicer presents himself as a keeper of Góngora's memory and asks for the patron's support and protection against those who may attack him and his edition.

> The name and memory of Don Luis is what motivates me to solicit the favour of your Highness, because I am afraid that I will cause so much anger in those who are against him, so that, since they cannot even write a draft, among all their writings, to promote his Fame, they will try to take vengeance on me, for having taken on the enterprise to comment on his Works [...] the only remedy would be to see myself at the Royal feet of your Highness, whose grandeur will create respect so that they will leave the erudite dust of this illustrious Man in peace and give me the space to finish publishing his Works which were so ill-treated in the last printed edition. (Pellicer 1630: 9)

How the poet would be remembered, and on whose authority, seem to have been questions fundamental to the activities of publishing and storing his works. In all cases, the issue of memory and storage is brought to the fore, fused with the relations of power and patronage in which these practices were embedded. First Pellicer is worried about the vengeance of Góngora's enemies and then he puts himself at risk for having taken on the task of commenting on his works. His only remedy is the protection (hopefully) to be granted him by Cardinal-Infante Ferdinand, so that the ashes of Góngora might rest in peace and Pellicer occupy himself with finishing the stabilising of Góngora's works, so 'incorrectly' printed in the Vicuña edition. The constant intertwining of body, memory and writing reveals the significance of this issue for Pellicer and his contemporaries. The object of the book functions as a mediator producing a certain status for the actor; through it, he becomes associated with the sovereign, and the sovereign in turn becomes associated with the erudition and knowledge that justify the practice of power. The action thus perpetually transforms the actors that it affects, and the relations in the network are not given but produced by such actions.

Pellicer returns to the faults of the Vicuña edition, after having compared the disregard for the material storage of Góngora's works with that of the Roman historian Sallust, whose manuscripts according to Pellicer were deliberately corrupted: 'It was not long ago that with similar strategies the Works of Don Luis de Góngora came out so dishonourably printed and with so many faults, and even without name, but they will come back copied from more reliable originals' (10). The implication of Pellicer's statement is that somebody had published the Vicuña edition with errors and anonymously, to distort the memory of Góngora. The material storage assumes a pivotal position as it is the posthumous guarantee of worthy and perpetual remembrance. Today it may be difficult to recognise the impact of such inconspicuous media objects. When a printed book is understood as a multiplication of an unquestionably copyrighted 'intellectual property' – an immutable mobile – the object itself can seem to have little significance on an ontological level. In this early modern network, however, it clearly has specific agency.

After the dedication in which Pellicer seeks the protection of Cardinal-Infante Ferdinand, there is a long section with the title 'To the learned *ingenios* of Spain, well-worthy of Latin erudition' which further embeds the object within a network of erudition.

> For the smallest Quill to comment on the greatest poet might seem arrogant [...] so I come to ask forgiveness for having taken on this enterprise, for the errors of my quill, and for the mistakes of the printing. (16)

The 'minor quill' of the twenty-eight-year-old writer and the possible errors of the technology of print are contrasted with the perceived enormity of the subject of the book. Once again the writing instrument assumes symbolic features and is depicted in intimate connection with the human body. The technographic aspect is thus as present here as in the poetry.

Pellicer has to justify to his readers why he is indeed qualified to comment on the poetry of Góngora and how his edition is worthy of the late poet's memory. He gives three explicit reasons that motivate him to his enterprise, the first having to do with the suitability of this poetry for learned comments. The insistence on Góngora's ability to imitate Greek and Latin phrases testifies to a rather different conception of aesthetic value than that of later modernity. Those imitations are considered to be objects of knowledge, allowing the commentator to exhibit his own erudition, which is precisely what seems to fuel many of the aficionados of Góngora.

Secondly, because of this erudition, the poetry is not confined to a separate sphere but is rather deeply embedded in a world where erudition and *ingenio* are the hallmarks of the nobility and a necessity for anyone interested in gaining respect and influence. Here, poetry is clearly associated with vast knowledge, which in turn is related to power and sovereignty. The book is thus a mediator between different actors, sustaining and constructing their relations; Pellicer associates himself with Góngora and knowledge on the one hand, and the brother of the King and sovereignty on the other. The third motivation given by Pellicer is the now infamous edition published by Vicuña:

> The third impulse was the sorrow with which I saw the Works of Don Luis so unworthily printed, perhaps as a result of an intervention from one of his Enemies, who were discontent with not having been able to discredit him in life, and decided to try to shame his name once he was dead, by making sure that his works were printed (which in manuscripts were sold at a very high price) with defects, alterations, lies and incorrectness, mixed up with a great number of apocryphal pieces adopted to Don Luis, so that they would diminish the credit he had earned from the other poems. In the end they were printed and came out, so full of horrors and darkness that if Don Luis himself was resurrected, he would not recognise them. (20)

This time Pellicer goes so far as to assume that the Vicuña edition was published at the instigation of one of Góngora's enemies in order to dishonour him. Pellicer's verdict on the edition is that the poems were printed 'with defects, alterations, lies and incorrectness' and that it included a large number of apocryphal poems, all made with the intent to damage the posthumous fame of the poet. Pellicer's words seem resonant with his contemporaries' verdict, but how bad was this edition really? Of three hundred and twenty-nine poems included in the Vicuña edition, only twenty-eight were not included in the Chacon manuscript, and out of these twenty-eight, nineteen are today considered to be by Góngora (1963: xvi). This leaves the Vicuña edition with nine poems that could be considered apocryphal. Furthermore, these nine poems were explicitly denounced as apocryphal in the second part of the Chacon manuscript. Interestingly, they form a block at the end of the Vicuña edition (fols 155-160), thus standing out from the rest of the book. It is thus probable that Vicuña had them inserted just before printing because he had a couple of extra folios to use in the book. Thus it was the price of paper – which in this case had been established by the secretary of the King as four *maravedis* per fold – that caused the book to be considered offensive to Góngora's memory. These nine apocryphal poems, which caused so much trouble, are probably the only ones that Vicuña himself actually collected (Góngora 1963: li).

The rest of the three hundred and twenty poems are all from before 1620 and would have been transcribed directly from a manuscript by someone who had access to Góngora's poetry. In the preface to the reader, the author writes of the material existence of the poems that 'they were archived in the library of Don Pedro de Cardenas y Angulo, member of the order of Santiago, twenty-four years of age and from Córdoba' (Góngora 1963: 9).. This Pedro de Cardenas, member of the Order of Santiago (in which Chacon was included after completing the manuscript, and into which Góngora got his nephew as a favour of the Count-Duke), was an early protector of the poet in Córdoba and perhaps the first editor of his works. In a letter to Don Francisco de Corral on 20 January 1620, Góngora writes: 'I am copying three or four drafts I have made these days: reasonable, because, as we are fasting, the brain is more unhindered. I attach them to your Mercy so that you can communicate them to don Pedro de Cárdenas y Angulo, whose hands I kiss' (Góngora 2000b: 346).

Góngora was thus actively sending the drafts of his poems to Cardenas, who formed a small archive of this material, letting other aficcionados copy from it. From this archive Salierne probably copied the manuscript that formed the basis for a hundred and fifty-five of the hundred and sixty folios of *Obras en verso del Homero Español*, which explains how the twenty-five-year-old Vicuña could print an edition including almost all the poetry Góngora had written (but not published) until 1620. The verdict of Pellicer that the edition of Vicuña contains 'many apocryphal' poems is therefore an exaggeration, probably due to his need to justify his own edition, although the inclusion and publication of the nine apocryphal poems was clearly scandalous to many, including the Inquisition.

In the preface, Pellicer also mentions that the manuscripts were highly esteemed and sold at a very high price, which seems to add to the shamefulness of the printed edition. The vast erudition that Pellicer deems it necessary to demonstrate in his edition shows that he struggled with the tension between the older medium of manuscript and the newer medium of print. His erudition thus serves the function of justifying the 'vulgar' medium of print. In proving his *ingenio*, Pellicer draws support from a vast knowledge of authors, explicitly stating that 'the authors I have seen are many, as can be verified later, and the Authorities infinite, and not from Polianteas, of which someone pretends to accuse my *Fenix* (Pellicer 1630: 21). The index of names cited in the book amounts to twenty pages with three columns, each divided into seventy-four different categories. These categories include, among other things, mathematicians, astronomers and Hebrew, Greek and Arab magicians. After this long list of authors, there is a page that announces 'The Life and writings of Don Luis de Góngora. Defense of his style by Joseph Pellicer de Salas y Tovar'. This is followed by a page containg a portrait of Góngora, accompanied by the same poem that is included in the Chacon manuscript. A couple of pages later Pellicer inserts a note to the reader where he explains that he had intended to include the biography of Góngora there:

> I had prepared to print here the Life of Don Luis de Góngora that I have written down, along with Eulogies of Celebrated Men, who in their writings honourably mention him. This has not been possible, because it was necessary to get a new licence from the Council to print it, and as this would cause delay, it would not be fair to the Book-merchant to detain the dispatch of the Book (48).

As discussed above, the 'Vida' was written by Paravicino and signed anonymously for the Chacon manuscript. Pellicer wanted to include it in his edition, but Paravicino resisted and asked Pellicer to leave him out of the project.

Paravicino was also a poet; like Góngora, he never printed his verses but only let them circulate in manuscripts. In the poetry books of the time it is not unusual to find verses by Paravicino next to those of Góngora, the Argensola brothers, Quevedo, or Lope. It was not until after his death that his poetic works were printed with the title *Obras Postumas, Divinas y Humanas de Don Felix de Arteaga* in 1642, an edition that was furthermore published under a pseudonym formed by Paravicino's second names, Felix and Arteaga. There is thus a clear affinity between Góngora and Paravicino beyond the friendship that led Góngora to name Paravicino as his 'testamentary'. The Royal Chaplain and the Royal Preacher both worked in the Royal Chapel for ten years and both experimented with innovating new writing practices in poetry and preaching, seeking and acquiring positions within the monarchy by means of their poetic skills, while avoiding the public medium of print (Blanco 2012c: 45).

One of the reasons for abjuring print seems to have been to avoid publicity and uncontrolled dissemination. In the preface to *Obras en verso del*

Homero Español, Vicuña writes that 'many verses are missing, some that the modesty of the author did not allow in public and others that he composed during the seven years since 1620' (Góngora 1963: 11). According to Vicuña then, Góngora did not want all of his poetry to be made public. Paravicino, in his letter to Pellicer, fears negative consequences and it seems that having his biography of Góngora anonymously signed was not enough protection, unless it were in a manuscript like the one produced by Chacon.

Furthermore, the nature of the exchange of objects these actors engaged in was supposed to be free of economic interest, unlike the profits from the business of printing, and was instead expected to be of very high *symbolic* value (Gutierez 2005: 110). Herein lies part of the explanation for Góngora's talk of the shame associated with the printing of his poetry. In the case of Pellicer, the situation was somewhat different. Although he was a poet, he acquired his fame as an erudite man by commenting on Góngora's poetry, among other things. Through these activities he acquired a reputation that would give him the position of Royal Historian in the service of King Philip IV. For Pellicer, publicity was not shameful but advantageous, which explains his eagerness to engage with various enemies.

Returning to the edition of *Lecciones Solemnes*, the note to the reader, saying 'I had prepared to print here the Life of Don Luis de Góngora, that I have written down', is fully explained. This page has been introduced in the centre of the last fold, but is not materially part of it and has thus been inserted subsequently, probably just before printing. Pellicer rewrote a version of Paravicino's 'Vida' that has survived in manuscript, and this was printed in edited form in Hozes y Córdoba's 1633 edition of *Todas las Obras de Don Luis de Góngora en Varios Poemas*.

The treatment of textual material by Pellicer also testifies to a view of authorship that differs from the modern concept. He uses the words of Paravicino as a matrix, adding and amplifying where he finds it necessary. The structure remains to a large extent the same, but with the added erudite references typical of Pellicer. The circulation of authorship is thus made complex in the network made up by Góngora, Chacon, Paravicino and Pellicer, with the anonymity of Paravicino leading Pellicer to appropriate the text for himself. The actors are all related through these objects, which work as mediators to construct the phenomenon of the author Góngora. One text was thus written by one actor, copied to a manuscript, locked up in a drawer, copied by another actor, mentioned in one edition, suspended in manuscript again, and then included, without the name of any author, in yet another edition, which in fact is related to the Vicuña edition of 1627 (Hozes 1633).

In the first phrase of the 'Vida', Pellicer declares his will to be part of the material memory of Góngora with the following words: 'to find myself in such an altitude that *my quill could make eternal the memory* of an *ingenio* that lived for the embellishment, reputation and honour of his fatherland' (Góngora 1921: 307). The insistence on writing as a cultural technique conferring eternity and memory on people or things is recurrent in the complex history of Góngora's poetry. Pellicer returns to the issue of the material storage and memory of the poet:

> The writings of this distinguished man were abandoned with the death of their author without anyone who cared for them, the originals getting lost and the copies beginning to disappear, and since he did not want to have them printed in his life with care, either they were printed with enmity or greed, in a hurry, with carelessness, with lies and with works which made his name resound with hatred. They came out so different from what they were before, that they were justly and reasonably withdrawn by judicious people (Góngora 1921: 307).

The process described here concerns the attribution of authorship and the construction of a literary work. As these documents make clear the process was complex and unstable, subject to conflicts and dependent on material factors. Góngora himself was reluctant to appear in the medium of print, and was far from the only poet who did not see his poetry in print during his lifetime. The demand to read him was great, but his poetry circulated from hand to hand, and Pellicer focusses here on what he refers to as *eternizar la memoria*, to make sure that Gógora's poetry will not get lost in fragments of manuscripts.

The recurring problem, however, which may indeed have affected Góngora's attitude toward print, was that every edition was, at least according to the contemporary readers, full of errors and in no way worthy of a poet like Góngora. Today, a printed edition seems the obvious way to fix and stabilise a text, but in the early modern era it frequently implied a corruption of the text far worse than that of a manuscript, as it reached a larger public and was associated with financial profit or even greed. To Pellicer, the Vicuña edition was so different from the manuscripts that he thought its censorship by the Inquisition justified. The problem seems to have been that the edition was not considered worthy of Góngora, and Pellicer's solution was to insert a vast stock of learned references and explications in his edition, which nonetheless was met with similar disdain.

Since Pellicer's 'Vida' is an amplification of Paravicino's version, it retains many of the arguments of the latter. After denouncing the unworthy Vicuña edition, Pellicer praises Chacon for preserving the poetry of Góngora in a suitable manner, describing its materiality and the physical context of the library:

> He copied all of them onto delicate calfskin parchment, in exquisite letters and expensive binding, in four volumes, and dedicated all of them to the name and protection of the

> Count-Duke of San Lucar, so that in his excellent and large library they could be conserved against oblivion, better than those of Homer in the precious box of that other prince, so that posterity could venerate them, and so that they could be respected among learned dust for centuries to come. For these volumes, a grand and religious quill wrote his Life in the front matter, whereby he legally fulfilled his duties as a friend, and also dictated for his portrait that stance which goes with the one I printed in this book, without wanting to declare his name (Góngora 1921: 307).

The 'delicate' calfskin parchment, the 'exquisite' letters and the 'expensive' binding, along with the protection of the Count-Duke, would preserve Góngora's works against 'oblivion' in the former's excellent and large library. The hyperbolic comparison of the storage in that library refers to Alexander the Great, who according to Plutarch was so fond of Homer's works that he decided to store them in a precious casket taken as booty from Darius (Plutarch 2004: 26). This reference also occurs in the sixth chapter of the first part of *Don Quijote*, in the episode of the book burning, and was a common reference at the time. Storage in the library of the Count-Duke would secure, 'among its learned dust', esteem and respect for Góngora. To Pellicer as to Paravicino, the Chacon manuscript stands out as the ultimate storage of Góngora's poetical works, in stark contrast to any printed edition. The *fama postuma*, which is often depicted as orbiting the globe, is here pinned down to technical storage capacity. Pellicer also indicates that Paravicino, 'the grand and religious quill', was the author of the 'Vida' and of the *octava* inserted under the portrait in the Chacon manuscript, reproduced in both *Lecciones Solemnes* and Hozes y Córdoba's edition of 1633. The *octava*, speaking for Góngora, contains the lines 'Pardon such copies of my learned mind', and 'there is no copy of me but my quill', thus reinforcing the idea of the manuscript as the one and only legitimate storage of the poetry.

Pellicer's edition of *Lecciones Solemnes* was hardly free from errors. Other commentators, such as Andrés Cuesta, García Salcedo Coronel and Martín Vázquez Siruela, lamented his mistakes. But competing commentators aside, the book was, like Vicuña's edition, denounced in five different letters to the Inquisition composed by actors connected to religious institutions. Fray Juan de Sossa thought that the 'book should be expurgated and withdrawn, because it can cause errors and illusions' (Artigas 1925: 211). Fray Alonso Vázquez de Miranda wrote:

> It is certainly a profanity going against the decree of the Tridentine Council, Item 4, to treat such matters on the vanity of a Poet whose works for the most part are lascivious and heretic, and to explain the fabulous concepts of Don Luis de Góngora

> painting the beauty of a woman, by referring to the beauty of the Trinity and the Angels, to sacred books and their meaning, to ideas of God and other supreme things, in vulgar language, by a man who is not of this profession. (Artigas 1925: 211)

Fray Vázquez de Miranda ordered the condemnation and withdrawal of the book because of references to sacred texts in discussions of profane poetry. He also insisted that real theologians should read the books and decide if they could be published, since Pellicer, on the face of it, had followed the rules, having his book approved by two theologians. Perhaps these violent reactions contributed to the fact that Pellicer never finished the second volume of *Lecciones solemnes*.

Until 1633, no edition devoted exclusively to Góngora's poetry could be printed, because of the withdrawal of the Vicuña edition, and perhaps also because of the suspension of licences for books of entertainment. Interestingly, it was the concern that this book was still being circulated that motivated the Inquisition to allow a new printing which would be submitted to the censorship of Padre Pineda:

> It is proposed that even if the Spanish Homer is prohibited, there is news that it circulates among persons who are not afraid of censorship and that there are many things in it which could pass without scandal. Therefore it can be printed after having been subjected to the censorship of Padre Joan de Pineda, with the name of the author, but without the dedication. (Manning 2009: 102)

This new legal status, after five years of prohibition, allowed Gonzalo de Hozes y Córdoba to print his edition of Góngora, *Todas las Obras de Don Luis de Góngora en Varios Poemas* in 1633. The publisher of this edition was the same Alonso Pérez that had produced Vicuña's edition, a fact never mentioned in the front matter of Hozes' book. *Todas las Obras* follows Vicuña's edition closely, but omits the poems censored by Pineda, and can therefore be considered to be a re-issue of the withdrawn *Obras en Verso del Homero Español*. This imprint soon became so popular that a second edition was produced in the same year, and one year later, in 1634, a pirate edition was printed in Seville by Manuel de Sande, who in 1624 had printed a pirated copy of Conde de Villamediana, another poet who like Góngora and Paravicino did not have his poetry printed during his lifetime (Moll 1984: 953). As the Inquisition document approving the printing signals, the demand to read and possess the poetry of Góngora was extremely high, fuelled by its limited circulation in precious manuscripts until 1627, and then by the withdrawal of the collected poems for five years.

Having refrained from printing Paravicino's 'Vida' in the first volume, Pellicer's plan was to include his rewritten version of the biography of Góngora in the second volume of *Lecciones Solemnes* that would 'soon be available'. As that edition was never produced, Pellicer's rewriting of the 'Vida' was included in Gonzalo de Hozes y Córdoba's 1633 edition, along with the portrait and octava that he had got from Paravicino, who had included it in the Chacon manuscript, although the printed versions derive from a copperplate by Juan de Courbes.

Pellicer's anonymous presence in this edition is in conflict with the approbation by Tomas Tamayo de Vargas, who had been assigned by the Royal Council to review the book and see if it was fit for publication. Tamayo de Vargas praised the edition, but at the cost of Pellicer's commentaries. After celebrating the poetry of Góngora and insisting that the poems should be made available to everyone – which it had not been hitherto – he writes, 'the time has come for all to enjoy them with no other ornamentation than their own perfection, and without the stains of glosses and purposeless additions, that until now have violated and obscured, rather than explained or illustrated them' (Góngora 1633: 4). Tamayo de Vargas thus indirectly participates in the condemnation of Pellicer's edition, saying that it violates and obscures the poetry of Góngora. Tamayo de Vargas may also have been responding to the fact that Pellicer took over the office of 'Mayor Chronicler of Castile' in 1629, a position he had no wish to give up. Thus in every material object of storage of Góngora's poetry, there are inscribed a number of complex actor-network relations. To a certain extent, every book affects the different positions of the actors, which also have political consequences. Chacon was granted entrance to the Order of Santiago after dedicating the manuscript to the Count-Duke and Pellicer acquired his new position as Chronicler after publishing his comments on Góngora, while Paravicino avoided the publicity of the printed book altogether, due to the effect it could have on his career as a Royal Preacher, a position he gained after organizing the poetic *certamen* on the occasion of the celebrations around the installation of the statue of the Virgin of the Tabernacle in the Cathedral of Toledo in 1618 (see Chapter 3).

However, this edition by Hozes y Córdoba did not manage to stabilise and store the poetry of Góngora 'adequately' either. Both José Pérez de Ribas and Juan de Salinas protested on seeing poetry they had written printed under the name of Góngora in this book (Carreira 1998: 92). From Pérez de Ribas there has survived a manuscript, usually referred to as 'El manuscrito Pérez de Ribas'. This codex, comprising various notebooks with poetry compiled during Góngora's lifetime, contains some corrections by Góngora himself. The interest of this document lies in the fact that it highlights the instability of his poetical works, even in manuscripts produced by his close friends and aficionados who had direct contact with him. On fol. 106, next to a poem that begins with the line 'Ia el trato de la verdad', there is written 'It is not mine' under a text that reads 'de Don Luis de Góngora'. As Dámaso Alonso has pointed out, these words were written by Góngora's own hand (Alonso 1978: 260). On another page, the same hand has written a note next to a *letrilla* attributed to Góngora – '*faltan*' – to mark the lack of the last two strophes of the poem, and next to the following lines, again, 'the following ones are not mine'. These last two lines that Góngora rejects are in fact included in the Chacon Manuscript, which shows that even this manuscript is not a stable text in the modern sense. The presence of Góngora's writing in the manuscript of Pérez de Ribas testifies to the way the material object containing what was conceptualised as poetry was unstable and in a constant state of renegotiation; here we can trace an emerging but not yet fully stable notion of authorship in which the poet himself needs to intervene in order to stabilise the poem. Thus the material object forces the actors, including the poet himself, to work through the problematic notion of authorship. It is in this sense illuminating to understand the conceptual object of poetry as an early modern cultural technique, including human actors and material objects in a process of annotation and rewriting, where the concept is preceded by the ontic operations that produce the symbolic work. A manuscript of poetry such as this one contains several examples of poems being crossed out and rewritten, which shows how the open-ended practice of poetry implied the use of quills and papers in a continuous process.

In manuscript 19.004 at National Library in Madrid, we find, in the fourth folio, a 'Scrutiny of the prints of the poetic works of don Luis de Góngora y Aragote'. As Antonio Carreira has convincingly shown, the author of this anonymous document was the same José Pérez de Ribas that protested upon seeing his poems in Hozes' edition of 1633 (Carreira 1998: 399). Carreira draws this conclusion from studying the numerous corrections of Góngora poems made by the anonymous author who, when commenting on the attribution of a romance starting with the line '*en la beldad de Iacinta*', writes 'If Don Luis claims that it is his, let us say he is mistaken'. Such assurance could only come from the person who wrote the poem, and as Carreira shows, the author is the same Pérez de Ribas that was the first owner of the manuscript discussed above.

Pérez de Ribas was an old friend of Góngora's, also from Córdoba, and highly familiar with his work. The document was probably written soon after the publication of Hozes y Córdoba's edition, *Todas las obras de Don Luis de Góngora en Varios Poemas*, since it cites and comments on the first edition of this book but not the second. The following is a transcription of the most relevant passages of the Escrutinio in Ms. 19.004 from Biblioteca Nacional in Madrid:

> Seeing the works of Don Luis de Góngora that have up to today been printed, one observes how inappropriate they are: they need to be reformed. […] his works have been printed in fragments by eminent men who are fond of them. We owe them gratitude for their intention, but not for what they produced; because the first one [Vicuña's *Obras en Verso del Homero Español*] came into the hands of the Author not with mistakes, nor

> drafts, but what is more, abominable errors; an offense without culpability, if not for its ignorance. The second one [Pellicer's *Lecciones Solemnes a las Obras de Don Luis de Góngora*] came with defences, or annotations, or whatever the attentive reader wishes to call them – great fatigue, great erudition, grand notes: they are certainly worthy of their author who in Spain is considered eminent; but it seems useless. [...] The third edition [Hozes y Córdoba's *Todas las Obras de Don Luis de Góngora en Varios Poemas*] that came out in print is admirable: for being made by a curious aficionad*o* from Córdoba, but at the same time appearing with so many offences, [...] This devoted *ingenio*, who assumed the major task of writing the Life of Don Luis, forgot to describe his effigy with the brush of his quill, perhaps more successfully than through the chisel on the copperplate. Because for Spain it is not necessary, since he was so known by everyone; but for posterity, and for Italy, France, The Low Countries, Germany, for all of Europe, for the Castilian and Portuguese Indias, where his name is so venerated; that they ought to build him statues of marble, of bronze, of eternities for his memory.

Pérez de Ribas thus adds a final and authoritative voice to the chorus of laments over the printed editions of Góngora. Vicuña's edition is dismissed as the work of an ignoramus, with too many faults ever to be accepted. Pellicer's *Lecciones Solemnes*, so full of commentary, is merely tiresome according to Pérez de Ribas, and will only confuse the reader. Hozes y Córdoba's volume in its turn is equally faulty and will have to be redone. The biography, portrait and associated poem are also dismissed as unsuccessful and unnecessary. The religious connotations of the words *ingenio devoto* could indicate that Pérez de Ribas was aware that Paravicino was the anonymous author of the biography and the *octava* under the portrait of Góngora.

Pérez de Ribas further notes that Góngora used to say that 'the best executor of my works is me. He also said: I want to do something not for the many' (13). These quotes indicate that Góngora's reluctance to use the medium of print was part of his poetic enterprise. 'To do something, but not for the many'. The best way to accomplish such a mission was, of course, to let the poems circulate from hand to hand, thereby ensuring that the readers were aficionados. Ironically, by sticking to the medium of manuscript, he ensured that interest in possessing the poetry would grow to such an extent that he ended up having done something for the many rather than for the few. But this also testifies to a striking historical difference in poetic writing practices. Today, it seems self-evident that whoever writes something wishes to be read, and generally by as many people as possible. For a poet like Góngora, who served as Royal Chaplain and was connected to powerful royal actors, poetry worked as part of the symbolic order of power relations.

Pérez de Ribas further insists on the practical use of Góngora's poetry. According to him, the accusations against the poet were usually the product of misunderstandings:

> Those who never met this *ingenio* considered him satirical. And [so did] even some who were devoted to him. What a deception! Looking carefully at his works one finds in all of them a general doctrine for all conditions, offices and professions [...]. So whether these, and others, are printed or not, they will not be erased from memory, nor through the agency of time, nor by the imitators of Don Luis (if he has any), in any way; rather, through centuries to come, and from people to people, his tradition will survive to the posterity of the world. (12-13)

Beyond the syntactic twists of Góngora's poetry, his contemporaries thus found a 'general doctrine' for any type of profession. His poetry was deeply embedded in the political, religious, juridical, scientific and artistic spheres, through the relations of human and material actors in this network, and not an autonomous object for aesthetic pleasure alone. As for the recurring issue of the memory of Góngora, to which almost all actors return at one point or another, Pérez de Ribas is sure that the printing of his poetry in the end will be insignificant, as the memory of it will not be blurred by anything but live on through the people who remember it. The object is thereby inscribed into a temporal régime of futurity specific to the early moderns (Hartog 2015). The end of this important document contains further information with regard to the ontic operations involved in the construction of the phenomenon of poetry:

> Note that there are romances and poems in it, which are in a state of confusion so that the reader might attribute them to the author he pleases. Because if there are indications, or if some are imitations (may this great man forgive me), if he has any blame it is leaving things so important to the selection of his aficionados: even this testifies to the extreme modesty which the nature of Don Luis manifested in his works. In fact one often could hear his friends trying to persuade him to print them to avoid this danger: 'Not my works, he said, I do not think they deserve it. If they shall be granted any luck, someone will have to do it after I am gone'. Not one, indeed, but there were and there will be many trying to do just that, but until now, all unsatisfactorily, as I have shown. This could be attributed to misfortune; because that is what it would be if merit is bereft of its reward. In time perhaps the best ones will co-operate to gather them accurately and have them come out, without errors and not in fragments. I hope that this volume will one day come into the hands of one of

> the few true aficionados, the good ones to whom one can entrust its legal care and have it printed, so that his name can be secured in its glory. (24)

After scrutinizing the printed editions of Góngora thoroughly, Pérez de Ribas comes to the conclusion that they contain so many errors that they will have to be rewritten line by line to serve their purpose of storing the poetry adequately. He further complains of the confusion arising when the reader attributes the poems to whomever he wishes. This clearly shows the tension between an emerging but not yet established notion of authorship and a cultural technique where poetry moves freely without the need of an author's name. This practice is still deeply rooted in a tradition where variants and multiple (or anonymous) authors seemed natural, and in spite of all Pérez de Ribas's complaints, the poems were materially stored in multiple variants. Only the poet himself, and his closest followers, could be sure to have the correct copies. And even among them, there seems to have been no stable material existence for this poetry.

Pérez de Ribas also recounts that Góngora responded to the demands of printing by claiming that his poetry did not 'deserve' it, at least not while he was alive. If someone wanted to do it after he was gone, it would be up to them. Góngora's utterance here must be understood as false modesty, as he evidently circulated his poetry through the network and received other compensation than purely financial profit. Góngora seems to have insisted that his poetry was disseminated discreetly, 'not for the many', and yet he acquired a reputation greater than any other poet of his time. This approach was made possible by the tension between the older medium of manuscript, to which was ascribed certain qualities, and a newer one considered to be for mass dissemination and for profit. The qualities of the manuscript – its singularity, concreteness, discreteness, physicality and ability to evade any censorship – seem to have differentiated this medium from print. Paravicino, Conde de Salinas, and Conde de Villamediana were all in a similar position. Where there seemed to be no limit to the number of books an author like Lope de Vega could print (his collected works, printed in his lifetime, comprises no fewer than twenty-five books), Góngora and others seem to have had a different conception of the material substratum of their poetry. Góngora frequently described Lope as a 'lower' poet, and in the 1622 'A Lope de Vega y sus secuaces' he invokes Lope's 'vulgar quill feather' and in the 1609 sonnet to Quevedo, known as 'Anacreonte Español' cited above, Góngora speaks of Lope's 'comic poetry'. Lope, although widely read and celebrated, was a playwright and did not come from a noble bloodline. Comic pieces were what made the most financial profit at the time, not least through printed editions. The 'comic poetry' of the 'vulgar quill' could thus be printed and widely disseminated without disgrace, but the quill of Góngora was considered to be unique ('*no hay de mi mas copia que mi pluma*'). The shame which Góngora in his letters associates with print, the insistence that it did not deserve to be printed – which can also be taken to mean that the print medium did not deserve his poems – and the recurring insistence on the part of Góngora and his editors that he never wrote anything heretical shows the instability of the conceptual object of his poetic works.

In the final words of the *Escrutinio*, Pérez de Ribas hopes that a future and more suitable editor will one day find the manuscripts and have them printed to guarantee the material storage and perpetuate the memory of Góngora. Not until the turn of the nineteenth century, however, when the Chacon manuscript fell into the hands of the scholar Foulché-Delbosc after two hundred and fifty years of oblivion, was such an edition produced. Following a century of philological work, readers today have a variety of excellent critical editions to choose from. But that should not obscure the fact that in this early modern network, there never existed any stable object of storage for Góngora's poetry. The one manuscript that would have served this purpose better than any other was stored in the library of the Count-Duke for the memory of future generations. In the end, we have to conceive of Góngora's poetry as deeply embedded in early modern life, where the poems were read and copied by hand, but never stabilised or fixed in any definitive form.

Historico-Philosophical Interlude 2

Walking into a gallery to view a painting today is a quite different experience from the viewing of artworks in early modern times. The institutionalised space of the museum sets up a specific pattern of interaction and distances the artifacts of the past. Even though many curators today do their best to overcome this distance by juxtaposing past and present, the artifacts seem to demand something from us that we no longer possess. The usual solution has been to provide an iconographic analysis, an interpretation, to get beyond the surface of the image to its core, its meaning. When the critic W.J.T. Mitchell started asking himself 'What do pictures want?', he was well aware that this question might seem absurd to the majority of his readers, based as it is on an understanding different from that of the inanimate object awaiting interpretation by a human subject (Mitchell 1996: 71). It is not only different from the prevalent understanding of images, it also seems to connect to an understanding of images that in the teleological account of History with capital H was left behind hundreds of years ago, after René Descartes 'discovered' that the mind, or *res cogitans*, was separate from the body and the material world, which it could therefore observe. The institutionalization of this Cartesian worldview has made it harder for us today to relate to cultural objects produced before it became dominant.

At the same time, however, the digital age seems to be producing dissatisfaction with this Cartesian self-reference (Gumbrecht 2014). At this point, we may be able to approach the cultural objects of the past from new and hopefully less anachronistic perspectives. The realization of the importance of the materiality of any given cultural object is one way in which the contemporary conception of cultural objects seems closer to that of the early modern era than that of intervening centuries. The materiality and associated practices differ, of course, being historically specific, but the relation between the human body and material object is in both eras pushed to the fore. This is not to say that viewing digital images on a screen has anything to do with entering an early modern gallery – the abundance of images in the former era, and their relative scarcity in the latter (even if early modern galleries were often filled from floor to ceiling) is a case in point – but in both cases an exclusive focus on interpretation and the attribution of meaning fails to do the objects justice. Rather, we must supplement our understanding of the symbolic with a description of objects in the real. In this sense, the ontic operations that make the symbolic possible can also point toward the agency of things.

Around 1600 in Spain, entering a gallery to view a painting, or opening a codex with a frontispiece with a portrait of the author, was an act that entailed a kind of magic. Two hundred years before the invention of photography, the material copying of a human effigy was a strange and almost uncanny affair. The relation between the human body and material object produced what Gumbrecht calls 'presence effects': 'The word presence does not refer (or at least does not mainly refer) to a temporal but to a spatial relationship to the world and its objects Something that is present is supposed to be tangible for human hands, which implies that, conversely, it can have an immediate impact on human bodies' (Gumbrecht 2003: xiii). It is this impact of the presence of objects on human bodies that is hard to account for in the subject/object paradigm that comes with a Cartesian worldview.

To overcome this paradigmatic view of cultural objects, the concept of cultural techniques proves useful. As Bernhard Siegert puts it: 'The notion of cultural techniques strategically subverts the problematic dualism of media and culture; it opens up media, culture, and technology to further discussion by highlighting the operations or operative sequences that historically and logically precede the media concepts generated by them' (Siegert 2007: 29). Writing and painting are in this manner understood as elementary cultural techniques, put to use in different manners to produce what we understand as a cultural object. The notion of cultural techniques is employed here to overcome prejudice of what a cultural object is, and to be able to form an understanding of its underlying operations and historically specific practices and conceptions. The following chapter investigates the cultural technique of subject constitution by analysing the portrait as a material object capable of storing a copy of the human being and producing presence effects. This is done with reference to a number of sources, including poetic writing about painting, precisely because it records the presence effects and underlying material operations of this cultural technique.

In early modern Spain, as we have seen, the issue of material storage assumed an important and privileged position. This can be seen in several contexts, of which the material trace of ephemeral being is perhaps the most important. The topos of *vanitas mundi*, for instance, insists on the ephemeral quality of human life by exhibiting its material traces. The best-known images in this tradition are the *Stilleben* featuring skulls which were popular in the Spanish Netherlands in the work of Flemish painters such as Harmen Steenwyck and Jan Davidsz. de Heem (see Figure 11), but the topos was widespread throughout the Spanish Empire, and is present in its poetry as well. The *vanitas* topos exhibits bones, skulls and ashes along with instruments of cultural techniques like pens, globes, watches and desks. This association of instruments and bodily remains evoked common problems of storage. If human life was vain, brief and transient, one way of overcoming

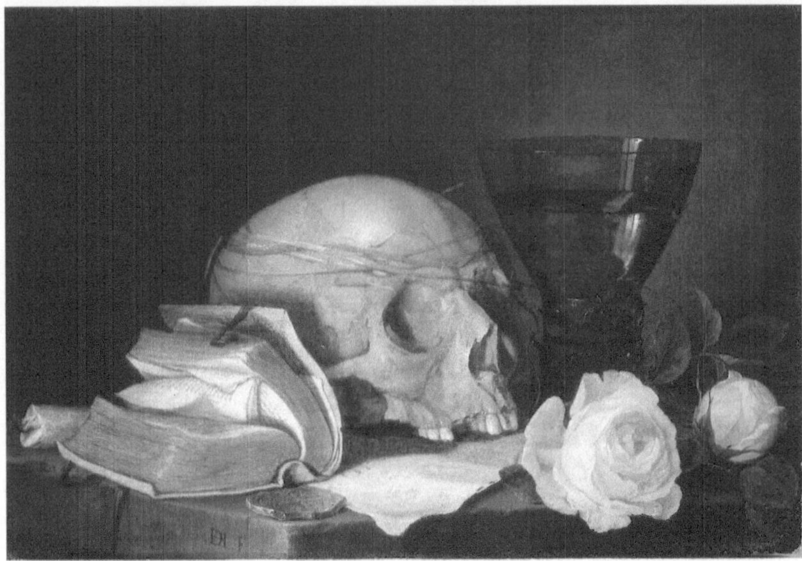

Figure 11. Jan Davidsz. de Heem, *Vanitas* (1629). Source: Wikimedia Commons.

it was to employ material objects and instruments that could 'freeze' time. Such was painting and such was poetry, and nowhere was this more visible than in the poems dedicated to portraits. This association sometimes goes so far as to understand the portrait itself as a relic, the material trace of a late human being.

Cultural objects such as portraits and manuscripts existed in specific spaces which allowed interaction with them. These spaces were galleries, cabinets and libraries, with no clear distinction between them. A typical gallery around 1600 in Madrid would contain all of these objects as well as precious stones, relics, scientific instruments, and other objects of knowledge (Bredekamp 1995). In them, people engaged with these objects in various ways that escape the modern paradigm of meaning and interpretation. These spaces could roughly be said to pertain to four different but overlapping and interacting 'spheres' in which the vast part of the culture and media discussed in this chapter moves. Peter Sloterdijk defines the sphere as 'the interior, disclosed, shared realm inhabited by humans – insofar as they succeed in becoming humans. Because living always means building spheres, both on a small and a large scale, humans are the beings that establish globes and look out into horizons. Living in spheres means creating the dimension in which humans can be contained' (Sloterdijk 2011: 28). Sloterdijk´s concept is here adopted and brought together with Gumbrecht´s 'presence' to discuss where and how the objects of this network move about.

First and perhaps most influential was the bureaucratic sphere of the royal court. This was the go-to place for anyone who wished to survive in the aristocratic environment, as it distributed virtually all attainable positions and favours (Gutierrez 2005: 115). Besides the King (Philip II, III and IV respectively) there was a *valido* or minister who acted out a large part of the power practice. (In the case of Philip IV it was the Count-Duke of Olivares.) These were social spheres as well as physical spaces, providing a scene for the spectacle of royal life, in which collections and galleries assumed a privileged position. The sense in which Gumbrecht speaks of Philip II as a master of *disimulo* is a case in point, where the agency of paper puts the secretary in a position of power. While artistic/poetic practices to a large extent took place within this sphere, there were also academies in Seville and other towns that provided additional spaces in a second sphere (the Count-Duke of Olivares frequented these in Seville before becoming a minister). This had to do with the fact that virtually no 'professional' writers or artists existed independently, but only through positions given by the Court, such as those of Royal Painter, Preacher, or Secretary. In the palaces of Archbishops, monasteries, and convents, the religious institutions constituted another sphere. These spaces were intermingled with those of the Court while occupying an inviolable position because of their sacred nature (San Lorenzo el Escorial is perhaps the clearest example, being both a palace of the King, a monastery, a library and a gallery). The positions within the Church however, were orchestrated from the Court, and mostly held by persons with a connection to it. Finally, there was the academic sphere, which primarily occupied the many universities of the era. In fact, Spain went from having just a few universities at the end of the fifteenth century to over one hundred in the seventeenth century (Kagan 1974: 63). In pointing out these spheres and spaces, my intention is by no means to separate them but rather to provide a physical framework for the subsequent discussion. All of these spheres and spaces were intermingled and interdependent. There was no such thing as power in itself, nor was there any independent creation of cultural media objects. The objects themselves bear witness to this, and the reconstruction of these physical spaces can tell us about how things and media operate as cultural techniques.

2

On Spheres and Spaces: In the Gallery

The Portrait and the Codex

Engravings constituted a large part of the visual culture of early modern Spain, and the most common place to find these engravings was in a printed codex (Civil 1969: 99). These frontispieces, as they are generally called, were an indispensable part of the verbal/visual system of the book, inscribing it within a network of actors. The mode of publication used for the Góngora manuscripts and printed books discussed in the previous chapter were part of a larger tendency in the 1620s in Spain. Poets published their work while still alive or someone else took care of it right after they died (as in the case of Góngora), and the inclusion of heraldic or architectonic *portadas*, euologistic verses and portraits seems to have played an important part in the increased interest in the material object of the book as storage and perpetuation of memory. The construction of these objects was often aimed at stabilising something unstable, at creating a difference between ephemeral and durable; visual portraits and biographies were crucial links in this operative chain.

The inclusion of author portraits in medieval manuscripts of the *chansonniers* was used to create authority in the construction of an author, in a shift from sacred to secular, while also bestowing a higher status upon the object itself (Galvez 2012: 102). There the portraits played an important part in validating the word as coming from a human rather than a divine subject. They could also lend authority to the sovereign through poetic praise and, conversely, validate the poetry itself by virtue of its association with the ruler. Author portraits on frontispieces were not uncommon in sixteenth-century printed books, but in the 1620s their presence increased notably in Spain, particularly in poetry books (Garcia Aguilar 2009: 125).

In 1625, only three years after Philip IV had ascended the throne, with his favourite the Count-Duke of Olivares as first minister, the Council of Castile decided to prohibit the printing and selling of novels and comedies, as they were considered morally dangerous to the youth of Spain (Cayuela 2011: 365). The council had the following advice to give the King regarding the printing of books of entertainment:

> Because the damage of printing books of comedies, novels, and other of the same kind, has been recognized as softening the habits of the young, it is advised that his Majesty orders the Council not in any circumstance to give licences to print such works (Moll 1974: 98).

This new legal protocol, explicitly prohibiting the printing of books of entertainment, coincided with an increased interest in publishing poetry. Poetry was not mentioned in the prohibition, but it seems reasonable to conclude that the more learned it was, the less harmful it would seem. Thus Pellicer's urge to enlighten the erudite readers of Spain about how learned the poetry of Góngora (and by extension he himself) was, can be understood in relation to the complex situation of literary publishing at the time. Exquisite manuscripts with extensive front matter could further be a way of establishing the material object as pertaining to the learned sphere rather than that of entertainment; portraits with euologic verses were therefore key to a strategy of imbuing the object with an 'aura' that the 'vulgar' prints lacked.

As John Elliott has pointed out, it is probable that the true motive behind the legislation was Olivares's fear of a literary opposition rather than the official reason ('softening the habits of the young') given in the document. Both Philip IV and Olivares were known as protectors of literature, and Olivares frequently appears as the dedicatee of books of poetry (as in the case of the Chacon manuscript). Thus it may seem ironic that the only poetic book withdrawn during the ten-year prohibition was Vicuña's edition of Góngora in 1627. The exemption of poetry from the prohibition had to do with its relation to sovereignty, and the dedications and portraits included in these objects were an integral part of the solidification of these relations of power (Gutierrez 2005: 119). The production of printed books of poetry rose during the prohibition and was increasingly reified as an object of economic value (Cayuela 2011: 372).

Front matter in general, and frontispieces in particular, have often been overlooked in early modern scholarship. The documentation around them is especially scarce in Spain, which leaves the scholar with a number of clues that have to be reconstructed in order to fully understand this early modern media practice. Behind the material object of a codex there are usually a number of actors collaborating in producing the particular media object, where the role of the 'author' is far less obvious than it is today. On the other hand, emerging notions of secular authorship were established through the presence of the portraits, thus making visually explicit something that today is taken for granted.

When Alonso de Villegas's *Flos Sanctorum* was published in 1589 he included a portrait of himself under which he explicitly explained the function of this visual inscription in the book:

> It having come to my attention, my Christian reader, that this Flos sanctorum has been reprinted several times without my authorization, and that the print runs come out filled with errors, some of them made on purpose, by people who, following their own opinions, say something different than what I say and have researched well; in order to avoid this damage, I had this portrait made by the scrupulous silversmith Pedro Angel, which will serve as my signature. So, wherever it appears, it will be understood that the print run was made under my command, and therefore will be more correct. (Bass 2008: 43)

The problems Villegas faced are similar to those lamented by the various editors and commentators of Góngora. In a time of emergent notions of authorship and intellectual property, still without copyright or legal protection, the portrait in the front matter of a codex could thus serve as a signature to help distinguish it from other copies. The portrait of Villegas constitutes him as a legal subject, connecting the human body and the object of the book.

The problem of attribution and ownership in a time before the establishment of copyright is also reminiscent of the dismay expressed by Miguel de Cervantes over the 'fake' *Don Quijote* by Avellaneda. When Cervantes published his *Novelas Ejemplares* in 1613, he did so without including a portrait or laudatory verses in it. Instead, he wrote an ironic prologue to the reader, in which he humorously explains the lack of a portrait, which is due to the inability of his friend to carry it out:

> This friend might well have created my portrait, which the famous Don Juan de Jáuregui would have given him, to be engraved and put in the first page of this book, according to custom. In that way he would have gratified my ambition and the wishes of several persons, who would like to know what sort of face and figure has he who is so bold as to come before the world with so many works of his own invention. My friend might have written under the portrait – This person whom you see here, with an oval visage, chestnut hair, smooth open forehead, lively eyes, a hooked but well-proportioned nose, & silvery beard that twenty years ago was golden, large moustaches, a small mouth, teeth not much to speak of, for he has but six, in bad condition and worse placed, no two of them corresponding to each other, a figure midway between the two extremes, neither tall nor short, a vivid complexion, rather fair than dark, somewhat stooped in the shoulders, and not very light-footed: this, I say, is the author of Galatea, Don Quixote de la Mancha (Cervantes 1881: 4).

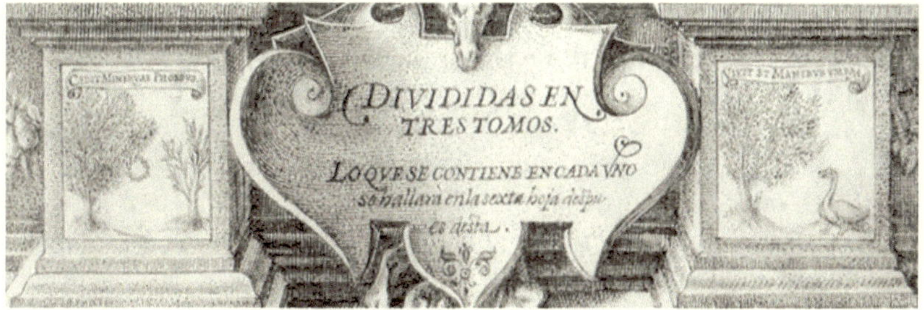

Figure 12. Detail of frontispiece of the Chacon manuscript.
Source: Biblioteca Nacional de España

Cervantes uses the ironic style that has become the hallmark of his authorship to comment on the practice of inserting an engraved portrait of the author with eulogistic verses placed below it. The irony stems from Cervantes inversion of this particular practice; instead of a portrait, he offers an ekphrastic description of a portrait, and instead of praise, he paints the picture of a toothless old man of average height. This person, he insists, thus making explicit the purpose of this practice, is the author of *Don Quijote.* The satire shows that this conception of the function of front matter was widespread enough for Cervantes to mock it.

Visual Representation in the Chacon Manuscript

As mentioned in the previous chapter, the Chacon manuscript contains a page with a portrait of Góngora, under which is placed an *octava* that technographically refers to its own writing process, thus creating a self-reflexive loop in this text/image hybrid object. The portrait, which is in fact painted with quill and ink on parchment, is based on a now lost oil painting by the Dutch artist Juan Van der Hamen, which belonged to a series of portraits of 'illustrious men' (Jordan 2005: 121). These portraits were often used in the front matter of a manuscript or printed book as frontispieces, serving as a visual inscription of an authorship that needed to be made explicit (Marias 2012: 47). In many cases the poet being thus portrayed composed a poem to accompany the portrait, thus creating an interesting and complex case of ekphrastic comment on the human body and on material storage in image or words. This ekphrasis is thus based on the visual representation of the same body that produces it.

The Chacon manuscript also carries a frontispiece with the dedication to the Count-Duke of Olivares and two emblems (see Figure 12). The one in the left corner shows two trees with the motto 'Phoebus gives way to Minerva' ['Cedit Minervae Phoebus']. This motto expresses that the first tree of Phoebus (or Apollo in ancient Greek mythology), which is the laurel tree that Daphne was transformed into according to the myth, and thus by association that of the poet's laurel crown, is replaced by the olive tree of Minerva (or Athena in ancient Greek mythology), which is then associated with the Count-Duke through his last name Olivares. It can thus be understood as a visual rendering, coded in mythology, of how the posthumous fame of the poet is handed over as a material object to the protection of the powerful Count-Duke.

In the right-hand corner there is an image of a swan under an olive tree with the motto *Vivit et manibus umbra* ('the shadow endures for the dead'), where the swan can be understood as representing the deceased poet now under the protection of the shadow of the olive tree (the Count-Duke). The swan has been associated with poetry ever since antiquity, where it was said to be the bird of Orpheus, or the bird he was transformed into, and furthermore, the feather of the swan, the quill, has an obvious connection to the poet here. This emblem expresses a movement from the fame (the laurel) of the poet and his quill, to the protection of Minerva, the goddess of poetry and wisdom. The emblem can thus be understood as an imperative to the Count-Duke, as he is identified with Minerva through the olive tree, to protect and care for the memory of (Góngora's) poetry. The olive branch is itself associated with immortality and renewal of life, and in the reading of this emblem it is connected to the afterlife of the poetry in the manuscript, vaguely reminiscent of the Phoenix, which is often associated with writing practices and material storage. The memory and immortality of the poet and his poetry are guaranteed by Minerva/Olivares through the manuscript. This verbal/visual representation is thus an illustration of the object in which it is contained, as evidenced by the recurring references in the front matter to the shadow and thus to the Count-Duke's protection of the memory of Góngora.

This visual representation served to a large extent to solidify the relation between the material object of storage and the human subject, which was far from stable, as indicated by the constant play of attributions and rejections of specific poems. The historically specific practice of inserting a visual representation of the author into the book must thus be understood as part of a network of actors in which the relations between Góngora, Olivares, Chacon, the codex, the library and the Court were made explicit.

The portrait of Góngora in the manuscript is based on a lost painting by van der Haamen, which portrays an aged Góngora in the sixtieth year of his life and was painted in 1620. Manuel Sanchez Mariana believes that the artist responsible for the portrait must have been someone with 'extraordinary skill in the technique of engraving' as it shows mastery of the point although it is made with a quill (Mariana 1991: xiii). Kirsten Kramer notes that the portrait in the manuscript functions like a 'second body' that duplicates the physical body, thereby changing the relation between model and copy from representation to substitution and embodiment (Kramer 2008: 69).

The portrait is placed in a sketched frame with exquisite adornments of angels, fruits and Góngora's coat of arms surrounding it (see Figure 13).

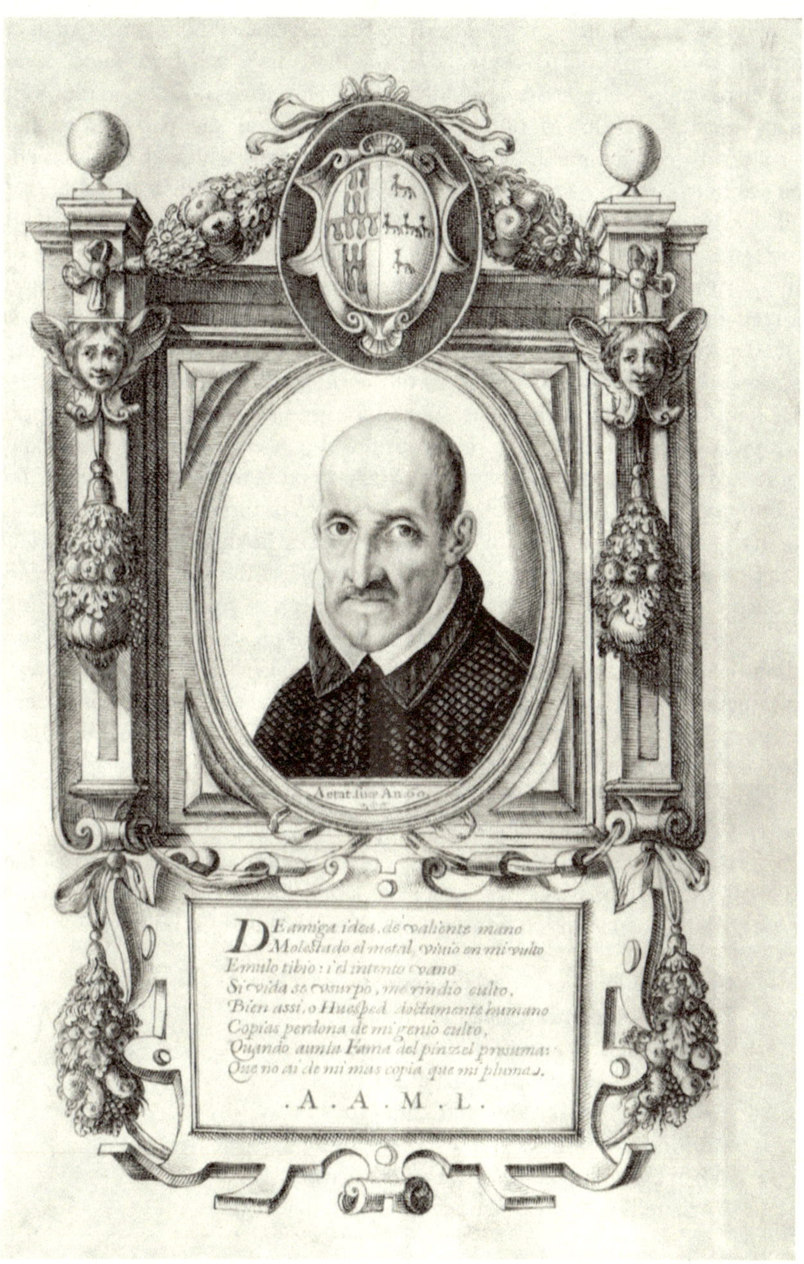

Figure 13. Portrait of Góngora in the Chacon manuscript.
Source: Biblioteca Nacional de España

Thus the parchment page activates different iconic levels that transcend representation. The three-dimensional frame makes the portrait look like a painting in a gallery, reproduced in copperplate, although it is in fact drawn with a quill on parchment. To say that this is a hybrid object is an understatement. The *trompe-l'oeil* effect of a frame drawn on the manuscript page creates an illusion of three-dimensionality on the two-dimensional surface of the parchment. At least three frames exist within the parchment page: that of the portrait, that of the coat of arms, and that of the poem, all of which are connected in an elaborate architecture. The fruits around the frame highlight the *trompe-l'oeil* effect, inviting the spectator to perceive of the portrait as breaking out of the order of representation of the codex and imagine himself standing in front of it.

Bernhard Siegert has traced the *trompe-l'oeil* of Dutch still life painting back to the illuminated manuscripts of the fifteenth and sixteenth centuries. He finds that the *trompe-l'oeil* effect in manuscripts arises from 'the competition with reading practices enforced by the printed book', in that Protestant reading practices tended to clearly separate the book from the reader's body, while 'the illuminated manuscript appealed to the presence of the reader by attempting to have the medium itself dictate the practices linking book and reader' (Siegert 2015: 189). In this sense the late example of the partially illuminated Chacon manuscript with its *trompe-l'oeil* portrait can be understood as resisting the detachment of print and insisting on physical presence. The portrait and the poem on the parchment create a presence effect by activating an array of functions simultaneously. By doubling as a wooden frame, the parchment page opens up a virtual *mise-en-abyme* of the imaginary and the real in which the distinction between material carrier and pictorial space has collapsed.

The presence of this portrait in the manuscript is far from coincidental; it reveals the necessity of establishing visually the relation between the human subject and the non-human material object, which together construct the portrait's subject along with the other paratexts. Just below the portrait is the *octava*, which creates an interesting effect of ekphrastic referentiality:

> Of a friendly idea and brave hand
> Disturbing the metal, lived in my face
> Tepid rival; and even if this vain attempt
> Stole [my] life, it worshipped me.
> Well so, O Host, erudite and human,
> Pardon [such] copies of my learned mind,
> When even Fame takes pride in the brush
> for there is no copy of me but my quill.
>
> [De amiga idea, de valiente mano
> Molestado el metal, vivio en mi vulto
> Emulo tibio; y el intento vano
> Si vida se usurpó, me rindio culto.
> Bien assi, o Huesped, doctamente humano

Copias perdona de mi genio culto,
Cuando aún la Fama del pinzel presuma:
Que no ai de mi mas copia que mi pluma.]
(Góngora 1628: 10)

This *octava* is directed at the portrait placed above it, acting as an instance of prosopopeia, giving voice to the inanimate object of the portrait. It is also an example of the ekphrastic competition between the medium of writing and the visual medium of painting. The *octava* speaks of a 'tepid rival' and a 'vain attempt', as if the portrait rivalled the writings of the poet by emanating from the same 'learned mind'. The painter, in the poet's rendition, has attempted to steal life by imitating nature in a dead material, a conception that alludes to Prometheus' creation of man from clay, a myth that was frequently associated with artistic practice. The Promethean creation parallelled that of the painter in attempting to create nature, something only God could do. This theme of the fragile materiality of the medium of painting then turns into a recursive loop back to the medium of writing. Where the painter's brush may well lead to fame, there can be no other copy of the 'mind' of the poet than his own quill. Taking into account the physical movement of poetry through manuscripts and printed books at the time, this insistence on the singular writing tool of the poet takes on a specifically material dimension. Furthermore, the poem in fact says that the 'quill' is a copy of the human being, which further contributes to our understanding of the conception of this tool.

Thus the notion of copies and authorship is activated through the different media and their respective materialities. Beyond the interpretation of the poem, which reflects a historically specific cultural technique – that of writing with quill, ink and paper – the connection between the human subject's mind/body and the material storage in various media (manuscript, print, painting, copperplate) reveals the tension between an emerging notion of authorship and the not yet controlled storage media that are supposed to contain it. The line 'Well so, O Host, erudite and human' furthermore establishes an explicit connection with the receiver of the manuscript, the Count-Duke of Olivares, whose erudite humanity (and monumental library) will serve as a host to the workings of the singular quill contained in this material object, like the shadow cast by the olive tree on the swan, which by way of synecdoche represents the quill used to pen the poems.

The uninformed reader of this parchment page in the Chacon manuscript may draw the seemingly plausible conclusion that the poem was written by the poet in question, that is, by Góngora, as it speaks of '*my* cultivated mind' and '*my* quill'. Interestingly, this is not the case. The *octava* is signed with the initials 'A.A.M.L.' which reveal that the author of the epigram is an anonymous friend ('Amicus Anonymus'), long thought by Góngora scholars to be José Pellicer, the writer and editor of the *Lecciones Solemnes* discussed in the previous chapter (Ponce Cardenas 2013; Mariana 1991). The biography of Góngora referred to as the 'Vida Mayor' (which, since it survives in manuscript, we know was written by Pellicer, and is not to be confused with the 'Vida Menor' included in the Chacon manuscript), gives us the answer to the question of the mysterious anonymous author of this epigram: 'A grand and religious quill wrote his Life for these volumes with the title of Preface, where he legally fulfilled his duties as friend, and also dictated for his portrait that stanza that is printed in this book, without wanting to declare his name' (Góngora 1921: 307).

The only 'grand and religious quill' that could be responsible for the epigram is Fray Hortensio Felix de Paravicino y Arteaga, and, given the fact that Paravicino himself writes in a letter to Pellicer about the biography of Góngora that he has written and keeps locked up in a drawer, there can be no doubt as to the identity of the author (Iglesias Feijoo 1983). Furthermore, the term 'legally fulfilled his duties' refers to the fact that Paravicino was one of the legal executors of Góngora's will in which the latter had given him the right to publish his poetical works, a task which this manuscript would accomplish.

Pellicer's words 'dictating for the portrait' show that Paravicino in fact wrote the *octava* for Góngora's portrait; all speculations regarding portraits of the Royal Preacher himself can be dismissed by the fact that there already existed several sonnets by Paravicino to portraits made by El Greco. The issue of authorship becomes complex as it develops around various human and non-human actors, through the cultural technique of establishing that actual relation between human subject and material object. In this case, a portrait of the poet has been placed in the front matter of an exquisite calfskin parchment manuscript, under which there is an epigram giving voice to the portrait and expressing the singularity of the quill of the poet. Still, the voice that speaks for the portrait is not composed by the poet himself but by his friend who prefers to remain anonymous. The reason for Paravicino's anonymity was discussed in the previous chapter, but what is of interest here is the instability of authorship. The singularity of the poet's quill can thus not be understood in the modern sense as emanating from his soul, but rather must be considered a technical practice mastered by those who, like Góngora and Paravicino, possess ingenuity. The written text ascribes subjectivity to the author (my quill, my face, etc.) in an act of ascription that is not dependent on any pre-existing category, as is made evident by the interchangeability of the poems and their relations to human bodies.

The Stolen Face

In fact, the portrait of Góngora by van der Hamen used in the Chacon manuscript already had a sonnet dedicated to it by Góngora himself when Paravicino 'dictated […] that stanza' (assuming that he did it when composing the biography, which Pellicer's testimony indicates). In the Chacon manuscript, the sonnet from 1620 bears the informative title 'To a

Flemish painter who made the portrait from which was copied the one at the beginning of this book':

> You steal my face, and the more indebted
> To your brush, twice exceptional,
> Is the ever spirited but brief canvas,
> In the colors it greedily drinks, [the more]
>
> I fear vain ashes for the brief canvas,
> Which I imagine as an imitator of the clay,
> Upon which (be it ethereal or divine)
> A light splendour entrusted speechless life.
>
> Noble Belgian, carry on your noble theft,
> For fire will spare its material
> And time ignore its texture
>
> The centuries an oak counts on its leaves,
> The tree counts them deaf, its trunk blind;
> Who sees more, who hears more, lasts less.
>
> [Hurtas mi vulto y cuanto más le debe
> A tu pincel, dos veces peregrino,
> De espíritu vivaz el breve lino
> En los colores que sediento bebe,
>
> Vanas cenizas temo al lino breve,
> Que émulo del barro le imagino,
> A quien (ya etéreo fuese, ya divino)
> Vida le fió muda esplendor leve.
>
> Belga gentil, prosigue al hurto noble;
> Que a su materia perdonará el fuego,
> Y el tiempo ignorará su contextura.
>
> Los siglos que en sus hojas cuenta un roble,
> Árbol los cuenta sordo, tronco ciego;
> Quien más ve, quien más oye, menos dura.]
> (Góngora 2000a: 532)

This sonnet revolves around the theme of Prometheus' theft of fire and his creation of man in clay as the active forces in the cultural technique of portraiture, where the face of the poet is conceived of as 'stolen' when the thirsty canvas drinks the colours of the brush. But the material canvas is transformed by the Promethean fire into a being of flesh, just like the human body made from clay, and may therefore be consumed by the same fire that produced it, turning it into 'vain ashes', an expression of the *vanitas* motif, the idea that every living thing will ultimately be consumed by time and die. This use of use of the word 'ashes' is interesting in that it relies on an older religious and mythological discourse of death to highlight the materiality of the portrait. The cultural technique of painting is thus understood and reworked through an older discourse of sacred and mythological ashes and bones, which creates an interesting juxtaposition of bodies and material objects.

Here, life appears as a fragile and limited thing that shall leave its possessor with the passing of time. The life-giving quality of the divine fire stolen by Prometheus from Hephaestus and Athena is thereby transferred to the material object of van der Hamen's painting. The portrait has thus become so alive that it may meet the same mortal fate as any living creature. But in its second half the poem performs an about-face, encouraging the painter to carry on his noble theft, for, after all, the material of the canvas will not be consumed so easily by time; it is depicted as an oak, which is alive, but is mute, deaf and blind and will last longer than man. The contemporary commentator García Salcedo Coronel explained the significance along these lines: 'it means that although the oak lives for many centuries, in the end it is still a tree which has no senses, and whoever has them more open, which is man, will endure less: as if to say in this portrait made of senseless matter, my memory will endure longer than in the human that the colors represent' (Salcedo Coronel 1645: 246).

The portrait is thus said to perpetuate the memory of the poet precisely through its non-human longevity, assuming a position of vibrant materiality (Bennett 2010). In this conception it is the senses of man that shorten life, and by being alive yet senseless the oak and the portrait will better endure the passing of time (Lara Garrido 1987: 142). This sonnet, then, records the production of the painting as it is being produced, describing the animation of the canvas as a living entity. The poet's understanding of the cultural technique of portraiture shows how the conception of it implied a blurring of the line between human and non-human material objects. Thus the fear of the destruction of the painting by the unforgiving motion of time is confronted with the idea that the portrait is alive and that the soul of the poet has been transferred to it.

As this sonnet already existed and was included in the Chacon manuscript with reference to the portrait at the beginning of the book, Paravicino's production of a new ekphrastic poem for the same portrait should be considered a significant action that reveals a historically specific relation between human body and material object in stark contrast to modern conceptions of authorship. If the 1620 sonnet by Góngora ascribes life to the portrait by van der Hamen, but concludes that its longevity will be due to the fact that it lacks the capabilities of hearing and seeing, Paravicino's *octava* emphasises the process of animating the portrait by ascribing it voice by means of prosopopeia (ironically, the original portrait *was* eventually destroyed by fire, or perished by some other means). The frontispiece thereby becomes a collective work of art involving Góngora, Paravicino and van der Hamen, where each part is integral but movable. The complex aesthetic product of portrait and poems creates a mirror-like world where the painter looks at the poet looking back at the painter through their different media *ad infinitum*.

Adding to the mobility of the ekphrastic complex is the fact that the *octava* by Paravicino is also included in the 1630 *Lecciones Solemnes* by Pellicer. There it stands below a portrait of Góngora (see Figure 14), but this time it is not the one painted by van der Hamen but the one painted by Diego Velázquez in 1622 and then engraved for the codex by Juan de Courbes. This version of the portrait includes a personification of fame, *Fama*, who trumpets far and wide, 'your name will be heard to the limits of the world' – a quote from Góngora's poem *Polyphemus and Galatea* – and the poet is crowned with the laurel of Apollo. This laurel is not visible in the preserved original oil painting by Velázquez but appeared in radiographic scans below the first layer of paint (Marias 2012: 49). The presence of the laurel indicates that the image was intended to be included in Francisco Pacheco's book of portraits, and was perhaps later converted into an oil painting on canvas (Blanco 2004: 200).

A Book of Portraits for the Perpetuation of Memory

Velázquez's portrait of Góngora was painted just two years after van der Hamen's and was commissioned by the renowned painter and writer Francisco Pacheco, father-in-law of the young artist, who wanted to include the portrait in his *Book of Descriptions of Real Portraits of Illustrious and Memorable Men* (Pacheco 1886: 134). Pacheco's account reveals that painting the portrait of Góngora was Velázquez's first step on the way to becoming a Royal Painter, which he later did. There is thus an intimate connection between the practices of poetry and painting and the practice of power (beyond the concept of representation), in which the celebration of power becomes the celebration of art itself (Blanco 2004: 199).

Pacheco's project to compile about a hundred portraits of illustrious men while including epigrams and biographies (*vidas*) shows the prevalence of the portrait as a medium of presence. As in the case of the *Hombres Ilustres* by van der Hamen (from which the portrait of Góngora included in the Chacon manuscript was copied), and of the frontispieces in various codices, this cultural technique produced subjectivity by materially recording and storing the memory of influential actors. The book thus becomes a verbal/visual archive which ascribes subjectivity and agency to human beings. The visual representation of a human being seems to have conveyed an idea of the presence of that very person, as in the ekphrastic poems indicating how the Promethean theft will create a copy that may rival nature and become a living being. Thus the portrait of a famous poet was a matter of recording

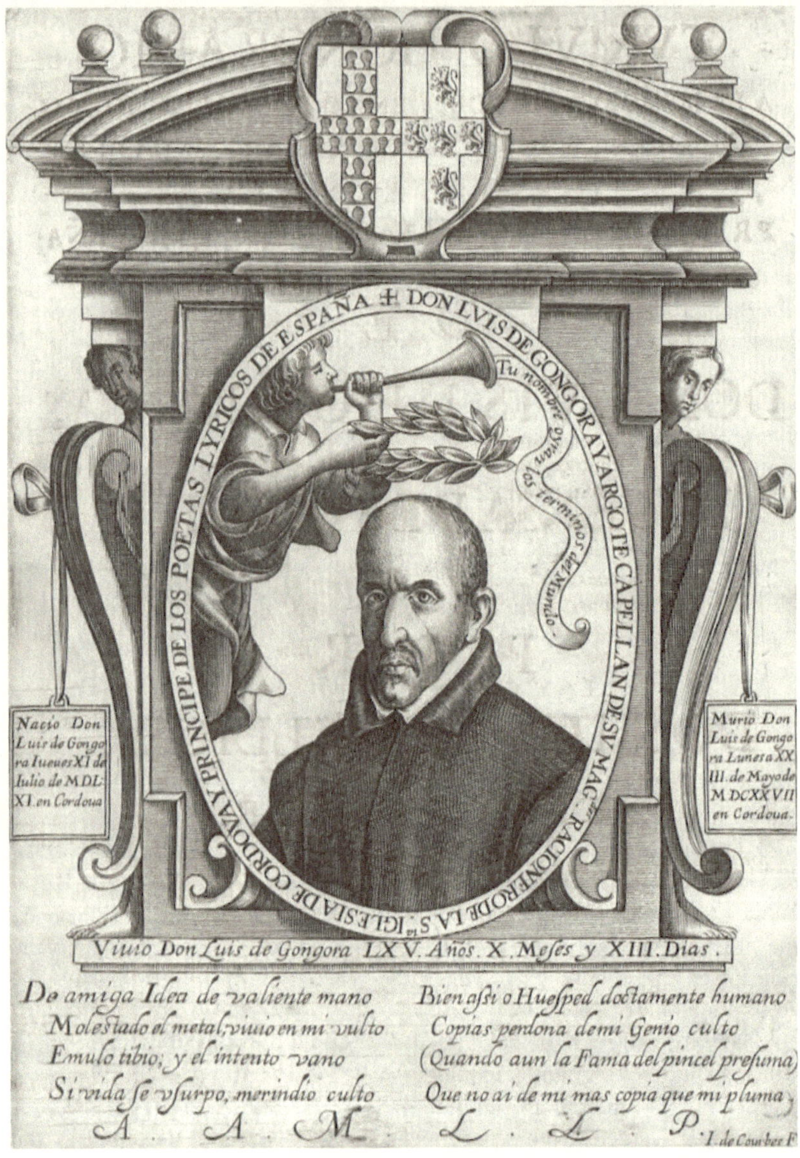

Figure 14. Portrait of Góngora in Joseph Pellicer, *Lecciones solemnes* (1630).
Source: Biblioteca Nacional de España

and immortalizing, while also constructing the human subject as author by establishing a connection between the effigy and the stored words, which were otherwise dispersed and ephemeral.

Pacheco's book project was never finished and only existed in manuscript form, which in the context of early modern Spain does not mean that it was not communicated and considered important. The manuscript opens with an elaborate frontispiece signed with the name Francisco Pacheco and the date and place, 'en Sevilla 1599', which is generally taken to be the year when the project was begun. This frontispiece, along with its overt verbal address to the reader shows that the book was intended for circulation (Pacheco 1985: 159). It would be too hasty, however, to conclude that it is only a manuscript prepared for printing. Rather, like the Chacon manuscript, the book may well have been intended to serve as a basis for later editions, but the manuscript itself was considered a medium that would find its readers in the library where it would be stored, or elsewhere by means of (duly restricted) circulation. The singularity of the object may further have increased its status, as the urge to see the 'memorable men' was great, and Pacheco thereby became the patron of a private archive or gallery.

The book contains the images of well-known poets, writers, artists and ecclesiastics, most of whom had a connection to Pacheco's home town of Seville, an important seat of intellectual life in early modern Spain. One of the portraits is that of the same father Juan de Pineda who wrote the extensive *censura* on Vicuña's edition of Góngora, a fact which testifies to the arbitrariness of the inquisitorial practice as an instrument of control. Every portrait in the book is accompanied by a biographical text (*vida*), praising the virtues of the person portrayed, and is generally followed by a verse eulogy, often directed at the portrait itself. The book is thereby constructed as a gallery and archive dedicated to the memory of these men, many of whom frequented the academies where poetry and painting were discussed (Civil 1988: 422). In this manner, Pacheco's book of illustrious men bears further resemblance to the Chacon manuscript in that the composition is similar. Both objects are manuscripts containing portraits with poetry directed at them, and the biography of Góngora referred to as the 'Vida menor' is constructed in the same manner as the biographies in Pacheco's book. The front matter of the Chacon manuscript could have fitted well into Pacheco's work, and though modern scholars have often been inclined to consider such manuscripts as a basis for printed editions, these aspects show rather that they were considered media in their own right. Collected and stored in an exquisite library, they were at least as important for any self-respecting aristocrat as an art collection. They could be taken out for reading by visitors, circulated from hand to hand and copied. The opening page of the book shows a grand architectural scene where Hercules, Julius Caesar, Hispalis (the Roman name for Seville) and Béthis (the river Guadalquivir that runs through Seville) occupy one corner each, and over them presides an allegory of *Fama* holding an illustrated book in her hand. That book could be understood as the book itself, which Pacheco hopes will gain him appropriate fame in the kingdom of Spain. By caring for the material memory of the most distinguished men, Pacheco also produces his own fame, just as Pellicer linked himself to the memory of Góngora in his *Lecciones Solemnes*.

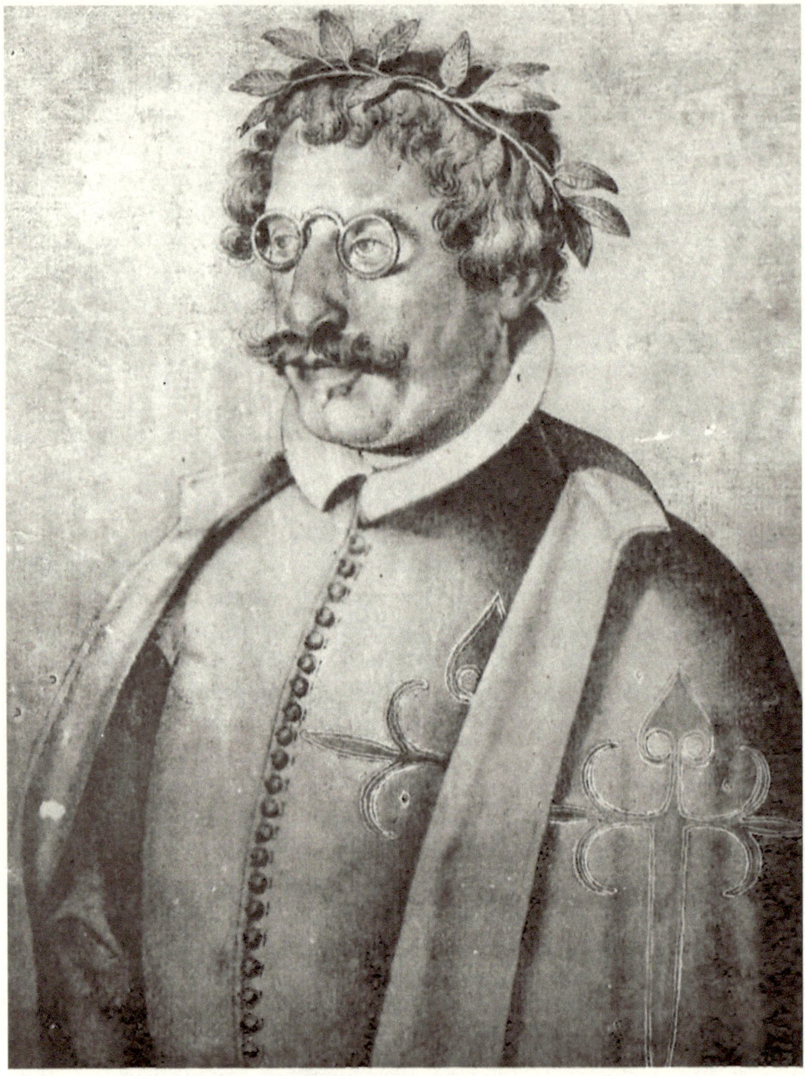

Figure 15. Portrait of Francisco de Quevedo in Francisco Pacheco, *Libro de descripción* (1886). Source: Hathi Trust

Pacheco intended to include about a hundred of his hundred and seventy portraits in black and red chalk and grey wash, along with frames, eulogies and poems for each portrait. Even though his book was never printed, it was known in Madrid and must have circulated in manuscript, and of course verbally through the different actors involved in the project (Cacho Casal 2010: 383). Pacheco asked painters, poets and scholars to contribute information, poetry and portraits to the book project, thereby making it a collective work, and large parts of the biographies were appropriated from other texts in circulation at the time (Cacho Casal 2007: 47).

One of those portrayed was Francisco de Quevedo (see Figure 15). In his famous poem *Silva to the Brush*, a poem that circulated in manuscript but was not printed until after the author's death, the poet celebrates the ability of the brush, standing metonymically for painting, to capture nature and perpetuate memory. Quevedo's poem was written at a time when the status of painting was under debate, with many commentators wishing to promote it from the level of craft to that of an art. Pacheco's book is explicitly celebrated in *Silva* by the following lines:

> For you, honour of Seville
> The learned, erudite and virtuous
> Pacheco, with a skillful pencil,
> Collects those sketches,
> Which have honoured the nations
> Without needing to confine their likeness
> To the real colors in order to be admired,
> Because from charcoal and lead
> they obtain their likeness, a soul and life.
> Second father of eminent writers,
> Since his rare drawings
> Confer on them a second being so true
> That the first does not fear death.
>
> [Por ti, honor de Sevilla
> El docto, el erudito, el virtuoso
> Pacheco, con el lapis ingenioso
> Guarda aquellos borrones
> Que honraron las naciones,
> Sin que la semejanza,
> A los colores deba su alabanza,
> Que del carbón y plomo parecida
> Reciben semejanza y alma y vida.
> Segundo padre de escritores claros,
> Pues sus dibujos raros
> Les dan segundo ser tan verdadero,
> Que no teme la muerte del primero.]
> (Quevedo 2009: 83)

Quevedo's lines here exhibit the conception of the portrait as a medium in which the material object is ascribed life and the painter becomes a creator of a human being (a second father) permitting mortal humans to live on after their death. *Silva*, which has been much commented upon, contains illuminating passages with regard to the function of painting and portraits at the time. The first lines for instance, provide the following information:

> The envy of death you remedy
> and wittily restore
> what it cruelly removes. Your are so strong,
> so mighty, that disdaining time's laws,
> and the shadows of antiquity,
> you restore, from ages long past princes,
> kings and queens, illustrious majesty and beauty,
> which, buried, flees from memory.
> Through you, arranged by you
> the living communicate with the dead.
>
> [Tu enmiendas de la muerte
> La invidia, y restituyes ingenioso
> Cuanto borra cruel. Eres tan fuerte,
> Eres tan poderoso, que en desprecio
> Del Tiempo y de sus leyes,
> Y de la antigüedad ciega y escura,
> Del seno de la edad más apartada
> Restituyes los príncipes y reyes,
> La ilustre majestad y hermosura
> Que huyó de la memoria sepultada.
> Por ti, por tus conciertos
> Comunican los vivos con los muertos.]
> (Quevedo 2009: 81)

The visual transference of a face onto a material canvas is thus seen as a cancellation of time and a perpetuation of memory, and painting becomes a cultural technique for communication and memory that can overcome the passing of time. These conceptions of early modern visual culture are important to the often-overlooked front matter. To Quevedo, the storage of the dead in material form is also a feature of the library, where he can converse with the dead. The first quatrain of his famous sonnet 'Desde la Torre' reads as follows: 'Retirado en la paz de estos desiertos, / con pocos, pero doctos libros juntos, / vivo en conversación con los difuntos / y escucho con mis ojos a los muertos'. ['Withdrawn to this solitary place, with a few but learned books, I live conversing with the dead, listening to them with my eyes' (Quevedo 2009: 56). In Quevedo's sonnet it is the 'learned press' that facilitates this peculiar conversation with the dead, in which he listens to the authors of the past with his eyes. The material object of the book is here perceived as a means of storage that can overcome the passing of time and the absence of physical bodies.

The title of Pacheco's book contains important information with regard to the scope of the project. Pacheco aims to show 'real' portraits of 'memorable men', evincing an intention to overcome the inevitable passing of time and the dead into oblivion. By supplying a 'real' visual portrait and a summary of the most important facts of the life of the person portrayed, along with the appropriate verses, Pacheco produces a material memory that he hopes will overcome unforgiving time. The difficulty of this aim is often reflected in the poetry, especially when it is directed at the portrait itself.

One of the first portraits in the book is that of Louis of Granada, a Dominican friar who rose to fame for his orations and writings during the latter half of the sixteenth century. Pacheco portrays him from the side, dressed in his Dominican vestments and with an appropriately religious air about him. After the biography, which details the circumstances of his life and writings, there is a sonnet dedicated to the portrait by Don Juan Infante de Olivares:

> You, who of the Laurel,
> and always green Grass,
> like a triumphant of the glorious city
> interwoven with one, and another Rose,
> envelopes your forehead in extended Fame;
>
> shine then, over the flowering branch of the firm trunk,
> where thus rests, with voice and feather,
> the scentful matter; being reborn of the flame.
>
> Two times immortal, two times I see
> Pacheco work on your perfections,
> and in these and always I admire you;
>
> If a Master of all, with excesses
> of light superior in elevated stars:
> then in this effigy, in flesh and hard bones.
>
> [Tu, que del Lauro, i siempre verde Grama,
> Cual triumfador de la Ciudad gloriosa,
> Entretexida de una, i otra Rosa,
> Ciñes la frente en dilatada Fama;
>
> Ilustra pues, la floreciente rama
> Del firme tronco, donde assi reposa
> Con la voz i la pluma, la olorosa
> Materia; renaciendo de la llama.

Dos vezes immortal, dos vezes miro
Ocuparse Pacheco en tus progresos,
I esas mesmas i mas siempre te admiro;

Si Maestro de todos, con excesos
De luz superior en alto giro:
Si en esta efigie, en carne i duros guesos.]
(Pacheco 1985)

After praising his extended *fama* with reference to the laurel crown (which is not in the portrait), Olivares creates an image of the deceased subject as being reborn through an extension of the laurel tree, in which Granada is said to rest on a branch, and then, as the Phoenix, with its voice and its feather (also referring to the voice and quill of Granada himself by association), is reborn through the flame. The word *olorosa* further refers to the smell of incense associated with the Phoenix. In this way, Granada becomes 'two times immortal' through the workings of Pacheco, in the visual portrait and in the words accompanying it. The last line then proceeds to describe the portrait as being made in flesh and hard bone. Thus the animated conception of the material object as a living entity is active here as well. To the early modern reader/viewer, this is not a just trope or a metaphor but rather something real and physical, as it is connected to divine creation (Bray 2009). If God creates nature through a divine idea, and then gives it form, the painter (that is, the Promethean thief) gives life to the canvas by transferring, or copying, life onto it. This can be hard to imagine today, in a visual culture where images are abundant, but the portrait of a human being around 1600 was conceived of as magical, inasmuch as it could store something absent in material form.

An interesting example of the concept of portraiture as perpetuation of memory is found in the case of the Andalusian poet Baltasar de Alcázar. Pacheco was a friend and admirer of Alcazar, and his biography recounts the life of a Renaissance man full of virtues and talents, ranging from languages to painting, from astronomy to poetry, passing through the secrets of nature, stones and metals, as well as geography. Alcázar seems to have possessed the quality of an *ingenio* to perfection in the author's view, being an admired poet but also learned in other skills. Pacheco opens his euology by stating that Philip II should have been as glad as the Emperor Augustus, who saw Virgil and Horace during his reign, for seeing Alcázar during his. Pacheco was also the editor of Alcázar's work after the poet's death, so his short biography gives an interesting testimony of the circulation of poetry in the medium of manuscript. 'The things that this illustrious man did live on by my diligence: because every time I visited him he wrote something down that he kept in the treasury of his lively memory' (Pacheco 1985: 120). Pacheco collected the poetry of Alcázar by asking him to recite it so he could take notes, whenever he visited him. Just as in the case of Góngora, the poetry seems to have been conceived as stored first in the human memory of the poet and thereafter recorded in the material storage container of the manuscript conducted by the aficionados who came into contact with him. According to Pacheco, Alcazar's accomplishments *live on* because they are recorded and stored appropriately, and are therefore exempt from oblivion and death. Alcázar's section of the book ends with a few lines by the poet Juan de Jáuregui directed at the portrait by Pacheco, lines in which the poet discerns the storing of the memory of Alcázar: 'thus in Pacheco's lines we see the reiteration of your being [...] in your image you become eternal, because he could eternalise you'. These lines insist on the repetition of Alcázar's being in the material form of the portrait where it becomes 'perpetual', which seems to be the explicit aim of the project. Pacheco has thereafter inserted a few lines by his own hand, directed at the portrait he has painted:

> If to imitate your glory
> I tried, Alcazar, in vain
> it is enough that my hand
> could extend your memory:
> and it is no small victory
> to have managed,
> by means of Art to
> defeat time's oblivion:
> may the sharp and singular *ingenio*
> celebrated in songs,
> Apollo, your glorious name.
>
> [Si de imitaros la gloria
> Procure, Alcázar, en vano,
> Basta que pudo mi mano
> Estender vuestra memoria:
> Y no es pequeño victoria
> Haber con l'Arte podido
> Vencer del tiempo el olvido:
> El ingenio agudo y solo
> Celebre cantando Apolo
> Vuestro nombre esclarecido.]
> (Pacheco 1985: 120)

Pacheco expresses how he used his hand to 'extend the memory' of Alcázar, thus 'vanquishing the oblivion of time' by means of art. This conception of the materiality of painting runs through many of the verses dedicated to portraits; portraiture is understood as a production of memory by means of storage in material form. Baltasar de Alcázar also dedicated poetry to the portrait of Pacheco that is not included in the book. Alcázar's verses are interesting in that they make explicit the connection between the divine and artistic creation that underlies this conception of the portrait as an animated object:

> With artificious quill
> he takes man out of his tomb,
> giving him life and fame,
> so that time will not destroy him.
> And so without equal he uses
> the office of God, to the effect
> that the one power
> is divided between both …
> And so it is not of a human intent
> what Pachecho paints for us;
> of another distinct matter it is
> of celestial foundations.
> Thus with invincible skill,
> to what is spiritual,
> giving it a lifelike portrait,
> he forms a visible body.
>
> [Con artificiosa pluma
> Saca del sepulcro al hombre,
> Dándole vida y renombre,
> Qu' el tiempo no lo consuma.
> Y así sin igual alguno
> Usa el oficio de Dios,
> Por estar entre los dos
> Partido el poder del uno.
> Y así no es de humano intento
> Lo que Pacheco nos pinta;
> De otra materia es distinta
> De celestial fundamento.
> Pues con destreza invencible
> Lo qu' es espiritual,
> Dándole retrato igual,
> Le forma cuerpo visible.
> (Alcazar 1910: 224)

In Alcázar's conception of the portrait, it presupposes a divine act of raising the dead from their tombs and giving them a second eternal life on earth. Pachecho uses 'the office of God' to produce something that is in the material world but is based on 'celestial foundations'. This conception goes back to the Neo-Platonic view of the natural world as the material form of God's divine idea; hence the painter resembles him in creating an animated material object based on the idea itself. It can be understood as an inversion of the medieval topos of *Deus Pictor*, in which the cultural technique of portraiture is granted a divine status that might serve to legitimise it.

This Christian view of the production of a portrait runs parallel to the mythological one expressed through the figure of Prometheus in Góngora and Paravicino's poems. While such an ability to produce a second copy of the divine creation is often praised, it also produces an ambiguity, as it can be understood as hubris, or an attempt to compete with God.

A Soul Lost Between Two Bodies: Paravicino and El Greco

The Royal Preacher Fray Hortensio Paravicino, who wrote the *octava* for the portrait of Góngora in the Chacon manuscript, also dedicated several sonnets to the art of his friend Domenikos Theotokopoulos, better known as El Greco (to whose tomb Góngora also dedicated a sonnet, discussed in the next chapter). Very little is known of the relationship between the Trinitarian Paravicino, the most famous preacher of the period, and the Cretan painter. The historical sources consist of little more than the two (or three) portraits El Greco painted of Paravicino, and the five sonnets the latter dedicated to the former (Cerdan 2013: 5). Around 1609 El Greco painted the more famous of the two portraits of Paravicino (see Figure 16), a painting that today is considered one of his most important. It has been described as the climax of El Greco's art and one of the most important portraits in art history (Jordan 1982: 201). El Greco is known for painting portraits where the sitter seems alive, and the one of Paravicino is a deeply sympathetic one, where the preacher and poet looks up from his chair holding two books – the smaller a book of poetry and the larger a work of scholastic theology – indicating the sitter's dual passions for poetry and preaching (Blanco 2012c: 30).

In this portrait, El Greco employed the full-length portraiture used by Raphael and Titian, in which the chair creates a frame around the body of the sitter, thus confronting the viewer with an interesting frontal perspective. Although the sitter is naturally still, the perspective created by the chair (whose upper line is at the height of the eyebrows) and the lively strokes of the brush create a sensation of movement that is characteristic of El Greco's style. This sense of movement in the portrait is precisely what animates it and gives the viewer a sense of physical presence.

> To the same Greek who painted the portrait of the author
>
> Divine Greek, do not be surprised at your work,
> for in [your] images, art surpasses being,
> but rather at heaven, for taking back,
> while sparing you, the life bestowed by your brush.

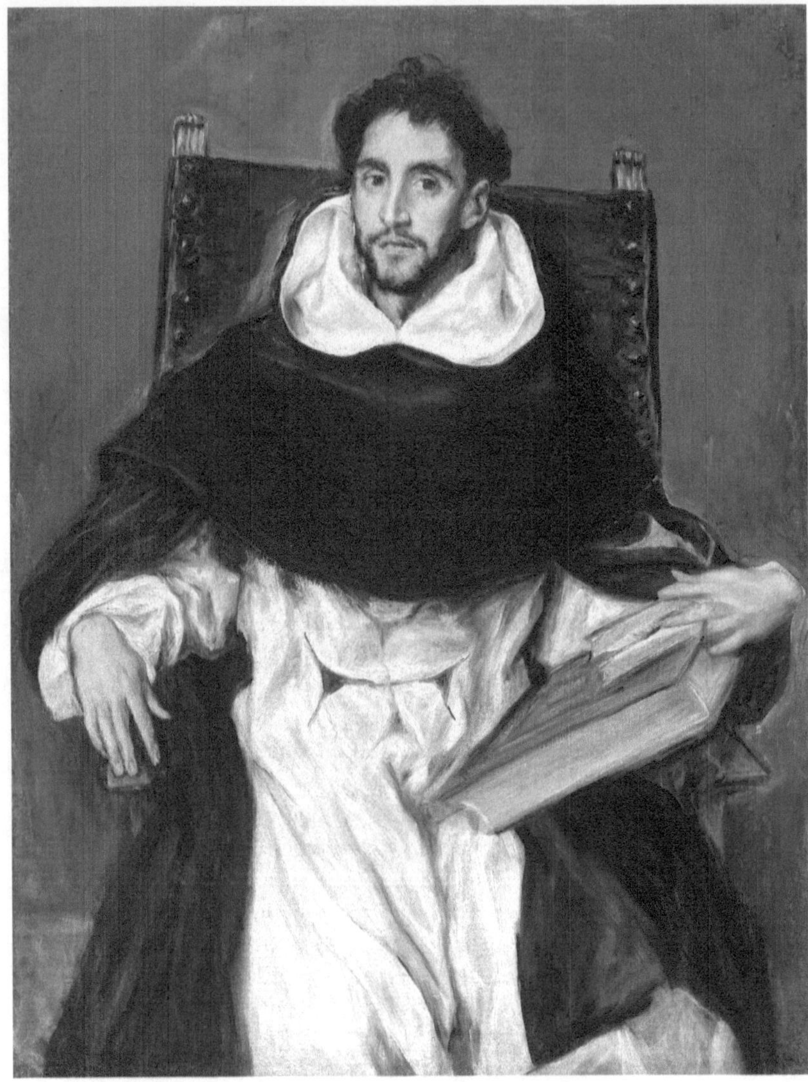

Figure 16. El Greco, *Portrait of Fray Hortensio Felix de Paravicino* (1609). Source: Wikimedia Commons

The sun does not spin through the heavenly sphere
as on your canvas, you just have to persist
to appear like God; let Nature enter
only to watch as she is overcome.

O rival of Prometheus, in your portraiture,
do not affect fire, leave that vital theft,
which grants such being even to my soul,

For with its twenty-nine years of life,
between your hand and God's, it stands perplexed,
not knowing in which body it should dwell.

[Divino Griego, de tu obrar no admira
Que en la imagen exceda al ser el arte,
Sino que della el cielo, por templarte,
La vida deuda a tu pincel retira.

No el sol sus rayos por su esfera gira
Como en tus lienzos, basta el empeñarte
En amagos de Dios, entre a la parte
Naturaleza, que vencerse mira.

Émulo de Prometeo en un retrato,
No afectes lumbre, el hurto vital deja,
Que hasta mi alma a tanto ser ayuda.

Y contra veintinueve años de trato,
Entre tu mano, y al de Dios, perpleja,
Cuál es el cuerpo en que ha de vivir duda.]
(Cerdan 2013: 8)

When Paravicino dedicated a sonnet to this portrait he focussed on its aspects of physical presence and liveliness. Some critics have commented on the conceit of the portrait as a living entity and the associated religious and mythological topoi (Bergmannn 1979; Lara Garrido 1987). But even if the painting is considered as a translation of the soul of the sitter to the canvas, it should not be forgotten that the conception of the soul of the human body appeared as something real in which most people believed beyond doubt.

The sonnet is based on the idea that the portrait is so alive that the sitter himself is in doubt over which body is his, the one made by God's hand or the one made by El Greco's hand. It revolves around the connections between being, image, art and nature. From the first quatrain, Paravicino expresses his ambivalence about the copying of the human body onto a material canvas. The first half of the sonnet alludes to the possible hubris involved in acting like God by creating a living entity. In the second half, the motif of Prometheus is introduced, in a manner reminiscent of Góngora's poem to his portrait. But where Góngora encourages the painter to carry on the 'noble theft', Paravicino is more doubtful and asks the painter to stop the 'vital theft', as it threatens to tear his soul apart. The last tercet expresses how after twenty-nine years of life on earth, his soul will no longer know whether it should inhabit his body of flesh created by God or the body created by El Greco in the portrait. These assertions coming from a Royal Preacher should be understood as the expression of a physical experience as well as a brilliant display of mythological and aesthetic concepts. The experience of the singularity of the soul caught in doubt is thereby expressed by the insertion of the portrait in the natural and divine order, which somehow produced it.

This concept of the portrait is quite distant from the Neo-Platonic theory of the physical world as a shadow of divine ideas, where the painter only creates a different expression of the original idea (Lara Garrido 1987: 137). Painting is understood as emulation of nature, and of divine creation, in that it uses the powers of God to affect the order of the world. It is this act of defiance of God's supremacy that links the painter to Prometheus in his theft of the divine fire to give life to the figure created from clay. At the same time, however, Prometheus is considered the real God in having made man from clay and given him life by the divine breath of air. As the contemporary mathematician and mythographer Juan Pérez de Moya put it in his *Secret Philosophy of the Pagan Gods*: 'The fire he brought from heaven, with which he gave being to the statue he had formed is the divine fire or animation which God gave to man. Therefore Prometheus means the allmighty God who created the world and man from nothing' (Moya 1977: 250). These early modern concepts of vital materiality are at stake in the poetic description of the portrait as an object animated through the cultural technique of painting. In this complicated relation between human and non-human, the portrait may be as active as a human subject, fostering a better understanding of the function of these objects in actual spaces during this period. This experience is linked to the religious sphere in which relics and other objects are understood to possess magical powers and are arranged to convey presence effects.

Like Góngora, Paravicino never printed his poetry and it circulated from hand to hand in manuscript. Only after his death was an edition printed, and according to modern philologists large parts of this edition are of doubtful attribution (Cerdan 2013: 6). Even today his poetry lacks a critical edition and must be understood as having existed in variants in different manuscripts, one of which was compiled by Francisco Pacheco, the author of *Libro de Retratos*, in which a hitherto unknown sonnet by Paravicino dedicated to El Greco was recently discovered. It is no coincidence that this particular sonnet was copied into Pacheco's manuscript, since he was working on his book of portraits for most of his career. While not explicitly dedicated to a portrait it should be read along with the four other sonnets by Paravicino directed to El Greco:

> Titiro the superior genius of Apelles
> sole artificer of the rival to Achilles,
> asked Phidias to borrow the copperplates
> and he took the points from Lisippus.

And in jealousy of the Greek's brushes
he entered deeply in his subtle efforts
thus correcting the profiles of a thousand centuries
of linen, canvas, bronze, marble, and parchment.

Here the myth becomes real, and here that
fatal disquietude of heaven will find
a sure Atlas for its pure lights.

So if Nature gets tired
of her continuous work, El Greco could
help her in bringing forth creatures.

[Títiro, el genio superior de Apeles,
Solo artífice al émulo de Aquiles,
Pidió a Fidias prestados los buriles
Y le usurpó a Lisipo los cinceles.

E invidiando del Griego los pinceles,
En sus esfuerzos se infundió sutiles,
Corrigiendo a mil siglos los perfiles
De linos, leños, bronces, mármol, pieles.

Aquí es verdad la secta, y aquí hallara
Del cielo ese fatal desasosiego
Seguro Atlante de sus lumbres puras.

Pues si Naturaleza se cansara
De tan contino obrar, pudiera el Griego
Ayudarle a sacar las criaturas.]
(Cerdan 2013: 8)

The sonnet opens with references to Greek antiquity, alluding to El Greco's geographical origin and cultural heritage. El Greco is then compared to Apelles, the only painter allowed to paint the portrait of Alexander the Great, here referred to as 'rival to Achilles' (because he was as unbeatable as the mythological hero) and to the most famous sculptors of Greek antiquity, Phidias and Lisippus. Paravicino then goes on to dwell on the technique of El Greco's painting as supporting the constantly moving heavenly sphere, just as Atlas, according to myth, supported it. The image of the heavenly sphere resting on the shoulders of Atlas and El Greco is eloquently transferred to the cultural technique of painting as dependent on tools and surfaces, which precede the abstract concept of the image they produce. El Greco, in Paravicino's poetical rendering, improves the world through his brush on canvas, wood, bronze, marble or parchment, making the natural world freeze

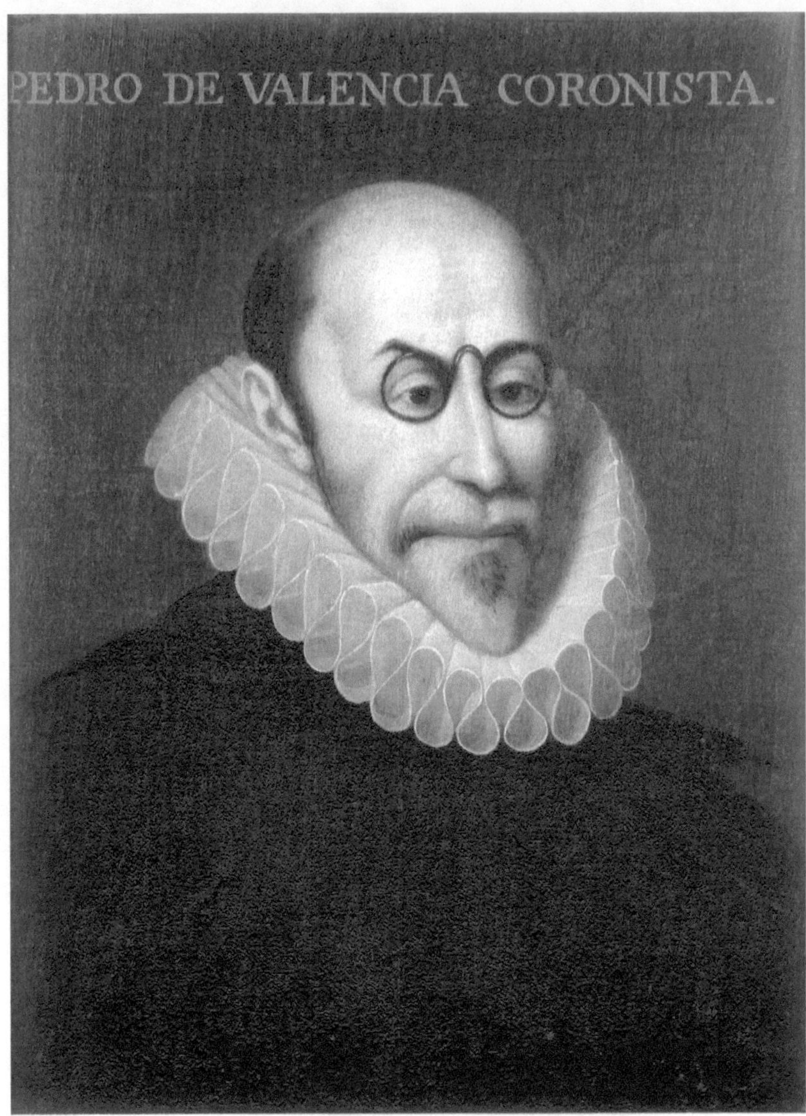

Fig. 17. Anonymous, *Portrait of Pedro de Valencia*. Source: Wikimedia Commons.

in time and become eternal. These extensive references to material support reveal the conception of art as producing presence in the physical world. The final tercet concludes with the assertion that if nature gets tired of 'working' (*obrar*, also referring to God's work), El Greco can help it produce creatures. This is the same concept of El Greco as an emulator of God that runs through the sonnet to the portrait, which opens precisely with 'Divine Greek, at your work'. Paravicino also wrote a sonnet to the portrait of Pedro de Valencia (see

Figure 17), the humanist who was the first commentator of Góngora's *Soledades* and who helped him improve the poem:

> This truth exhaling in worn out colors
> entrusting eternities to the canvas
> is a theft from death, as much as
> to the day of virtue, a lasting dawn.
>
> A relic it is, not a copy of that burning
> sun of sciences, which in cold shadow,
> splendidly pleasant, challenges the
> constant sameness of the origin itself.
>
> Great Valencia, it is not the brave brush of Philip,
> which animates your illustrious face but your genius,
> so efficient in its very idea.
>
> You always live by yourself, always present
> you will last through every century, in every climate
> Oh, let Spain last and see such glory!
>
> [Esta en caducas tintas espirante
> Verdad, que al lino eternidades fía,
> Tanto a la muerte es hurto, cuanto al día
> De la virtud crepúsculo durante.
>
> Reliquia es, no copia del flamante
> Sol de las ciencias, que entre sombra fría,
> Soberbiamente grata, desafía
> Del mismo origen la igualdad constante.
>
> Valencia grande, no el pincel valiente
> De Filipo, tu bulto ilustre anima
> Tu genio, si eficaz aun en su idea.
>
> Siempre vives por ti, siempre presente
> Serás a todo siglo, a todo clima.
> ¡Oh, dure España y tanta gloria vea!]
> (Cerdan 2013: 10)

In this sonnet Paravicino conceives of the painting not as a living entity but as a sacred relic of the deceased Valencia. It can thereby be understood as a variation on the previously discussed takes on the animation of the material object. In Góngora's sonnet the poet fears the death of the living portrait but concludes that it will live on like an oak as it lacks the human senses that shorten life, while in Paravicino's sonnet to El Greco's portrait the preacher's soul is caught in doubt over whether to inhabit his carnal body or the portrait. Here, the portrait is already a relic, understood as the sacred remains of a holy person. In this sense, a physical relation is established between object and human body. It is the *genio* of Valencia that lives on through the painting, and by extension his memory, which, in defying the original similarity, is even better than nature itself.

The use of the religious concept of the relic to understand the materiality of the painting is specific to this era in Spain where secularization was taking place in the sphere of art. It can be understood as a tendency with two directions. On the one hand, it may operate as a means of elevating the status of painting, an issue that was much debated during this time. On the other hand, and more importantly perhaps, it testifies to a 'secular' use of sacred terms for a new concept of the materiality of art and poetry alike. The recurring references to material support reveal a historically specific understanding of art and poetry as an intervention in the natural order. They are evoked as cultural techniques capable of overcoming the problem of absence and death in ephemeral human life. This is evident from the *vanitas mundi* topos, where skulls, bones and ashes are juxtaposed with tools like pens, clocks and globes. These objects are not only metaphorical but also actual and physical.

Paravicino's conception of the portrait as a relic can furthermore be understood as a poetical rendering of the physical experience of the material object as possessing supernatural or divine power. As Paravicino was the most famous preacher of his time and certainly believed in the power of relics, this sonnet should be understood as having been produced under a discursive order in which the materiality of the painting is more than just the support of its content. Like a relic, it possessed magical powers and produced presence effects on its viewer, who, like the pilgrims coming to the reliquary of a church, felt that they had come into contact with the physical effects of the object. Rather than explaining its inherent meaning, Paravicino uses poetry to convey this specific physical presence of the object.

Keeping the Object Close to the Heart: the Miniature Portrait

The practice of dedicating poetry to portraits was thus widespread in early modern Spain, and in many cases the poems can be understood as an investigation of the ontic operations and ontological status of the object in question. This practice can be traced to their increased presence in the aristocratic milieu of the era. Around 1609, Góngora dedicated a cycle of no less than thirteen poems to the Marquis of Ayamonte, at whose estate he spent a few months in search of support and patronage. The poems' implicit aim is to praise the Marquis, but they all revolve around historically specific events taking place rather than the noble bloodline of the subject. Three of the sonnets are dedicated to the frustrated voyage of the Marquis and his wife to Nueva España, today Mexico, where he was to serve as Viceroy of the Spanish Empire. The trip across the Atlantic never took place, as the Marquise decided that she did not want to leave Spain. Those poems all focus on ships and the drama of the ocean expressed through mythological references. One of the sonnets, however, is dedicated to the portrait of the Marquis' wife, which he showed to the poet when he was passing through Córdoba in 1606:

Illustrious Marquis, two times illustrious,
by your blood and by your intellect
illustrious two times more, and another hundred
by the light, you generously show me

of the two suns offered by the most exquisite brush
from their luminous firmament
to your illustrious bosom (boldness
that, even ending in ashes, would not seem too costly).

What blessed eagle, lord,
ever penetrated the region of her beauty
to copy for you the shining rays of her forehead?

Feeding your eyes on painting
at night you walk, illuminated
night which hardly could be dark with two suns.

[Clarísimo Marqués, dos veces claro,
Por vuestra sangre y vuestro entendimiento,
Claro dos veces otras, y otras ciento
Por la luz, de que no me sois avaro,

De los dos soles que el pincel más raro
Dio de su luminoso firmamento
A vuestro seno ilustre (atrevimiento
Que aun en cenizas no saliera caro);

¿Qué aguila, señor, dichosamente
La región penetró de su hermosura
Por copiaros los rayos de su frente?

Cebado vos los ojos de pintura,
En noche camináis, noche luciente,
Que mal será con dos soles obscura.]
(Góngora 2000a: 243)

The poetic eulogy records specific events: in this case the reaction of the poet when shown a portrait. It also testifies to the practice of the portrait as a visual medium of communication. The poet, who had not met the Marquise, was able through the stored image of her on a material surface that was small enough to wear, to get an impression of her physical presence. The circumstance of the composition of the poem shows that the portrait in question must have been a miniature portrait (Ponce Cardenas 2013: 145). To be specific, according to the sonnet, it must have been carried in a necklace, lying on the chest of the Marquis, close to his heart.

The miniature portrait was popular in the early modern era, and the practice of carrying such material objects close to the body was widespread. They appear as agents in several dramatic works of the time, such as those of Calderón, Tirso de Molina, and Shakespeare. In Quevedo's sonnet 'Portrait of Lisi on a Ring', the poet has encapsulated the whole universe in a miniature portrait of his beloved placed on a gold ring. Sor Juana Inés de la Cruz also wrote a poem to a miniature portrait on a ring: 'On a Ring She Portrayed the Countess of Paredes'. As has been shown by Patricia Fumerton, the miniature portrait played an important part in the most intimate of political affairs (Fumerton 1991: 67). When introduced around 1560, miniature portraits were often kept in bedrooms or private chambers, and showing them was a most intimate affair, conveyed only to a person one could trust. In time they began to be worn in gold lockets as a necklace. This is why the Marquis showing the portrait to Góngora was an event worthy of recording in a sonnet, as it was a symbolic practice establishing the connection and intimacy between the two. By describing and praising the miniature portrait, the poet simultaneously describes his intimate connection with the Marquis, whose protection and favour he hopes to obtain.

Such miniature portraits were usually painted in oil on copper, or sometimes on silver, bronze, or wood (Colomer 2002: 65). They were small enough to hold in the palm of a hand, and carry close to the body, in a necklace or otherwise, which seems to have been their main purpose. The miniature portrait was associated with affection, memory, and presence, in a more intimate manner than larger official portraits. They were also highly valued, as an anecdote of Queen Elizabeth I of England reveals; when asked to give away one of her miniature portraits portraying the Earl of Leicester to her half-sister Mary, who was supposed to marry him, she refused and would rather give her a ruby the size of a tennis ball (Fumerton 1991: 70).

Góngora's sonnet employs poetical discourse to verbally record and magnify the presence effect of this miniature portrait of Ana Felix de Zuñiga y Sotomayor, wife of Francisco de Gúzman, Marquise of Ayamonte. The first quatrain establishes the theme of light that runs through the whole composition. The splendour of the Marquis, through his noble blood and through his enlightened mind, is then transferred in the second quatrain to the classical (Petrarchan) image of the eyes of the beloved as two suns.

This transfer happens precisely through the demonstration of the miniature portrait, whose light is 'generously' shown to the poet. The second quatrain then turns to the painter who dared to come close enough to these two shining suns to capture them. This reference to the myth of Phaethon, who dared to ride the chariot of the sun to prove he was the son of Zeus, but lost control of it and was struck by a thunderbolt, represents the painter as having risked being burnt to ashes when 'stealing' the glowing suns from their 'original firmament' of the face, which is also a reference to the Promethean theft, present in several poetic conceptions of the cultural technique of portraiture discussed above.

The painter has transferred these glowing suns to the 'bosom' of the Marquis, a direct reference to his keeping the material object close to his body, in a necklace. The subsequent tercet is constructed as a rhetorical question in which an eagle, which was believed to be the only bird that could look into the sun, has penetrated this region of her beauty to 'copy the rays of her forehead'. The poet thus insists, through expanded mythological and hyperbolic imagery, that the painting of a portrait was a courageous, or even dangerous, act of copying. This peril also stems from the risk of commiting an act in defiance of God. In the last tercet, Góngora uses the syntactical rephrasing called hyperbaton (by the use of the Greek accusative form), to be able to say that the Marquis aliments or feeds – *cebar* – his eyes with the painting. Unusual as this expression may seem, it creates a striking image of the lover looking with a trance-like gaze at the magical material object that suggests the essence of his loved one. It also ascribes both ontological and grammatical agency to the object, which feeds the eyes. Finally, the Marquis can proceed through the dark night in the illumination from the shining portrait, an instance of the *chiaroscuro* technique that is frequent in Góngora's poetics (Deleuze 1991: 45). Showing the miniature portrait to the poet was in a sense letting his eyes feed on the Marquis's beloved (and to some extent a homosocial act). The viewing itself becomes an intimate and coded practice, producing physical effects of presence on the human being. Once decoded, the sonnet can thus be read as a testimony of the physical effect of the material object on the human subject, where the line between active and passive is thoroughly blurred.

Diego de Silva y Mendoza, Count of Salinas and Viceroy of Portugal between 1616 and 1622, was another highly esteemed aristocratic poet who never printed any of his poems. The cousin of King Philip III, through his noble descent he acquired an influential position in the Spanish Empire. Góngora visited him in 1604 and dedicated a couple of sonnets to his estate in Ribera del Duero. Like Paravicino and Conde de Villamediana, the Conde de Salinas admired Góngora's poetry and cultivated a personal relationship with him. These poems circulated solely in manuscript and were generally written within the Court, where poetical skill became a hallmark of power and influence. In manuscript 17.719, known as *Cancionero de Mendes Brito*, now held in the collection of the National Library of Spain, there have been copied three sonnets dedicated to a specific portrait. The title of this manuscript is 'To the portrait of the Duchess of Hijar, his daughter-in-law, that was sent to him in Portugal, before she married his son':

> Copied caregiving power,
> I have faith in you; if love I could give you,
> the same love would avenge you for
> a vivid silence and a painted hearing.
>
> It would not be alike nor a copy
> if what causes sentiment, sentiments would have;
> but it would talk, listen and respond
> if the highly regarded must be courteous.
>
> I only recover with great damage,
> because love is born blind among colors,
> adoring a delicious folly.
>
> I drink the very thirst in the remedy
> which coded in itself stones and flowers;
> I get lost all the more in being shown the way.
>
> [Trasladado poder de dar cuidado,
> Yo fe te doy; si amor darte supiera,
> El mismo amor vengado me tuviera
> De un callar vivo y de un oir pintado.
>
> No fuera parecido ni traslado
> Si lo que da a sentir, sentir pudiera;
> Mas hablara, escuchara y respondiera
> Si es que ha de ser cortés el bien mirado.
>
> Sólo con mayor daño me remedio,
> Pues ciego nace amor entre colores,
> Adorando un sabroso desatino.
>
> Bebo la misma sed en el remedio
> Que cifró en sí las piedras y las flores;
> Piérdome más mostrándome al camino.]
> (Ms. 17.719: f. 237v)

A portrait of the Count of Salinas's prospective daughter-in-law had been sent from Madrid to Portugal in order to confirm the future alliance between the two families. The tradition of having the parent accept the son or daughter-in-law was thereby arranged by means of a material object that acted as a substitute of the living person, to whom the father replied by writing sonnets. As with the miniature portrait of the Marquise of Ayamonte shown to Góngora, the material object is here understood to convey the physical presence of an absent person. In this sonnet the poet celebrates the almost magical power of the portrait to convey a presence that confuses. The power of this material copy leaves him in a 'vivid silence and painted hearing' as he enters into dialogue with it and imagines how it would interact. The second quatrain revolves around the object's lack of senses, another variation of the trope expressed through the image of the oak in Góngora's 'To a Flemish Painter'. As it triggers a sensory reaction in the viewer, it should be able to use its own senses, transforming into a living object able to talk, listen and respond. This sonnet is further testimony to the early modern concept of the vital materiality of the portrait, which is able to convey the presence of a human being. It is not understood as a mere representation, but rather material agency of nonhuman things (Bennett 2010).

The Fragility of Life and the Capacity of Storage

The Conde de Villamediana, another nobleman whose poetry circulated solely in manuscript until his death, and who was also an associate of Góngora and part of this network, dedicated two sonnets to a portrait and one to its painter. His take on the theme is quite Neo-Platonic; and the portrait the sonnets are dedicated to is that of his beloved: 'in this the weakness of art is evident with life and death so painted, rather offended than beautiful' (Rozas 1965: 56). In his account, art fails to store the presence of a human being, as the only true portrait of the beloved is the dawn itself. The first verses read:

> These that I see are certainly offenses,
> made to your high perfections,
> because they do not fit anywhere but in hearts
> where Cupid paints them; in mine I read them.
>
> Art never equals a great desire
> and so what is offered is only a draft
>
> Ofensas son por cierto éstas que veo,
> hechas a vuestras altas perfecciones,
> porque no caben sino en corazones,
> donde las pinta Amor; en mi las leo.
>
> El arte nunca iguala un gran deseo,
> y, así, cuanto aquí ofrecen son borrones.
> (Rozas 1965: 56)

This sonnet is more conventional in its conception of the portrait, but the theme of time and death is still present. The first lines of the second sonnet read: 'These that I see are certainly offenses, made to your high perfections, because they do not fit anywhere but in hearts where Cupid paints them; in mine I read them. Art never equals a great desire and so what is offered is only a draft'. In this conception the portrait is a failed attempt, but not as in previous cases because of the demiurgical aspect of the lady but because of the inability of the material object to equal the sentiment of the lover/poet. Nevertheless, the word *borrones* is revealing of the conception. It usually refers to a written draft on paper, frequently used by Góngora in his letters to describe the state of his poetry in manuscript, and also in Quevedo's poem to Pacheco discussed above. As the *borrones* are imperfect material versions of the poems read aloud or kept in the physical memory of the poet (*borrar* means to erase), so the portrait becomes an imperfect copy of an absent original. As discussed in the previous chapter, the poetry frequently existed in variants, due to extensive copying from manuscript to manuscript, but also because poets constantly reworked and changed their poems (Dadson 2012: 77). The complex configuration of material storage was thus present in poetry and painting alike. The perpetuation of memory, as a means of overcoming the passage of time leading to the death of the human body, was the problematic promise of these media objects. The sonnet by Villamediana is itself an example of this process; the lines cited above come from the Mendes Britto Manuscript, the same codex that contained the poem by the Conde de Salinas quoted above, but in a later version from another manuscript the poem has changed. Ironically, in this version the word *borrones* has been replaced by *razones*, Amor is writing instead of painting in the heart of the lover, and Art is no longer merely unequal to desire but firmly vanquished by it. The last line of the quoted version of the sonnet expresses how the beloved is herself 'the most perfect portrait made by God', whereas the later version has omitted the divine presence in favour of an original portrait painted in the heart of the lover by the hand of the beloved (Tassis y Peralta 1969: 114). Interestingly, the human being in the first version of the poem is understood in a Neo-Platonic manner as a portrait made by God, the essence of which is an idea, while the second version is focussed on the physical presence and traces of sentiments in the human body. These alterations can be read as the transition from a Neo-Platonic worldview to one focussed on presence and materiality.

In a sonnet dedicated to a painter, Villamediana developed his view of the ability of painting to animate the material object and to overcome oblivion:

> Do not only admire that your hand defeats
> the matter of being with which it admires,
> but that Art in its lying
> can condemn truth itself to shame,

whose miracle of discovery begins
in the bravery of the lines drawn up,
an ingenious parallel by which the
wrath of time today turns to oblivion.

Reason deems it a lifeless thing,
where persuaded delusion
idolises feigning as if it were true.

O miracle of Art, that has been able,
conferring voice and movement to a canvas,
to leave it with sentiment bereft of him.

[No solo admira, que tu mano venza
El ser de la materia con que admira,
Sino que pueda el Arte en la mentira
A la misma verdad hacer verguenza,

Cuyo milagro a descubrir comienza
En el valor con que las lineas tira
Paralelo capaz con que la ira
Del tiempo hoy del olvido se convenza.

Tener cosa insensible entendimiento,
Haze donde el engaño persuadido
Por verdad idolatre el fingimiento.

O milagro del Arte, que ha podido,
Dando a una tabla voz y movimiento,
Dexar sin el en ella el sentimiento.]
(Tassis y Peralta 1648: 54)

This sonnet to a painter presents another understanding of the 'true lie' of art, capable of overcoming oblivion by freezing time and animating a material object with voice and movement. In Villamediana's conception of painting, its persuasive power to act in the real is also its strength, as it enables physical communication in the present. This miracle of art, that it is in Aristotelic terms imitation but can exceed what it imitates both in terms of aesthetic beauty and in terms of longevity, is the central topos of this poem. The poet here effectively mixes a skeptical attitude, inherited from antiquity, with a celebration of the miraculous force of this vibrant matter to convey physical presence and communicate. In spite of the insistence on deception through words like 'lie', 'delusion' and 'feigning', the last quatrain accepts and celebrates this persuasive power of the material object, which then assumes voice and movement, creating sensory activity without possessing physical senses. Here, as in the poems discussed above, it is the problem of life's fragility that finds a possible if problematic solution in the vital materiality of the object.

'A corpse, some dust, a shadow, mere nothingness'

The printed books of Góngora were widely disseminated during the seventeenth century, both in Europe and in the colonies. In Nueva España, today Mexico, Sor Juana Inés de la Cruz kept books by Góngora in her library, along with the most recent research, like Kircher, Kepler, Giordano Bruno and Copernicus. From her convent, she wrote a number of poems, the most famous of which, *Primero Sueño*, is a cosmological and epistemological investigation of being and perception, often compared to Góngora's *Soledades*, which she had undoubtedly read (the title given by the first editor states that she wrote it in imitation of Góngora). Sor Juana de la Cruz is the most famous Hispanic poet and intellectual of the early modern era, and it has often been said that, being a woman, a precondition of her writing was that she became a nun. On the other hand, an ecclesiastical association was common among the male poets of Spain such as Góngora and Paravicino. While the religious sphere guaranteed her independence from marriage, it also provided the physical space of a vast library and supplied time for writing. Sor Juana also composed a treatise on women's right to study and cultivate the mind, the *Letter in Response*, a reply to a priest who had criticised her for writing poetry. Through her many admirers in New Spain, she obtained patronage that enabled her poetry to be printed and circulated in the Spanish courts (Prendergast 2007: 28).

> This thing you see, a bright-colored deceit,
> displaying all the many charms of art,
> with false syllogisms of tint and hue
> is a cunning deception of the eye;
>
> this thing in which sheer flattery
> has tried to evade the stark horrors
> of the years and, vanquishing the cruelties of time,
> to triumph over age and oblivion,
>
> is vanity, contrivance, artifice,
> a delicate blossom stranded in the wind,
> a failed defense against common fate;
>
> a fruitless enterprise, a great mistake,
> a decrepit frenzy, and rightly viewed,
> a corpse, some dust, a shadow, mere nothingness.
> (Cruz 1997: 193)

Este, que ves, engaño colorido,
Que del arte ostentando los primores,
Con falsos silogismos de colores
Es cauteloso engaño del sentido;

Éste, en quien la lisonja ha pretendido
Excusar de los años los horrores,
Y venciendo del tiempo los rigores,
Triunfar de la vejez del olvido,

Es un vano artificio del cuidado,
Es una flor al viento delicada,
Es un resguardo inútil para el hado;

Es una necia diligencia errada,
Es un afán caduco y, bien mirado,
Es cadáver, es polvo, es sombra, es nada.

Like her fellow poets in Spain, her portrait was painted and often included in the printed volumes of her poetry, like the *Fama, y obras posthumas del Fenix de Mexico, decima musa, poetisa americana*, printed in Madrid in 1700 (see Figure 18). As in the frontispiece of Pellicer's *Lecciones Solemnes*, a laurel crowns the poet, while Minerva trumpets her fame. Sor Juana's poetic work is filled with references to visuality and techniques of observing. In *Primero Sueño*, one finds mirrors, lenses, magic lanterns and prisms, and in the sonnet above it is the ontological status of the object seen that is in focus.

This material object, a copy of a human body, is for Sor Juana a deceptive artifice, as it pretends to be alive but is in fact made from what she perceives as dead material. The attempt of the portrait is precisely to freeze time, to store the human body in material form and overcome death and the passing of time. But in Sor Juana's conception of the cultural technique of portraiture, it is a failed and vain attempt, and in the end nothing more than 'a corpse, some dust, a shadow, mere nothingness'. This last line, as has often been pointed out, is a direct reference to Góngora's famous sonnet 'Meanwhile to match your hair', in which the ephemeral beauty of a young woman is said, with the passing of time, to turn into 'earth, to smoke, to dust, to shadow, to nothing'. Where the portraits of Góngora and Paravicino may well succeed in their God-defying act of overcoming death and the passing of time by means of storage in a material object, Sor Juana has no such faith in the portrait. In her conception of the material object of the portrait, there is a tension between the unforgiving character of time and the possibilities of storage in a material object that may overcome this aspect of earthly existence. The poetry of this era stages and reworks the relation between human and object, where the material object may store the spirit of the living, and thus, in a sense, assume a life of its own.

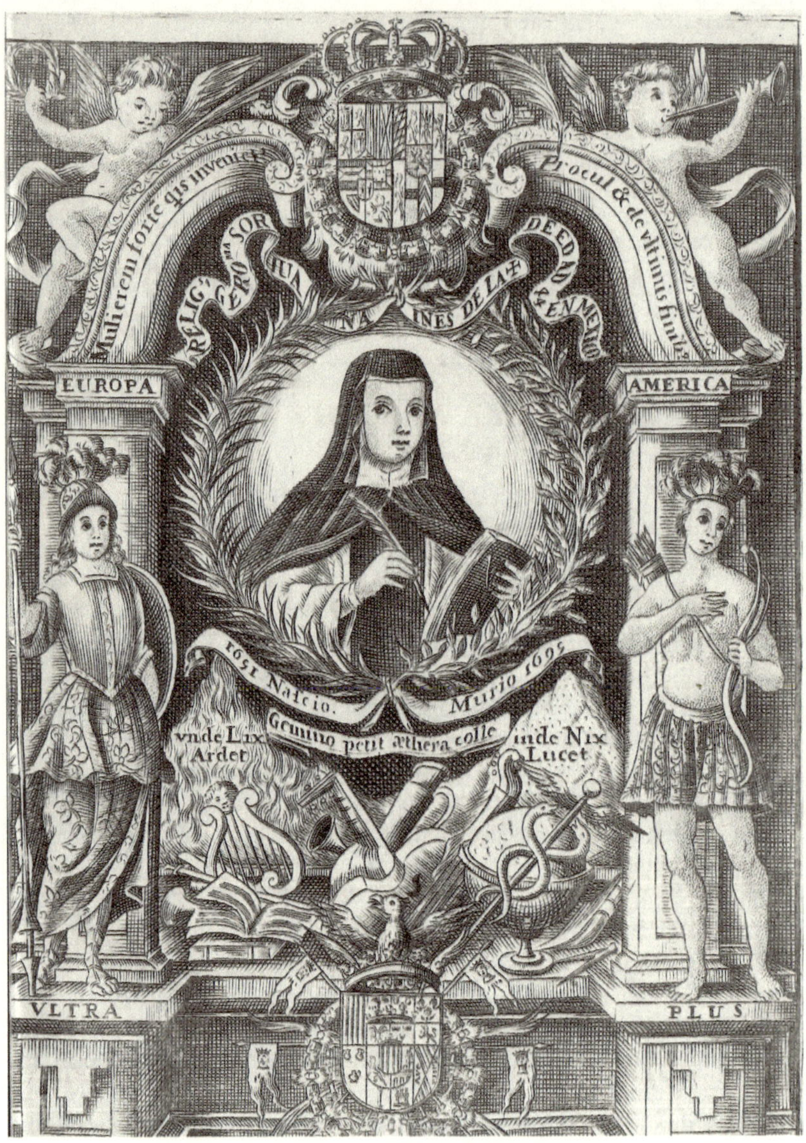

Figure 18. Frontispiece of *Fama, y obras posthumas del Fenix de Mexico, decima musa, poetisa americana*, Sor Juana Inés de la Cruz. (Madrid: Manuel Ruiz de Murga, 1700). Source: Internet Archive

The Splendour of the Collection in Early Modern Spain

In early modern Spain the status of painting was under re-evaluation. What had been considered a mechanical art with decorative purposes, like fine carpentry or other tasks focussed on physical rather than intellectual labour, was now launched by certain actors as a divine and creative act and therefore to be considered as a liberal art form (Brown 1978: 102). This transition had already taken place in Italy during the sixteenth century, but in Spain the process was prolonged throughout the seventeenth century, and only slowly did visual art win recognition as the Court acquired larger and larger collections of paintings, while treatises and poetry on the status of visual art circulated (Martín González 1993: 17). The art of portraiture had long been considered the lowest and perhaps most mechanical genre within the visual arts because of its 'lack of invention', and this cultural technique of storing the human body on material canvas was a focal point in this new conception of painting (Woodal 1997: 5). In addition, it presented an intrinsic problem in ontological terms, as it aimed in copying the human body to act as its substitute and overcome the unforgiving passage of time, a theme that preoccupied many actors in this network marked by a sense of *vanitas mundi*. On the other hand, portraiture, since the sixteenth century, had become a vital part in the political sphere of the court where it played an ideological role in the symbolic practices of power and sovereignty.

The strategies employed in this elevation of the status of painting are interesting not least in that they are often intertwined with the art of poetry. Thus the ancient relationship between the 'sister arts' was put in focus in order to understand the art of painting as dependent upon the same or similar forces as poetry. In discussing the relationship between poetry and painting, a matter thoroughly researched by scholars within the humanities, the focus is often on the abstract meaning of a certain execution of the different art forms. By comparing a painting of Diana with a poetical treatment of the goddess, interesting conclusions can certainly be made as to the verbal/visual techniques of rendering an iconographic motif. The 'plastic' quality often ascribed to Góngora's poetry, for instance, has led some scholars to look for resemblances to actual paintings of the era (Wagschal 2005: 102). What is of interest to me, however, is rather poetry and painting as cultural techniques producing certain ontological concepts. The constant references to canvas, brush, wood, copper, quill, paper, and press in this discourse are not coincidental. Rather, they reveal a deep preoccupation with the ability of certain material products to store or, to use a term more commonly employed during the time, to *eternizar*. The cultural techniques of painting and poetry were thus often understood through their materiality and were employed for storage and perpetuation of memory.

Painting had long been praised for its ability to make the absent present. As Leon Battista Alberti wrote in his *De la Pittura* in 1435, 'a painting lets the absent be present, but also it shows [to] the living, after long centuries, the dead' (Alberti 2013: 44). This idea of the presence effect of painting was a recurring topos in Spain around 1600, expressed in theoretical treatises as well as in poetry. It is active in Góngora's 'A un Pintor Flamenco', in its insistence on stealing a face, and in Quevedo's 'To the Brush', where 'the living communicates with the dead'. At the core of this conception of painting is the notion of it as a means of overcoming the passing of time and making eternal something or someone that will inevitably be lost. This conception is also conferred upon poetry by the same token, in words or in images; if they are recorded on a material surface such as paper or canvas, the living can communicate with the dead, and the absent can become present. It was also part of the political strategy of Philip II and other powerful noblemen (such as the Count-Duke of Olivares) to employ paper as a substitute for the presence of the human being.

The collecting and exhibiting of paintings and precious objects was on the rise during this period, perhaps to some extent as a result of the elevation of the status of painting from a mechanical to a liberal art brought about by actors like Pacheco. As mentioned above, this elevation coincided with a symbolic practice of power in which the portrait played a significant role (Woodal 1997: 3). The building of El Escorial by Philip II, which served as a monastery, mausoleum, and palace (with the vast library of the Paper King containing numerous precious and even forbidden books as well as an impressive art gallery and a great collection of reliquaries) was a major event at the time. The palace, which took twenty-one years to complete, was extremely costly and considered a monument of great importance by contemporary sources. Góngora praised the edifice in a sonnet around 1589, referring to it as the eighth wonder of the world and the second temple of King Solomon:

Sacred, high, golden columns,
wiping out the red glow of the clouds,
Apollo fears you as [he would fear]
the most brilliant suns, and heaven
[fears you as] most cruel giants.

Lay down your rays, Jupiter,
do not hide your own, Sun;
they are lanterns of a temple,
which for the greatest martyr of the Spaniards
was erected by the greatest king,

Religious grandeur of the monarch
whose royal hand controls the new world,
while the eastern bows down to him.

May time spare, may fortune respect,
the beauty of this eighth wonder of the world,
the years of this second Solomon.

[Sacros, altos, dorados capiteles,
Que a las nubes borráis sus arreboles,

Febo os teme por más lucientes soles,
Y el cielo por gigantes más crueles.

Depón tus rayos, Júpiter, no celes
Los tuyos, Sol; de un templo son faroles,
Que al mayor mártir de los españoles
Erigió el mayor rey de los fieles,

Religiosa grandeza del monarca
Cuya diestra real al nuevo mundo
Abrevia, y el oriente se le humilla.

Perdone el tiempo, lisonjee la parca,
La beldad desta octava maravilla,
Los años deste Salomón segundo.]
(Góngora 2000a: 110)

Góngora's praise of the physical grandeur of El Escorial through mythological imagery is, of course, indirect praise of the monarch himself. But the focus on the material structure is far from coincidental as it reveals the conception of the edifice as a monument of mythical proportions. The focus on material objects in relation to a human subject is a recurring theme in the poetry of Góngora and others of the time. It is thus a matter of poetic writing as a means of recording the physical presence of material objects like paintings, edifices or tombs and their effects on and relation to human beings. This is practice must be understood within the context of an era obsessed with the material and preoccupied by the *vanitas* of human existence. Góngora's sonnet blurs the line between the human and the non-human by associating the scale of the edifice, reaching so high that it goes through the clouds and threatens to outshine the sun of Apollo, with the person of the King. The reference to King Solomon in the last line has been much debated by Góngora scholars (Chaffee-Sorace 2010: 32). While many have interpreted it as expressing the wisdom of Philip II, Antonio Carreira has insisted that it refers only to the edifice, as a 'second temple of Solomon' (Carreira 1998: 64). The comparison between Philip II and King Solomon is based solely on the fact that both monarchs erected grand temples. As Carreira notes, Sebastian Covarrubias in his dictionary from 1611, under the entry 'Escvrial', calls the palace a second Temple of Solomon. As a matter of fact, sculptures of four Hebrew kings had been placed at the entrance of the building, in a clear reference to this conception of the palace as a second Temple of Solomon. Furthermore, Philip II is said to have identified himself as a second incarnation of King Solomon, of which the building of El Escorial was a spectacular material outcome in the symbolic practice of power and sovereignty. It was thus Philip's building project, not his wisdom, which caused the comparison with the Old Testament king.

By the time of Philip IV, the collecting of paintings and precious objects in grand galleries had risen to prominence among the courtiers and aristocrats of Spain. When Charles I of England was executed in 1649 after the Civil War, his vast collection of art was sold to cover the crown's debts. The Spanish ambassador Alonso de Cárdenas bought many of the most valued paintings in the collection, such as Raphael's *Holy Family* and works by Tintoretto, Titian and others, at the order of Luis de Haro, the nephew and successor of the Count-Duke of Olivares as first minister of the King. This event, which has been described by Jonathan Brown as 'the sale of the century', was the culmination of the huge interest in Spain in collecting and possessing material objects like paintings, books, and precious objects. Diego Velázquez, who by then had established himself as Royal Painter of the court, curated the collection bought from England (Brown 1995: 99). The reign of Philip IV, generally known as a time of financial crisis and decline, was also a period in which the status of painting underwent a transformation as a result of the investments made in artistic artifacts. According to Brown, Philip IV was unequalled as a collector of pictures among the royal families of seventeenth-century Europe, while his grandfather, the Paper King, had been the 'richest and greatest art patron of the second half of the sixteenth century' (97). The expansion of the Spanish Empire and the economic wealth it produced went hand in hand with the growing interest in collecting and possessing highly valued material objects. Philip II, the Paper King so fond of his writing desk, held a collection typical of the sixteenth century, including, besides rare books and manuscripts, tapestries, jewelry, mechanical instruments, and some 1500 paintings: the largest number held by any individual during the sixteenth and seventeenth centuries.

During the reign of Philip III (1598-1621), it was his minister the Duke of Lerma who continued this practice by acquiring 1431 paintings in the short period between 1599 and 1606, which he collected in galleries in the royal domiciles. Most Spanish collections of the time included Italian and Flemish masterpieces, as a reflection of the territorial acquisitions of the kingdom. Peter Paul Rubens came to Madrid in 1603, and in a letter he testifies to the practices in the Spanish court with reference to the Duke of Lerma: 'For he is not without knowledge of fine things, through the particular pleasure and practice he has in seeing every day the splendid works by Titian, Raphael and others, which have astonished me by their quality and quantity, in the King's palace, in the Escorial and elsewhere' (Saunders Magurn 1955: 33). During the régime of the Count-Duke of Olivares this collecting practice spread through the Court and was also conceived of as an important means of communication between aristocrats (Brown 1978: 126). Having a large collection of fine art in a gallery became a hallmark for any ambitious aristocrat during this period, and the possession of poetical manuscripts, such as the one by Góngora dedicated to Olivares, should be understood similarly, as providing the collection with truly unique objects. The presence of the material object was habitually at least as important as its content or 'meaning', whether it was a codex, a painting or some other valued artifact. The pictures were also used as tokens of exchange, and by the 1630s 'it was becoming widely known that gifts of pictures to the Spanish monarch were obligatory for those who wished to gain or maintain his favor' (Brown 1978: 131). The presence of artistic and literary artifacts was therefore not a matter of mere adornment at a Court obsessed with riches, but was integral to political practice itself. Fernando Bouza (1998: 207) maintains that the capability of governing was closely related in this period to artistic and literary practice. The capacities associated with the cultural techniques of poetic writing and fine painting, which took on a historically specific configuration of intellect (*ingenio*) and execution, were considered as material proof of the social status and the right to govern of the ministers and aristocrats. Thus the material object was an integrated tool in the political practice of sovereignty. When investigating the poetical and artistic production of the time, this aspect should not be overlooked, as it constituted a vital part of these practices. Somewhere in between the supposed agency of the human subject and the material object produced by a historically specific cultural technique, we find the interrelated practices of power and artistry, mutually dependent on each other, distributed through a network of actors.

Gallery-hopping in Madrid

Francisco de Pacheco, in his *Libro de retratos*, describes the life and virtues of Gonzalo Argote de Molina, who according to Pacheco had a vast collection of precious objects, such as paintings, rare books and manuscripts, arms and stuffed animals:

> He made in his estate of Cal de Francos (with great selection and at a high cost), a beautiful museum, gathering rare and foreign books of histories, printed and written by hand, splendid and extraordinary horses, of fine race and different skins, and a large number of antique and modern arms, which established marvelous correspondences between different animal heads and famous paintings of myth and portraits of famous men, made by the hand of Alonso Sánchez Coello, created marvelous connections [in the collection]. To the extent that his Majesty, being in Sevilla in 1570, saw himself obliged to come in a disguised wagon, arranged by Don Diego de Córdoba, to visit such a celebrated cabinet. (Pacheco 1985: 135)

This collection, which clearly bears the mark of the early modern *Wunderkammer*, was so impressive that the King himself had to come and visit it. Such 'cabinets of curiosities' included various forms of collecting, from exotica to portraits of royalties and rare books (Morán Turina & Checa 1985). Pacheco's account testifies to the widespread collecting that flourished in early modern Spain, and it was not just the King who aimed at possessing a collection of impressive material objects.

The 'museum' in Gonzalo de Argote's house seems to have been typical of the academic sphere that constituted a vital part of the material culture around 1600. The word *museo*, which is the first one employed by Pacheco, is defined in a Spanish dictionary from 1734 as 'the destined place for the study of Science, human letters and liberal arts' and it is added that 'it is also used for the place where one keeps various curiosities, pertaining to the sciences: like certain mathematical artifacts, extraordinary paintings, antique medals' (*Diccionario* 1734: 636). These spaces were intimately associated with erudition and knowledge, a sphere where poetry and painting coexisted with mathematical instruments and antique objects. It is in this context that Pacheco mentions the 'museum'; among the learned virtues of a memorable man such as writing poetry or preaching, he also possessed a vast collection of objects that seem to be the material counterpart of these abstract capabalities. Pacheco gives a similar account of Francisco de Medina, a learned man who, besides possessing vast knowledge, eloquent speech and being of the right religious nature, also held a 'a rich museum of rare books, and things never seen from antiquity and the present day'. Pacheco mentions this in passing, as if to say that Medina also possessed material objects on a par with his vast mental knowledge. It is in such a context that poetical manuscripts and portraits existed as objects not only symbolizing power and erudition but as producing these qualities. These material objects were not lifeless, dead things to the actors of this network, but rather an integral and material counterpart of the discursive order.

The Italian-born painter Vicente Carducho moved to Madrid at a young age to help his elder brother with the frescoes and paintings for El Escorial. During his career he produced several commissioned works for royal palaces and monasteries. He is perhaps best known, however, for his treatise on art, *Dialogos de la Pintura*, published in 1633, a few years before his death. Along with Pacheco's *Arte de la Pintura*, it is generally considered the most important Spanish treatise on painting from the era (Roe 2014). It is constructed as a classical dialogue between master and apprentice, and its overt ambition is to achieve an elevated status for painting as a liberal art. In the fourth book, however, Carducho mentions Góngora in a discussion of the sister arts of poetry and painting, and affirms that 'in his works one admires the greatest science, because in his Polyphemo and Solitudes it seems that he overpowers that which he paints, and that it is not possible for another brush to achieve what his quill draws' (Carducho 1633: 122). Carducho is one of the first in a long tradition to understand Góngora's poetry as visual, painted or plastic (Wagschal 2005).

In the eighth and last dialogue of this book, Carducho describes some of the most important galleries and collections in Madrid. The apprentice tells of several days of visiting royal galleries, which he describes in some detail. The interesting aspect of this chapter is that it allows a reconstruction of the practices and conceptions of the gallery of paintings. As Christiane Kruse has argued, not only the production of works of art, but also the viewing of them can be understood as a cultural technique (Kruse 2010: 198). This understanding of image-viewing as a cultural technique is based on the insight that artifacts can constitute 'objects of knowledge' (Bredekamp 2003; Latour 1989; Krämer & Bredekamp 2013: 23). In conceptualizing image viewing as cultural technique however, it is worth insisting on this practice as historically specific, that is, dependent on a contemporary understanding of these objects and their use. As is made evident in the poetry discussed above, the early modern conception of the portrait was rooted in the idea that the material object could be animate and have agency. Portraits as well as instruments, sculptures, and other artifacts constituted objects of knowledge, which at the same time possessed a form of magic in that they could have certain effects on the human body that came into contact with them. This explains in part why the attraction of the gallery, museum or cabinet increased around 1600 in Spain. At the same time, however, these objects were tools in technical and symbolic practices of power. In the following passage the apprentice in Carducho's book recounts his experience of visiting an unnamed royal gallery:

> Where I saw that they were dealing with paintings, sketches, models and statues with abundant information on the originals by Rafael Corezo, Titian, Tintoretto, Veronese, Palma, Baífan, and other famous men (from bygone and present times) from this Court, traded for each other; and I stopped to see how they were dealing with them, and they were discussing with great passion and very scientifically with the best Artists present, along with many other particular *ingenious* persons, Lords and Gentlemen, spending long time with this virtuous entertainment [...] There were writing desks, pyramids, balls of jasper and glass, and other curiosities for Oratories, offices and cabinets (Carducho 1633: 17).

The apprentice is overwhelmed by the richness of the gallery, and lists the impressive objects he has seen. Throughout the text, however, he emphasises how the '*ingenious* persons' were dealing with the objects in a very 'scientific' manner. The objects of knowledge listed include, besides originals by famous painters and sculptors, writing desks, pyramids, glass balls, and other objects for 'Oratories, offices and cabinets'. The space where the intermingling spheres of the academy and court meet in an abundance of tools could be described as a laboratory for cultural techniques. The writing desks are mentioned again when the apprentice recounts his visit to the next gallery, that of the Marquis of Leganes:

> Where vision and reason were delighted in seeing (beside the mass of rich writing desks, extraordinary clocks, singular mirrors) so many and such good antique and modern Paintings, so estimated by His Excellency, and praised by all who have knowledge in these matters. There I admired seeing them in such great harmony and order and with so much variety that it may well deserve appropriate and learned studies, along with the halls of the same house, where could be seen, like in Athens in the Schools of Archimedes, spacious tables filled with globes, spheres, regular bodies, and other mathematical and geometrical instruments (Carducho 1633: 148).

The apprentice also saw extraordinary clocks and singular mirrors, which along with the paintings exalted his 'reason'. He also emphasised that the objects were extremely well ordered and in the right place, a proposition in stark contrast to the popular modern understanding of the *Wunderkammer* as a whimsical and unordered room of excess. To this witness, the objects were rather reminiscent of the rooms he imagined Archimedes to have used for his teaching with their abundance of globes, bodies and geometrical instruments. The rooms in which the portraits of early modern Spain were incorporated should be understood as spaces of knowledge in which the objects by their physical presence worked on the human mind through its inseparable fleshly body. In another gallery the apprentice saw relics of saints stained with blood from martyrdom, which constituted another form of essential knowledge through material objects.

A Mute Choir of Living Dead: Reliquaries as Sites of Archival Magic

In 1607, on his way to the estate of the Marquis of Ayamonte where he would spend a few months in search of patronage, Góngora stopped in Seville and was received by the Archbishop Cardinal Niño de Guevara in his palace (Jammes 1967: 256). The Cardinal, who served as Grand Inquisitor of Spain between 1599 and 1602, was portrayed by El Greco in 1601 (see Figure 19), in a painting that may well have been in one of the galleries of the palace. New galleries had recently been built and in them the Cardinal hosted a grand collection of paintings, relics, books and other objects of knowledge. The gallery of the *prelado* in the palace had been redecorated in 1604 in a new iconographic program destined to elevate the status of the Catholic Church and the ecclesiastical life of Seville (Blanco 2004: 200). The new design

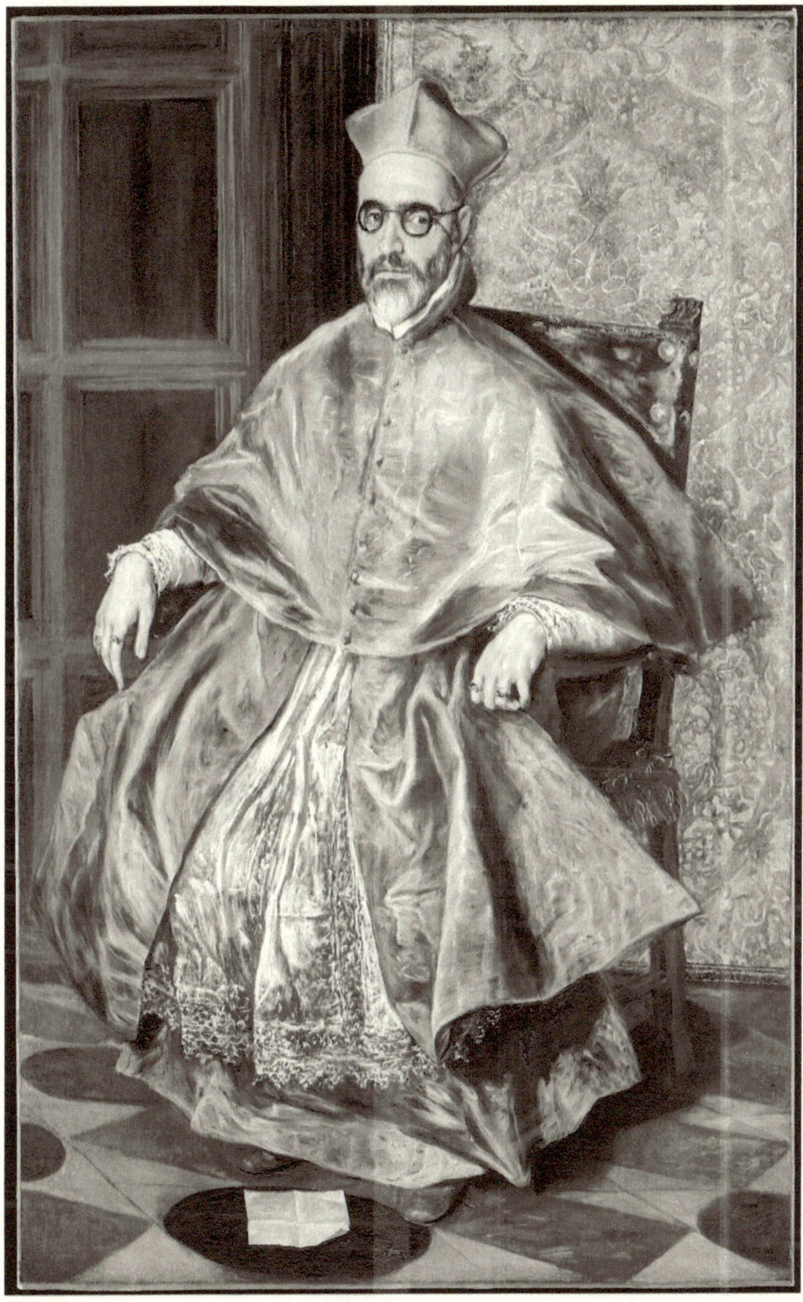

Fig. 19. El Greco, *Portrait of Cardenal Fernando Niño de Guevara*, (c.1600).
Source: Metropolitan Museum of Art, New York

included a ceiling fully decorated with framed paintings of oil on canvas which were incorporated into a wooden grid frame. The Archbishop's new design was explicitly conceived after the Council of Trent as an expression of counter-reformation in response to growing Protestantism in northern Europe (Fernández Lopez 1991: 134).

In the first five years of the seventeenth century, not only the Archbishop's palace but also the Casa de Pilatos and the house of the poet Arguijo in Seville were painted in a similar manner, framing different scenes of Christian history and the apocalypse in a specific iconographic program. The ceiling of the Pilatos has been attributed to Pacheco, while the authorship of the Arguijo and the Archbishop's palace remains anonymous. All of the painted ceilings follow Dürer to some extent (Valdivieso 1979: 15). This is particularly visible in the series of the Apocalypse, where Dürer's famous *Apocalypse of Woman*, which depicts Mary guarding Jesus against the seven-headed dragon, resembles the corresponding motif here. From the same much disseminated series of woodcuts, Dürer's *St John Digesting the Book* (see Figure 20) is of evident relevance to our understanding of Góngora's 'pellucid paper' in depicting a scene from the tenth chapter of the Book of Revelation, in which St John of Patmos is met by an angel descending from the clouds, handing John a scroll and commanding him to eat it.

Cardinal Guevara's new iconographic program and ingenious design should thus be understood as part of a tendency in the Sevillan art sphere, which in turn took its inspiration from Italy in general and from Michaelangelo's decoration of the ceiling in the Sistine Chapel in particular. Góngora visited the palace just two years after its completion, and the poem he wrote records the physical effect of entering this extremely rich gallery. It is also worth keeping in mind that the religious debates to which the Council of Trent (and hence Guevara's new iconography) was a solution, concerned the veneration of saints and relics which Protestants had condemned in their reformation. The iconography of the ceiling consists in seventy paintings distributed in twenty registers creating specific visual narratives. The motifs taken from the apocalypse are also alternated with the shields of arms of the Guevaras and the Niños, thereby culminating in the insignia of the Cardinal's archbishopric. The centerpiece depicts the Archangel Michael fighting demons, representing the Roman Catholic Church defeating the Protestants, and the surrounding registers are all allegorical depictions of the glory of this church and its priests.

> Oh you, any pilgrim entering here,
> if mute you admire, stop in awe
> before this wealth illuminated, [famous]
> for its glass, and more illuminated still for its divine brush,

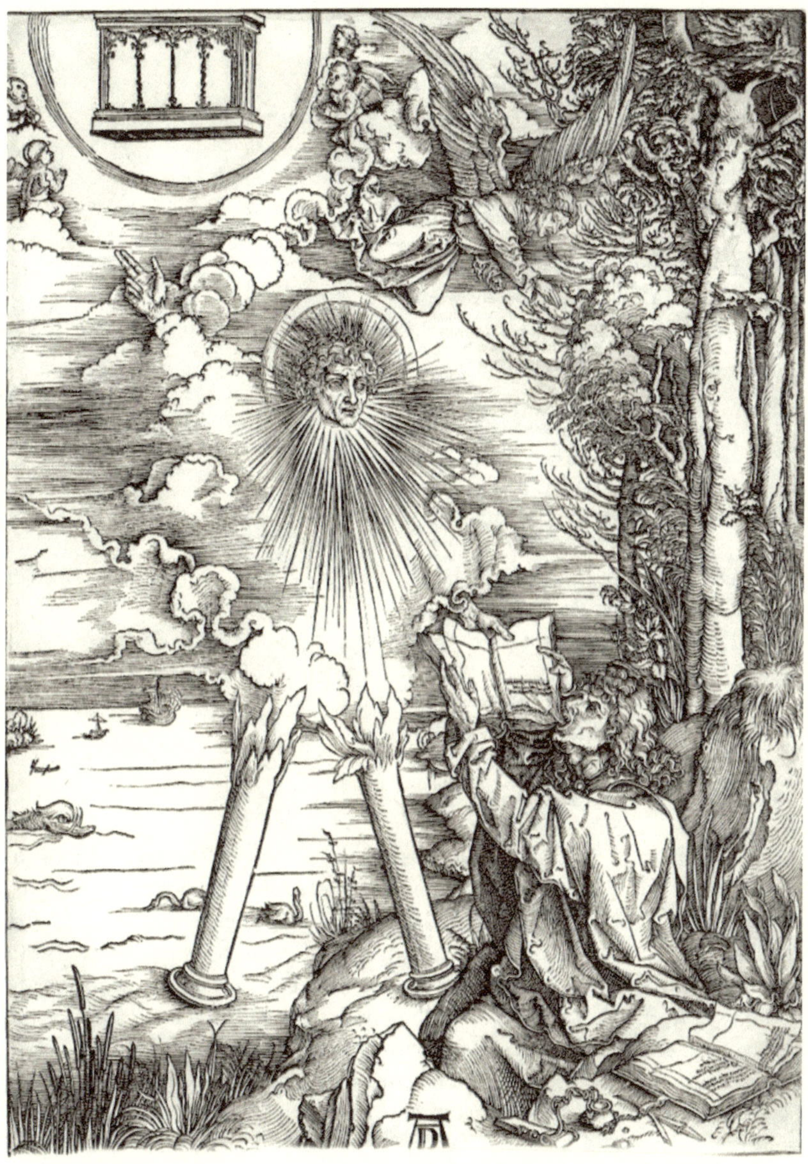

Figure 20. Albrecht Dürer *St John Digesting the Book* Source: British Museum.

celestial Thebaida, holy Aventine,
where today you are offered with rare grandeur
by the heroic Cardinal de Guevara
a restraint for desire, an end of the road.

Here you see the citizens of the desert,
the pilots of Peter's galeon;
and the chest, where until the last day,

their clothes are kept, even if broken,
of some celestial courtiers.
Adorn them with flowers, stranger.

Oh tú, cualquiera que entras, peregrino,
[Si mudo admiras, admirado para
En esta bien por sus cristales clara,
Y clara más por su pincel divino,

Tebaida celestial, sacro Aventino,
Donde hoy te ofrece con grandeza rara
El cardenal heroico de Guevara
Freno al deseo, término al camino.

Del yermo ves aquí los ciudadanos,
Del galeón de Pedro los pilotos;
El arca allí, donde hasta el día postrero

Sus vestidos conservan, aunque rotos,
Algunos celestiales cortesanos.
Guarnécelos de flores, forastero.]
(Góngora 2000a: 251)

The first quatrain reads as an inscription to a passing stranger coming to visit the splendid gallery, a common trope in classical and archaic Greek epitaphs and inscriptions on tombs, which gained a new significance in this Sevillan ecclesiastical context. The stranger or pilgrim (*peregrino* can have both meanings) is then encouraged to stop in silent wonder to admire in the bright room (where *cristales* refers both to the windows and the stained glass of the gallery) the illuminated paintings from a divine brush. The theme of light moves from the windows and stained glass to the light of the paintings, which facilitates the vision of the pilgrim who has entered the room. The second quatrain then establishes the gallery as a 'celestial Tebaida' and 'sacred Aventine', the former referring to the hermit monks who during the sixth century resided in the Egyptian region of Thebaida, and the latter to one of the seven hills on which Rome was built. These references to historical sacred sites are a poetic rendering of the paintings contained in the gallery; some of them depicted Holy Fathers of ancient Egypt, in the first tercet referred to as *padres del yermo* ('fathers of the desert') and others showing the popes of the Roman Catholic Church (Salcedo Coronel 1644: 202). The first tercet directs the vision to these paintings, which act as living entities; the pilgrim sees the citizens of the desert and the pilots of Peter's galley, i.e. the holy fathers of Tebaida, and the popes, who in succession of Peter are often said to navigate the Barque of St. Peter, a metaphor for the Catholic Church. The poet then directs the vision to a chest that contains the relics of holy persons and saints, kept to the last day, on which they were believed to be resurrected and would once again wear their clothes. According to Salcedo Coronel, this line does not refer to clothes but to the bones of the saints, understood as clothes of the souls, that they will need again on the day of the universal resurrection (200). The torn clothes of the sonnet are scattered bones, relics of the saints waiting to be resurrected. In another sonnet, dedicated to the Bishop of Jaén, Góngora writes, 'miraculous tomb, mute choir of living dead, of silent angels, Heaven of bodies, wardrobe of souls' (2000: 253).

Among the seventy paintings in the iconographic program, several are emblematic depictions of birds with moralizing messages, which in fact can help our understanding of the materiality of media. Aside from the swan and the dove, the eagle, the peacock and the phoenix are all recurrent images in Góngora's poetry. In the ceiling of the Archbishop's palace the eagle is to be understood according to the biblical interpretation as the bird able to fly closest to the sun and thus see the light of God. The peacock is accompanied by a Latin biblical quote (1 Peter 1:24) that reads 'all flesh is like grass and all its glory like the flower of the field'. The text and image produces the emblematic peacock as the much repeated symbol of vanity and recalls the transitory nature of fleshly and material being of humans on earth. The phoenix, finally, is depicted on flames surrounded by a quote from the Psalms (117:17) 'I will not die, I will live to sing the works of Jahve'. In the poetic renderings of Góngora and others, the moralizing values of the Old Testament conception of certain birds is transferred to the phenomenon of poetry and its materiality. This enmeshment of the oldest sacred allegories with contemporary practice can be understood as an early expression of secularization within the heavily disciplined Catholic discourse network. That the moralizing value of these birds transfers rather smoothly into early modern poetics can be explained in light of the materiality of paper: the scriptorial ontology of Christianity (the world as book and heaven as inscribed with divine messages) is transferred to early modern poetics through its materiality. Guevara's iconography and relics coalesce with Góngora's poem in a temporal notion of resurrection and afterlife, which in the case of poetry becomes an archival impetus towards longevity beyond the transient life of the human body.

The gallery contained a number of portraits of famous men, a collecting practice that had become widespread in Spain since the series of portraits of philosophers and theologians that adorned the walls of the library in Philip II's palace El Escorial. Mercedes Blanco reads this sonnet as an elevation of the status of painting by means of the poetical juxtaposition of portraits and relics, the most sacred object within the Catholic Church (Blanco 2012c). The brush of the painter thereby literally becomes divine through its association with the most sacred objects. The effect of the paintings can also be understood as equalling that of the sacred object, not only in terms of status but also with regard to perception and ontology.

While the gallery of the Cardinal assumes a privileged position because of its association with the Catholic Church, gazing at various objects is reminiscent of entering a *Wunderkammer*. Many of the museums, cabinets, and galleries contained sacred and religious objects along with non-religious paintings, books, and scientific instruments. The definitive separation of such objects occurred later, and their coexistence as objects of knowledge was common in early modern spaces (Bredekamp 1995). In Counter-Reformation Spain around 1600, relics and cabinets assumed increasing importance. Many of the relics that had been dispersed throughout Europe were brought back and welcomed with solemn processions (Morán Turina 1985: 174). The collection of the Escorial contained many objects of various origins and purposes. To cite one example, it had a grand collection of relics that were placed in the most privileged parts of the monastery, but it also had one of the largest collection of books prohibited by the Inquisition for their profane or heretical character. The library's collection included books on subjects including magic, necromancy, occultism and alchemy (Taylor 2006: 139). The strict separation between religious and profane brought about by the Inquisition was only enforced on those under suspicion or otherwise out of favour with the court and the Church.

Cardinals like Niño de Guevara, politicians like the Count-Duke of Olivares or kings since Philip II all housed collections of this type, as a physical space for the experience of knowledge. It is in this context that precious codices like the Chacon manuscript or the *Libro de retratos* of Pacheco were exhibited, along with portraits and instruments. It is thus no coincidence that Góngora and other contemporary poets dedicated several sonnets to portraits, galleries, monuments and buildings, as they all formed the material part of the contemporary sphere of knowledge. The experience recorded in many of these poems is indeed one of wonder and exaltation in the contact with the physical space and material objects which embodied knowledge and seemed to possess a power that few people would recognise today. Relics were obviously assumed to possess a power beyond their symbolic value, but so did many of the more profane material objects of knowledge like portraits, manuscripts, stones or instruments. The material objects produced presence effects, of which poetry became a record, as it aimed to capture and store the physical and sensory experience in words.

According to the collector of a contemporary *Cancionero*, Conde de Salinas wrote the following sonnet after visiting the Sanctuary *Nuestra Señora de la Salceda* (see Figure 21), where his brother Pedro Gónzalez de Mendoza was guardian (Gaillard 1988: 59). Gónzalez de Mendoza would later become Archbishop and publish a history of the Sanctuary in which the engraving below was included.

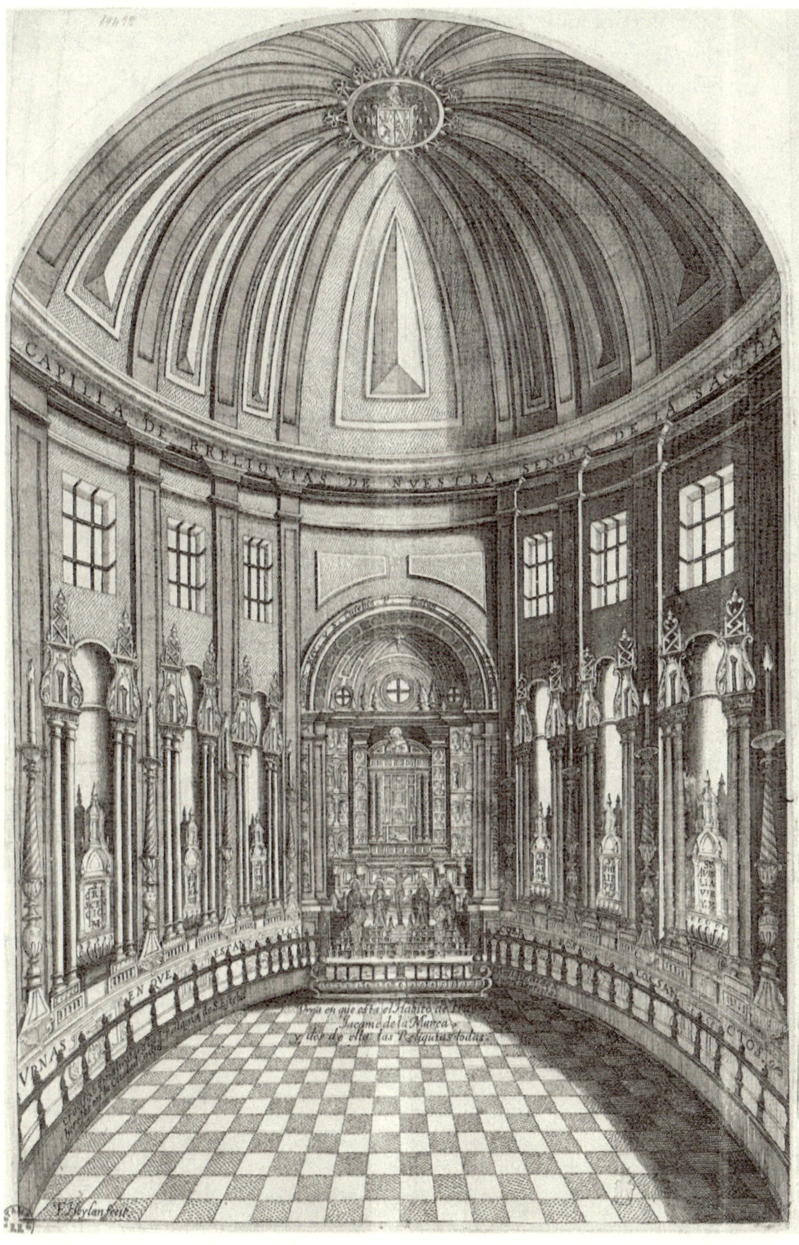

Figure 21. Reliquary of Nuestra Señora de la Salceda. Engraving by Francisco Heylan, from Fray Pedro Gonzalez de Mendoza, *Historia del Monte Celia de Nuestra Señora de la Salceda* (Granada, 1616). Source: Biblioteca de Andalucia

Testimonies of faith, saintly archives,
righteous veneration, due rewards
triumph over time, protection of the afflicted,
anxious sounds, comforted tears;

pains turned into devoted chants;
admirable sanctuary of the select,
more victorious the more defeated,
since you persisted in aiding so many;

out of that fire of love, golden ashes
finally grazed upon the stone of Christ;
righteous melting pot distributing palms;

miraculous tomb, mute choir
of living dead, of silent angels,
heaven of bodies and path of souls.

[Testimonios de fé, archivos santos,
justa veneración, premios debidos,
triunfo del tiempo, amparo de afligidos,
oídas ansias, socorridos llantos;

trocadas penas en gozosos cantos;
admirable sagrario de escogidos,
más victoriosos cuanto más vencidos,
que os perseguisteis socorriendo a tantos;

de aquel fuego de amor, cenizas de oro
en la piedra de Cristo al fin tocadas;
justo crisol que distribuye palmas;

milagroso sepulcro, mudo coro
de muertos vivos, de ángeles callados,
cielo de cuerpos y camino de almas.]
(Silva y Mendoza 1985: 85)

The first quatrain establishes the reliquary as a 'saintly archive', where testimonies of faith are kept. Archives were increasingly used for record-keeping during the early modern era, and the establishment of Europe's first file archive in Spain the Archivo General de Simancas, as well as the document regulating it written by Philip II in 1588, are important for understanding this notoriously blurry notion (Vismann 2008: 99).

The rapidly growing archive of Simancas and the fast developing administration of the Spanish crown should be understood as encompassing a humanist-influenced politics of knowledge, which during the reign of the Paper King reached huge proportions (Grebe 2010: 26). But the word *archivo* was also used to refer to a general media practice of storage that did not necessarily encompass the regulating power of the national archive in the service of the state, although any use of the word in an era which instigated an enormous archival apparatus of files and documentation must of course be understood in connection with this *dispositif.* In his dictionary from 1611, Sebastian Covarrubias defines an archive as 'the chest or cupboard where the original scriptures, privileges and memories are kept' (Covarrubias 1611: 91). In the preface to the first printed edition of Góngora's poetry by Vicuña, discussed in the previous chapter, the author states of Góngora's poetry that 'the archive of it was the library of Don Pedro Cardenas y Angulo'. 'Archive' was thus used to designate the material record of memory, like the phrase *ad perpetuam rei memoriam* placed at the end of Roman documents to signal their permanence and perpetuation of memory.

In Salinas' sonnet, the relics act as 'saintly archives' and documents of faith. Instead of a verbal reading, as with a written document, the poem stages a physical sensory reading of them, in which the poet hears 'anxious sounds' and 'comforted tears'. The last tercet is an almost literal copy of the last tercet in Góngora's sonnet to the reliquary of the Bishop of Jaén, in which he speaks of the bones as clothes of the soul. The only change made by Salinas is the replacement of 'wardrobe' with 'path', so that the last line reads *camino de almas* instead of *vestuario de almas*. Salinas should rather be seen as reusing and appropriating the stanza of his friend Góngora, because it created the sonnet he wanted to achieve. It can also be understood as revealing that Salinas had Góngora's poem in his mind (or memory) when visiting the reliquary in his brother's sanctuary. The saintly archive of the chest was thus conceived of by both poets as a 'mute choir of living dead' presenting the visitor with a highly physical archival experience.

Shining Diamonds and Speaking Portraits in Villamediana's Cabinet

Mute voices and speaking silence are also present in Góngora's sonnet from 1621 to Conde de Villamediana, 'Celebrating his taste for diamonds, paintings and horses'. Villamediana hosted one of the greater collections of jewels and paintings in the Spanish court, many of which he had brought home from his sojourns in Italy. He was a passionate collector who mounted his diamonds in lead to augment their shine, which was a new practice at the time (Salcedo Coronel 1644: 238). He also had a great collection of horses which he never sold but kept in their stables until they died, or offered them as gifts – and horses, according to Carducho in *Dialogos de la pintura*, formed an integral part of many noblemen's collections, on a par with paintings, stones, books and instruments. After Villamediana had been murdered in 1622, his estate was auctioned. When the Prince of Wales and the Duke of Buckingham unexpectedly arrived in Madrid to look for art, they went to the estate sale of the late Villamediana from which they acquired Titian's *Woman with Fur Wrap*, among other paintings (Brown 1978: 114). In a letter from 1622, Góngora testifies to the exquisite and eccentric lifestyle of his friend: 'Villamediana shined greatly, as always at a high cost, and this time to the extent that even when dropping a bag of diamonds worth six hundred escudos while on horseback, he would rather just lose the gems than seem common or lose the race' (Góngora 2000b: 398). The sonnet to Villamediana's collection has since the very first commentaries been interpreted as an expression of Góngora's great affection for his friend, interestingly expressed through the material possessions in his famous collection. Góngora's praise of Villamediana's cabinet is an interesting juxtaposition of jewels, paintings and horses, where are all animated and assume mythical proportions.

The stones hidden from others by the Orient,
raw competitors of the brightest star,
are shown to you in lead by their lode,
if they are not already fastened to the brightest metal.

How much in your cabinet the brave brush
be it domestic or foreign,
simulates voices, being mute and make up
a talkative silence in their painted vocals.

Limbs [were] hardly given to the purest breath
of the wind by their fertile beautiful mother,
[and] their colors, splendour of Betis by Iris;

when – he breathing fire, she smoke –,
they chew gold in their hard bridle,
oh generous splendour of gentlemen.

[Las que a otros negó piedras Oriente,
Émulas brutas del mayor lucero,
Te las expone en plomo su venero,
Si ya al metal no atadas más luciente.

Cuanto en tu camarín píncel valiente,
Bien sea natural, bien extranjero,
Afecta mudo voces, y parlero
Silencio en sus vocales tintas miente.

Miembros apenas dio al soplo más puro
Del viento su fecunda madre bella,
Iris, pompa del Betis, sus colores;

Que fuego él espirando, humo ella,
Oro te muerden en su freno duro,
Oh esplendor generoso de señores.]
(Góngora 2000a: 555)

This sonnet to the collection of Villamediana is based on optical phenomena and the physical experience of precious objects and animals in the gallery. The first quatrain revolves around the diamonds, the precious stones that outshine the sun, which Villamediana mounted in lead or gold ('the brightest metal'). The second quatrain moves on to the Spanish, and foreign, paintings held in the gallery (like Titian's *Woman with Fur Wrap*). These paintings, here metonymically referred to by the instrument, the 'brush', simulate voices and 'talkative silence', whose sounds are painted in colour. The material object of the painting is once again ascribed a silent voice, which is also reminiscent of the 'mute choir' in the reliquaries. The tercets describe the splendid horses of Villamediana with mythical imagery as being born of the wind, an association to their velocity. These horses, which got their colour from Iris, breathe fire and smoke while chewing their golden bits, controlled by Villamediana. The sonnet stages a hyperbolic and spectacular scene of vision and optical illusion through paintings, diamonds and horses. The gallery of Villamediana is conceived of as a privileged place of vision and sensory experience, described in detail with reference to cultural techniques.

Historico-Philosophical Interlude 3

> Memory, Mother of the Muses – the thinking back to what is to be thought is the source and ground of poesy. This is why poesy is the water that at times flows backward toward the source, toward thinking as a thinking back, a recollection.
>
> Martin Heidegger, 'What Is Called Thinking'

The 'historical reality', as Rodriguez-Moñino called it, of early modern Spanish poetry was to a large extent ephemeral rather than durable. The physical existence in manuscripts alongside printed books, *correr manuscrito*, meant that the recording of poetic discourse was in frequent lack of stability during the lifetime of its producer. Rather, it was stored in the cognitive memory of the poet, or so it was thought, as in the case of Góngora. The manuscript copies were of course the material storage and memory aid, but there seems to have existed a conception of poetry as primarily stored in the cognitive and individual memory of the poet (where it was subject to all the alterations of human cognition).

The material copies, on the other hand, were just that: *copies.* Góngora and others often use the word *borrones* to refer to them, meaning 'jottings'. As soon as the poet passed away, however, the need for durable material storage became urgent. This process can be conceptualised as a feedback loop between *communicative* and *cultural* memory (Assmann 2008). The poetry was kept in individual cognitive memory and primarily communicated orally, aided by the medium of paper, while after death it had to be confined to the materially stored documents in a library that guaranteed long durability. To complicate matters, it should be added that the poetry on the one hand often recorded specific events (as discussed in previous chapters) thus constructing a form of memory for the ephemeral, and on the other hand was based on the cultural memory stored in books and libraries. This fusion of cultural and communicative memory, of ephemeral and durable, is at the heart of poetry during this era. While it should be clear that it is impossible to maintain this binary opposition between cultural and communicative memory, between oral and written, the notions are useful as tools for sketching the complexity of this process of storage and perpetuation of memory (Carruthers 2014: 276).

The cultural techniques of poetic writing and painting during this era can further be understood as practices related to the problem of the ephemeral quality of life itself. As the popularity of the *vanitas* and *memento mori* topoi show, there existed a preoccupation with the temporal transience of earthly life to which techniques of storage in material media provided one potential, though problematic, response, a preoccupation that religious notions like salvation, eternal life and resurrection had earlier taken care of (Schneider 2003: 76). The task that poetry set itself around 1600 in Spain was, to a large extent, the ancient task of recording and preserving events and things worthy of memory for posterity. The written record of poetry thereby became an artifact that could be saved and reactivated at any time and place, independent of the original circumstance of its production.

In the eighth book of Homer's *Odyssey*, Odysseus is having dinner with the Phaeacians when Alcinous brings the bard Demodocus to the table to sing for them. The blind bard then sings about the Trojan War, and Odysseus 'drew his purple mantle over his head and covered his face, for he was ashamed to let the Phaeacians see that he was weeping'. Hannah Arendt interprets this scene as the beginning of history, in that Odysseus hears the bard sing about events he has lived through. The reconciliation of the song with reality comes about, according to Arendt, through tears of remembrance. Odysseus then turns to Demodocus and praises him for his affiliation with gods and muses and adds, 'For well and truly do you sing of the fate of the Achaeans, all that they did and suffered, and all the toils they endured, as if perhaps you had yourself been present, or had heard the tale from another' (Homer 1995: 307). The bard thus appears as historian in a primal scene of history consisting of the meeting between memory and poetry, authenticated through Odysseus who lived through the events, in which the absent is made present (Hartog 2000: 389).

The Homeric epics are a clear example of this long tradition of equating poetry and memory (cultural and collective), and in Sappho we may trace an awareness of how writing can transgress the boundary between life and death (Svenbro: 1993). As Jan Assmann puts it, 'the original task of the poet was to preserve the group memory' (Assmann 2011: 39). And as the researches of Milman Parry and Albert Lord demonstrated almost a century ago, oral poetry is always already technical, because it was based on mnemotechnical systems without which it could not exist (Parry: 1928). There is thus no 'pure' social or cultural memory independent of cultural techniques.

Mnemosyne, who gave birth to the Muses, guaranteed the storage and permanence of poetry, and poetry in this sense served memory as a recollection of that which (in Heideggerian terminology) is no longer 'ready-to-hand' (*zuhanden*), thus making the absent present. Through the 'present-at-hand' (*vorhanden*) of poetry, the absent almost becomes ready-to-hand. The relation between memory and poetry is a double-sided process concerning first the verbal recollection or gathering of something absent, and second the gathering and storage of that verbal memory itself, which later can be made present *through* this particular mode of storage. In early modern Spain, poets were historians and historians were poets, working toward the construction of cultural memory and its perpetuation.

While poetry around 1600 in Spain was understood as a memory practice in and of itself, it frequently addressed other material memory objects. In the previous chapter the focus lay on the cultural technique of portraiture as a means of storing the ephemeral human effigy, and in the next chapter it shifts to other objects of material storage such as monuments, tombs, and vessels. An important aspect of this practice of storage is the temporality into which memory is inscribed. The conception of 'eternity' at which the material memory aims is quite different from the modern historical awareness of the 'future', dominant since the nineteenth century. The spatial and temporal frames of memory will therefore be highlighted in this chapter.

Early modern Spanish poetry was often focussed on the transient nature of earthly existence, the unavoidable passage of time leading to death and destruction; thus this poetry aimed to freeze time, storing objects and events for posterity. Poetry and painting alike record and perpetuate that which is ephemeral and transient, linking it to the notion of eternity and the perpetuation of memory through its very materiality.

One of Góngora's first poems from 1582, 'Meanwhile to match your hair', can be read as typical of this attitude:

> Now while to match your hair
> bright gold must know it seeks in vain
> to mirror the sun's rays, and while amid the fields
> with envious gaze the lily regards the whiteness of your brow;
>
> and while on each red lip attend
> more eyes than wait on carnation,
> as if intent on plucking it, and while
> your graceful neck outdoes bright crystal
>
> with disdainful ease enjoy them all,
> neck, hair, lip and brow, before
> the gold and lily of your heyday,
>
> the red carnation, crystal brightly gleaming,
> are changed to silver and withered violet, and you and they together
> must revert to earth, to smoke, to dust, to shadow, to nothing.
> (Góngora 2007: 24).

[Mientras por competir con tu cabello
Oro bruñido al sol relumbra en vano,
Mientras con menosprecio en medio el llano
Mira tu blanca frente el lilio bello;

Mientras a cada labio, por cogello,
Siguen más ojos que al clavel temprano,
Y mientras triunfa con desdén lozano,
Del luciente cristal tu gentil cuello,

Goza cuello, cabello, labio y frente,
Antes que lo que fue en tu edad dorada
Oro, lilio, clavel, cristal luciente,

No sólo en plata o víola troncada
Se vuelva, mas tú y ello juntamente
En tierra, en humo, en polvo, en sombra, en nada.]
(Góngora 2000a: 27).

This poem celebrates the beauty of a woman's hair, forehead, neck, and lips by means of her body's classical competition with nature, whose every aspect she outshines, encouraging her to enjoy this beauty now, since, with the passing of time, it will turn into 'earth, smoke, dust, shadow, nothing'. This harsh ending complements the initial *carpe diem* with *vanitas*, a topos that gained popularity precisely in the transition from the sixteenth to the seventeenth century. In contrast to the classical *carpe diem*, which encourages the audience to capture the moment while it lasts and therefore is life affirming, the *vanitas* is more sombre in its reminder that everything, no matter how happy or beautiful, will eventually become dust and ashes.

The poem sets out to capture precisely that beauty which will soon be gone, thereby constructing a memory of it. This attitude, present in much writing from the time, can be read as a poetics of memory striving to overcome the passing of time and the transformation of matter into dust by means of material storage through ink and paper. This early poem by Góngora is one of the most commented on in his poetic production, and its last line was widely imitated during the Spanish Golden Age (Senabre 1994). Some critics have even insisted that this poem inspired the *vanitas* motif in seventeenth-century still life painting (Wagschal 2005: 114). It therefore provides a good point of departure for digging into the relations between poetry, memory, media, and death.

3

Poetry as Memory Practice: In the Face of Death

The Library of the Count-Duke of Olivares

The destination of the Chacon manuscript was the library of the Count-Duke of Olivares. In the preface of the manuscript quoted in the first chapter of this book, Chacon writes of the urgent need for the protection of Olivares after Góngora's recent decease: 'It [a supposed pirate volume] can only be dispelled by the rays of a favour stemming from I do not know what, if not your grandeur, or your Excellency's erudition now when you have desired these works for your Library' (Góngora 1628: 2).

The memory of Góngora, which according to Chacon 'lives in his works', was obviously more than ever in need of the protection of the Count-Duke, due to its unstable material existence after his decease. Chacon was thus asking the most powerful actor of the Spanish Empire, next to the King himself, to protect the memory stored in this material object by accepting it and keeping it in his library, as the Count-Duke himself had asked. The library of the Count-Duke appears as a privileged place of storage and a guarantor of long durability in the construction of memory.

Libraries were in fact generally considered important instruments in the practice of political power in early modern Spain. The construction of the library in El Escorial, one of the world's most exclusive and well-stocked at the time, marked the beginning of an era obsessed with the material object of the book (Bouza 1989). Some poets, like Quevedo and Lope de Vega, conceptualised this bibliophilia as ornamental erudition for people who never actually read the books (Noble Wood 2011). Libraries were material symbols of economic and intellectual status, which were obligatory for those who wanted influential positions in the Court or Church. When Pellicer, who also edited Góngora's works, published the posthumous *Obras* of Anastasio Pantaleón de Ribera in 1634, he wrote on the title page, 'Published from the library of Joseph Pellicer', as if to inform the reader that the manuscript copy of this book was held in his own private library. In the same year, Lope de Vega published his *Rimas Humanas y Divinas del Licenciado Tomé de Burgillos* with the following information on the title page: 'Not taken from any library (which in Spanish is called Bookshop) but from papers of friends and his own drafts'. Lope's affirmation can be read as a commentary on the habit, exemplified by Pellicer, of boasting about erudition by including references to books and libraries. Pellicer and Lope epitomise two opposing attitudes to early modern media. To Lope, who printed as many books as he could, media were means of communication, while to Pellicer they were part of a symbolic practice of power and erudition. Pellicer was appointed 'Mayor Chronicler', first of Castile, then of Aragon and finally of King Philip IV himself in 1640, so his efforts clearly aligned him with the power-structures of the time. Many considered Lope, on the other hand, a 'vulgar' poet who wrote and published for profit, a particularly shameful attitude in seventeenth-century Spain.

Libraries were instruments of power, deposits of knowledge and part of a symbolic practice necessary for sovereignty (Bouza 2004). The connection between the material objects of paper and parchment and the practice of power was intimate from Philip II onwards. The buildings themselves testify to this, as is exemplified by El Escorial. Access to relevant information and cultural memory was a vital part of the symbolic practice of power, especially so in a monarchy that legitimated its sovereignty through erudition. That the library of the Count-Duke of Olivares was an exclusive and important one should therefore not come as a surprise.

Olivares started creating his library in 1621 in emulation of the one founded by Philip II in El Escorial (Ponce de Leon 2013). It came to be one of the most important and richest of the era. His first librarian, Father Lucas de Alaejos, became the prior of El Escorial in 1627 and was succeeded by the poet Francisco de Rioja. When the Jesuit priest Claude Clement, famous for his influential library manual published in 1635, visited Olivares' library the same year he commented that 'it is one of the most excellent, for the number of books in it as well as for the selection of the best books of every kind, very worthy of a visit and whose fame is everywhere; there is in it an uncontrollable longing to augment it day by day, because of his singular affection for studies' (Elliott 1986: 49). John Elliott writes that 'everywhere he travelled, Olivares would leave in his wake a trail of plundered monasteries, which Juan de Fonseca and Francisco Rioja, his advisors on such matters, had systematically stripped of their most precious bibliographical treasures' (Elliott 1986: 26).

A document attributed to a Venetian ambassador in Madrid during the reign of Philip IV recounts the habits of the Count-Duke. This document was translated into Spanish by a contemporary, and exists in various manuscripts; my quotation is from MS. 10409 in the Biblioteca Nacional. The ambassador opens his account, probably written for his home court, by comparing the Spanish monarchy to the Book of Revelation:

> The Spanish Monarchy is that mysterious book of the Apocalypse, in which it seems easier than elsewhere to read the eternal letters, indicative of the rites and communal practices,

> but all the more difficult to understand its internal deliberations; the orders and political intentions jealously kept in drawers under the secrecy of the Council (MS 10409: 7).

The metaphor of the Book of Revelation chosen by the ambassador is probably not incidental. The Count-Duke was known to have grown up with the cultural technique of writing as his primary weapon; his father, Enrique de Guzmán, had been known as 'El Papelista' for his abundant production of memoranda and declarations as ambassador of Rome during the reign of Philip II, the Paper King (Marañon 1935: 677). The secretive monarchy employed documents, writing and communication to build and protect the political empire. Olivares himself was known as the 'Archduke of copyists' who spent the majority of his time as a minister in his office, at his writing desk, turning papers (Marañon 1936: 169). He even had permission, a *cédula real*, to take any documents, papers or books of the state and keep them in his own private library and archive. As Aleida Assmann points out: 'The archive is not just a place in which documents from the past are preserved; it is also a place where the past is constructed and produced. The latter process depends partly on social, political and cultural interests, but it is determined as well by the prevailing media and technologies. The archive first came into being through the material, fixed form of writing that codified information for later usage and thus laid the foundations for extended bureaucracies of power' (Assmann 2011: 13). These foundations for extended bureaucracies of power were founded in the early modern Spanish Empire, first by Philip II, the Paper King, and then by the favourite of each successor, the Duke of Lerma and then the Count-Duke of Olivares, through their care for and development of the material storage forms of archives and media. In this historically specific practice, poetry assumed a privileged position precisely because of its association with power and memory through the cultural technique of writing (Gutierrez 2005).

According to the inventory of the first librarian of 1627, the year before the Chacon manuscript was included, the library of the Count-Duke contained about 2700 printed books and 1400 manuscripts (MS 9/5729). This is a large number for a private collection, and in the case of Olivares we can assume that the objects were both exhibited and read. According to the contemporary witness Francisco de Melo, the Count-Duke cited ancient authors as if they were still alive (Marañon 1935: 683). The vast majority of the books, however, were on history and geography, from which the Count-Duke obtained the relevant knowledge for governing. A special room was used for maps and geography into which Olivares invited soldiers and politicians to study the visual representations of the world. The maps were ordered and collected from around the world, consisting both of detailed representations of contemporary territories and of ancient maps detailing the lands of the Greeks and Romans. The inventory of the library is structured in two parts, by authors and by themes. Under the entry 'Geography' is a vast selection of contemporary and antique works, allowing the minister to form a global vision of the world from his library and office.

The number of literary books was limited, however, even if there were a number of poetical books. Novels and drama were extremely scarce, while the manuscripts and printed books of poetry seem to have formed a select corpus (Marias Martinez 2011: 482). This may also have had to do with the fact that learned poetry was considered knowledge (and even memory) while novels and drama were understood as entertainment. The place of the Chacon manuscript in this collection seems self-evident: an exclusive parchment manuscript dedicated to the Count-Duke himself with what was considered the most erudite and difficult poetry of the time. As I have already explained in Chapter 1, in 1625 the Council of Castile, under the command of Olivares, passed a law forbidding the printing of 'books of comedies, novels, or others of this genre'. Even if many printers and booksellers tried to side-step the prohibition by pretending that their books had been produced in other regions, the prohibition had a clear effect and was part of a political program in which control of the flow of information seemed essential. The same year as this prohibition was effected, Olivares obtained royal permission to take whatever books or papers he pleased from the official state archive: 'may the Count of Olivares, Duke of Sanlucar la Mayor, have at his disposal the books and papers of various matters that H.M. has sent him and commands will be delivered to him and that he has gathered or will gather and may keep in his house to be stored in its archives or wherever he finds suitable' (Marañon 1935: 683). Olivares thus simultaneously prohibited the dissemination of printed books of entertainment and made sure he had full and unlimited access to the archives of the empire. When the nephew of Pope Urban VIII, Francesco Barberini, visited the Spanish Court in Madrid in 1626, Olivares had him produce an 'apostolic mandate' which excommunicated anyone who removed or helped to remove a book from his precious library. This parchment document, which was placed where it 'could be seen and read' in the library, aimed at the conservation of 'the large quantities of books of different scientific matters, history and letters of very high esteem' (Bouza 2011: 341).

The importance that the Count-Duke placed upon the cultural technique of writing and the deposits of cultural memory was immense. In his will of 1642, written shortly before he fell from grace in the Spanish Court, Olivares writes extensively about the destiny of his precious library, which by then contained the Chacon manuscript:

> And it is my will that the library that I have gathered remains united, and I immediately unite it, by virtue of the faculties I have for it, integrating, incorporating and adding it to the estate of my house in San Lúcar and the others I leave, so that it cannot be

> sold, donated or removed in all or in part and it shall be placed at the location I choose for my funeral. And to show the esteem I have of it and so that it may never be dissolved, I demand that the person who inherits the house and come into possession of this library, has to do so legally in the presence of the Assistant of Seville or Corrector of the Habit named by his Majesty, and in the presence of the persons I decide to name as librarians, and has to promise to honour this and never dissolve or remove all or part of it, as stated above, but rather add to and enrich it [...] – But I declare that neither Patron nor Prior nor the protectors can be anything more than mere administrators to protect and conserve it, with no right to make even a small use of it without the approbation of the general administrators, which have to reside in this Court. – For the governing, use and conservation of this library I leave orders and constitutions in writing separately. (Marañon 1935: 687)

Olivares firmly insists that his precious library was not under any circumstances to be dissolved or sold. For this purpose he set up a typical bureaucratic apparatus involving various actors and declared that the cost of maintaining this library should be taken from the fortune he left. To guarantee its durability, he set up various impediments, so that a future owner could never sell any part of it, and he drew up orders and constitutions for this library in a separate document. There should be no doubt that the library played an important role for this actor, but what is even more interesting is the intimate relation between the library and his own impending death. The library was to be stored at the place of his burial. It must therefore be understood as more than just a database. Rather its materiality was intimately connected to his fleshly body and sovereignty, and at the time of his death his concern for the books was one of his main concerns. There was an intimate connection between material storage media, the practice of power, and death. When he fell from grace and was removed from the Court in 1643, Olivares's books were moved from the Alcazar of Madrid and shipped to his new home in Loeches. His contemporaries interpreted this relocation of the Count-Duke's library as a sign that his removal from the Court was permanent, which further testifies to the identification of him with his library, and of his library with power and sovereignty (Elliott 1986: 655).

Unfortunately for Olivares, however, neither threats of excommunication nor the bureaucratic scheme stopped his wife from getting rid of the books after his death. In her will she ordered that they be sold and dispersed to different monasteries and religious institutions (Elliott 1986: 690). This would also be the last sighting of the Chacon manuscript for nearly three hundred years.

Media, Ashes and the Materiality of Death

Books, paintings and libraries were considered to be related to death and absence by virtue of their ability to store and make present the voices and effigies of the deceased. This symbolic association can be seen in most *vanitas* paintings, where they often share pictorial space with hourglasses, burning candles and skulls.

Marcel O'Gorman has recently argued that modern technology is imbued with striving for immortality, and that there is a direct link between technics and death (O'Gorman 2015). Some critics meanwhile have described modern culture as thanatophobic and highlighted the relative absence of discussions of death in media and cultural theory (Gere 2016). If western modernity succesively developed this thanatophobic supression of death and mortality, death is ever-present in the early modern period, when media seem to call death to mind, rather than suppress it.

Accordingly, death plays a central role in the conception of media and storage culture in early modern Spain. The *vanitas* motif is one example of this tendency to equate death and the ephemeral with material objects and storage capacity. In the early seventeenth century, a series of actual deaths of public officials gave occasion for the production of cultural memory through poetry and monuments, often in connection with one another, as epitaphs for the tomb itself. As Giulia Poggi points out, it was actual deaths and the accompanying ceremonies, rather than the philosophical or abstract category of death, that inspired the funerary sonnets of the Spanish Golden Age, especially when those deaths gave rise to expressions of a collective character (Poggi 1993: 788). Under these circumstances, Góngora's funerary poems often focussed on the materiality of death rather than on the biography or virtues of the deceased (Gornall 1978: 115).

When Philip II died at El Escorial on 13 September 1598 at the age of 71, memorial services were held, and tombs and monuments erected in almost every major city. The official mood was one of great sadness and national grief, while modern biographers have detected a hidden sense of relief among Philip's subjects, who were tired of the rule of the bureaucrat Paper King (Parker 1978: 198). Whatever the reactions of individuals may have been, the death of the King produced rituals and ceremonies, as well as a large number of printed books. By 1610 at least forty-one books had been printed relating to the death of Philip II, many of which also reproduced memorial writings (Vargas-Hidalgo 1995). The death of the King underscored the inevitable transformation of all human life into 'earth, to smoke, to dust, to shadow, to nothing', and thereby referred to a common conception of death. The event itself was used to legitimise the succession by relating the exemplary and holy death of the monarch in his spectacular palace, the Escorial. One commentator insisted that Philip II had died in Escorial 'in the same way a silkworm constructs its cocoon, and lies dead within it, so that the new majesty of his son might emerge just as another silkworm springs from the cocoon to renew the days and works of the predecessor entombed therein' (Porreño 1942: 18). The material framework of the Escorial with its library, galleries and mausoleum was thus conceived of as integral to the symbolic practice of sovereignty.

The decease of an official person of the magnitude of Philip II produced a vast number of material traces, all of which contribute to the construction of the cultural memory of the monarchy. In Seville, various monuments were erected with inscriptions, and by the Cathedral a mausoleum of enormous proportions was constructed which included an exact copy of the monastery of San Lorenzo of el Escorial. This mausoleum alone was considered important enough to be the subject of a book by Francisco Jeronimo Collado (1611) and Cervantes (2003: xxvi) dedicated a sonnet to the monument. Many critics have argued for the ironic character of this sonnet, as Cervantes was a former soldier and so felt more comfortable with the power practice of Philip's predecessor, Carlos V, than the paperwork of Philip II, while others have seen in it honest praise of the deceased ruler (Ludovik Osterk 1999). The sonnet, which ends with the line 'he left, and there was nothing', is enigmatic in a sense proper to the poetry of this era, to such an extent that attempts to extract a subjective experience from it will always be problematic. With regard to the importance conferred upon these memorial practices, it is interesting to note how Cervantes expresses himself in his *Voyage to Parnassus*. The canonical *Don Quijote* is described as 'a pastime for the melancholic and sulky chest', while the sonnet to the monument of Philip II is valued in the following way: 'I composed the sonnet – the highest honour among my writings – which begins, my God I'm stunned by this grandeur' (Cervantes 2001: 56).

As Jan Assmann explains, 'memories of the dead are the primal form of cultural memory' (Assmann 2011). Many early forms of writing were epitaphs inscribed on stones, often directed at the passer-by, and constructed as an imperative to memory. This connection between death and material storage was revived in the early seventeenth century and brought to its extreme form by an ever-present awareness of the ephemeral quality of life and an insistence on the material forms of memory. A good example of the tendency to equate material storage, death, and resurrection are the two sonnets Góngora wrote for Luis de Cabrera's *Historia de Felipe II*, printed in 1619 (though without these sonnets by Góngora). According to the Chacon manuscript, Góngora wrote them at the request of a friend, without having met Cabrera nor read his book. However, it is possible that Góngora had seen the manuscript copy of the book, as Biruté Ciplijauskaité points out (Góngora 1981: 166). The reference to 'envy' in the eleventh line of the first sonnet also echoes Cabrera's words in the front matter: 'may his praise be preserved for posterity in a perpetual and agreeable confession of envy, so that the glory and veneration of Your Highness may celebrate them' (Cabrera 1619: 7). The sonnets were written for the 'beginning' of the books, and thus formed part of the early modern paratextual practice of opening a book with laudatory verses, preferably by a poet of some magnitude, which along with the dedication, and in many cases a portrait, would help to legitimise an authorship that was still without legal copyright and needed to be made explicit.

Once again, Cervantes' ironic verses may illustrate this case. *Voyage to Parnassus* opens with a sonnet entitled 'The author to his quill', in which Cervantes, for lack of a laudatory sonnet dedicates a sonnet to his own writing quill in much the same way he substitutes ekphrasis for portraiture in *Exemplary Novels*: 'Well you see that they have not given me any sonnet to illustrate the cover of this book, so come, you, my unsharpened quill and produce one, even if lacking in discretion' (Cervantes 2001: 16). Beyond this ironic comment on the practice of opening books with laudatory verses, the sonnet also testifies to a conception of the writing quill as an animated object, addressed imperatively with the pronoun *vos* as a grammatical subject.

In the printed version of Cabrera's book published in 1619 (although the licence and taxation are from 1615), there is no poem by Góngora, nor any other poet. Góngora's two poems for Cabrera's two volumes therefore had a peculiar material existence. Written for a book that the poet may not have seen, and subsequently not included in that book, they were disseminated primarily in manuscript form. Of the twenty-eight preserved versions of this poem, twenty-five are from manuscripts and only three from printed books, (edited by Salcedo Coronel, Hozes and Vicuña), all of which have the first sonnet inserted on the first page, almost as if their editors wanted it to refer to their books as well. However, even if Góngora, as Chacon states, had not read Cabrera's book when he composed the sonnets in 1614, he definitely read it later, as he sent a copy to Francisco de Corral on 30 July 1619, just months after it had been published.

The biographical fact supplied by Chacon, that Góngora never actually read the book, seems telling in this context. What Góngora, or any other poet, personally felt when composing a particular poem is not of concern here, nor was it so to contemporary readers. This is important to bear in mind when reading any poetry of this era, but particularly when discussing dedicatory verses to books or tombs. The poet does not strive primarily to convey his personal feelings at the decease of a particular person (although a personal sentiment can of course be present as well), rather he is producing a form of writing that attaches itself to a certain discursive order. The first of the two sonnets, written in 1614 for the first volume of Cabrera's book, reads as follows:

> In this volume lives he, who rests
> in that marble, a king forever glorious;
> his ashes there find rest and
> from them he is reborn here today.

With your quill he flies, and it makes you
learned Cabrera, in our age, famous;
with his [feathers] you make him victorious
over the French, Belgian, Lusitan, Thracian.

Feathers of such a Phoenix, and in your hand,
which time could ever consume them and
which envy offend you, if not in vain?

May it write what they saw, such a grand quill,
of the two worlds each hemisphere,
of the two seas each foam.

[Vive en este volumen el, que yace
En aquel mármol, rey siempre glorioso;
Sus cenizas allí tienen reposo,
Y dellas hoy él mismo aquí renace.

Con vuestra pluma vuela, y ella os hace,
Culto Cabrera, en nuestra edad, famoso;
Con las suyas lo hacéis victorïoso
Del Francés, Belga, Lusitano, Trace.

Plumas de un Fénix tal, y en vuestra mano,
¿Qué tiempo podrá haber que las consuma,
Y qué envidia ofenderos, sino en vano?

Escriba, lo que vieron, tan gran pluma,
De los dos mundos uno y otro plano,
De los dos mares una y otra espuma.]
(Góngora 2000c: 423)

The first quatrain juxtaposes the medium of the book and the marble tomb, both of which are said to contain the remains of the deceased king. The depiction of the ashes that rest in the marble and acquire new life in the volume (the ancient term for a scroll, here used for the codex) is a transformation of the Phoenix myth, whereby the King, like the bird, can be reborn out of his ashes by means of the object of the book. As the contemporary commentator Salcedo Coronel puts it: 'Don Luis says, speaking of Philip the Prudent, that he lives in that History, because in it is preserved the memory of his glorious virtues' and further that 'the same Philip is now reborn out of his ashes in this volume, which makes eternal his memory' (Salcedo Coronel 1644: 5, 7). The book is conceived of as the container of the memory of the dead through its juxtaposition with the marble tomb; the King is reborn like the Phoenix through the cultural technique of writing, here intimately associated with memory. Marble, a reference to the materiality of the tomb, is a metonym, which, according to Salcedo Coronel is 'taking the matter for the materialised' (6). This type of material metonym is not uncommon in the poetry of the era and, beyond its rhetorical function, it testifies to discursive practices of coupling symbolic and material in cultural techniques; the material object produces the symbolic work. The whole sonnet is constructed around such material metonymies based on the myth of the Phoenix where writing quill, book, marble and ashes are used to produce a physical understanding of material memory objects.

In the second quatrain the focus lies on the quill, which in the extended metaphor of the Phoenix is said to allow Philip to fly and thereby make Cabrera famous. This understanding of the book as on the one hand producing and containing memory of the deceased and on the other granting fame to its writer is reminiscent of the conception in Pacheco's *Book of Portraits* discussed in the previous chapter. The last two lines of the second quatrain create an interesting metaphor of feathers and power. Building on the previous two lines which refer to the quill of Cabrera, they state that Philip, with his feathers became victorious over his enemies, which is of course the history contained in the book. This imagery expresses how Philip II, the Paper King, built his empire with feathers, which besides being a metaphor of power and an allusion to the wings of fame, is also the material of quills, and thus reveals a link between this cultural technique and the practice of power (Salcedo Coronel 1644: 7). This metaphor is made possible by the mythological reference to the Phoenix, which generally symbolises rebirth but also the empire and in Góngora's sonnet the cultural technique of writing with quill. In the tercets, the equation of the feather as an instrument of writing and political power is further developed; the feathers of this Phoenix, in the hand of Cabrera, can never be consumed by time; consequently, they work toward the perpetuation of memory into eternity that underlies the conception of material storage media. The final lines recount how the grand quill of Cabrera writes (about) what the empire saw: the two worlds (the new and the old) and the two seas (the Mediterranean and the Atlantic/Pacific).

The deputies of Aragon, who felt that the second volume of the book related certain historical facts in an unflattering manner, withdrew it, whereafter it remained unpublished until 1876. However, Góngora wrote a sonnet for each of the volumes, and the one cited below was intended for the second:

> Secondary feathers are, oh reader,
> all letters contained in this heavy volume;
> feathers forever glorious, not those of the bird
> whose tomb is so aromatic:

but of that one, whose holy ashes today
is sealed in gentle peace by a piece of porphyry,
for a great Phoenix goes into a small marble,
so haughtily denied to our feet.

Today reborn, then, from his deeds,
the Phoenix – the world – owes to Cabrera,
all beautiful feathers, however secondary,

beating the air; to Cabrera, a second and Spanish Livy,
made eternal, if not crowned by
as many laurel leaves as Philip is by stars.

[Segundas plumas son, oh lector, cuantas
Letras contiene este volumen grave;
Plumas siempre gloriosas, no del ave
Cuyo túmulo son aromas tantas:

De aquel sí, cuyas hoy cenizas santas
Breve pórfido sella en paz süave,
Que en poco mármol mucho Fenix cabe,
Si altamente negado a nuestras plantas.

De sus hazañas, pues, hoy renacido,
Debe a Cabrera el Fenix, debe el mundo,
Cuantas segundas bate plumas bellas;

A Cabrera, español Livio segundo,
Eternizado, cuando no ceñido
De iguales hojas que Filipo estrellas.]
(Góngora 2000a: 423)

This second sonnet follows the general idea and imagery developed in the first, with the focus on the Phoenix, ashes, and marble. The reference to 'secondary feathers' in the first line refers to the fact that it concerns the second of the two volumes, and the memory of Philip II is thus reborn a second time with this book. In the first two quatrains, the late king is depicted as the Phoenix reborn from his sacred ashes by means of Cabrera's writing (the feathers are explicitly attributed to Philip, not to the bird reborn from aromatic ashes in Arabia). In the first two lines, the feathers of the bird/king are associated with the letters in the heavy or grand volume/book. This association is rooted in the connection between the written letters and the writing quill, the feather of Cabrera, which here revives the feathers of Phoenix for the memory of the King, whose feathers are also the traditional symbol of power and the carrier of fame. The second quatrain dwells on the materiality of death, the great ashes encapsulated in the small marble or porphyry container; the limited size of the tomb is juxtaposed with the grandeur of the King by the line 'a great Phoenix goes into a small marble'. This line reminds the reader, in the mode of *vanitas*, that even the ashes of such a grand ruler as Philip II fit into a small urn. The last two tercets dwell on the image of the Phoenix produced by Cabrera, who makes the ephemeral memory of the King eternal, thus also making his own memory eternal by producing as many leaves of laurel to crown his head (*hojas*, translated here as 'leaves', also means 'pages') as the late king is crowned by stars in the sky.

The focus in the two sonnets on the materiality of death, on ashes and marble, reveals an interesting conception of storage. Rather than celebrating the late king's ascension to heaven and his afterlife in the divine realm, Góngora describes the material storage and inscription of memory on earth. The sky is only present as an extended metaphor of the fame produced by Cabrera's writing, and the mythological imagery supplied by the Phoenix reveals a preoccupation with the earthly afterlife through memory.

'The anthropological heart of cultural memory is *remembrance* of the dead', writes Aleida Assmann (2011: 23). This aspect of cultural memory has its roots in Egyptian and Greek antiquity, and was revived in the early modern era as the secular practice for overcoming the oblivion of death. The Greek and Roman preoccupation with *fama* and earthly afterlife shifted with Christianity to a focus on the salvation of the soul and the divine afterlife in heaven, during the middle ages, and then to the Neo-Platonism of the Renaissance (even if many poets were still preoccupied with their *fama*).

The founding myth of mnemotechnics told by Cicero in *De Oratore* recounts how the poet Simonides used a spatial memory to identify the bodies of the dead guests after a banquet in which the roof had collapsed; already there the poet and poetry are linked to remembrance of the dead. Simonides's mnemotechnical system was interpreted as the triumph of human memory over the loss of death and destruction (Cicero 1942: 465). As Assmann further notes, 'immortality of the name is the secular variation on immortality of the soul. It does not require family members, priests, monasteries, or acts of charity, but singers, poets, and historians. Religious *memoria* concerns personal memory and the salvation of the soul, whereas worldly fame entails social remembrance by posterity' (Assmann 2011: 29). Assmann describes how the poet became the gatekeeper of memory and fame in ancient Greece by the ability to immortalise through poetry, an ability that was reinforced by the invention of alphabetic writing, which worked primarily in the service of the perpetuation of memory. 'Physical death could be overcome by immortalizing the name and deeds of the individual, and in such a culture the poet was to possess a special gift (or magic power) of long-distance communication, thanks to which he could address even the unborn generations of the future'. In early modern Spain, this aspect of ancient memory culture and cultural memory was brought to the fore again, as medieval conceptions of the salvation of the soul slowly started to give way to a secular form of memory practice in which the earthly afterlife acquired through cultural memory seemed more urgent. The Christian practices of caring for the soul of the deceased were, of course, still present, but they were complemented by a new attention to material forms of cultural memory, in a process that can be understood as an early phase of the secularization of memory. This process took the form of an extreme focus on material traces rather than spiritual transcendence in poetic writing in general, and in funerary poetry in particular. Thus the materiality of death tends to displace the transcendence of the soul, and the spirit is understood as contained in material objects such as paper, parchment, canvas, marble or copper: an entire series of materials processed through cultural techniques. The long-distance communication proper to these media, were also what made them instruments of power in the bureaucracy of the Spanish Empire. The material storage medium was on the one hand the guarantor of memory after death, and on the other hand an integral part in the symbolic and actual practice of power, as in the case of the Paper King and his successors.

Fully Immersive Spectacles of Memory: the Catafalque of Queen Margaret

In October 1611, the Spanish Queen, Margaret of Austria, died in labour at San Lorenzo el Escorial. Rodrigo Calderón, a *valido* of the Duke of Lerma, the minister of King Philip III, was later accused of having used witchcraft to kill the Queen. As when Philip II died, most of the major cities in Spain held funerary celebrations consisting of the erection of catafalques or funerary monuments and the inscription of poetry. These ceremonies constituted major public events of multimedia celebration at which poetry, monument, music, lights, and procession worked together in a grand celebration of mourning and death (Page 2009: 429). The city usually had to borrow money to produce the spectacle, which was not only an obligation but also a moment of pride for the local community.

In Góngora's native Córdoba, a 'majestic and splendid' tomb was constructed by Blas de Marabel: 'and after offerings of various models of the tomb had been made by local and foreign persons, one was considered the most splendid and majestic, which we would later see put into practice and constructed in the right form, by Blas de Marabel, Grand Master of Fabrics in this City and its Bishopric, a man famous for his art' (Gúzman 1612: 3).

The catafalque was built of wood and painted to resemble marble in a three-tier arrangement with poetry, emblems, figures, and a large number of candles on each level. Góngora wrote three sonnets, a stanza in *octava real*, and two *décimas* for this ephemeral monument. The primary historical source of documentation for the event is a book printed in 1612 in Córdoba by the widow of Andrés Barrera, and edited by Juan de Guzmán, entitled *Relación de las honras que se hicieron en la ciudad de Córdoba a la muerte de la serenísima*

Reyna Señora nuestra, doña Margarita de Austria. This book is both a collection of the poetry used on the catafalque and a description of the monument and procession. Regarding the purpose of this production of cultural memory, Guzmán writes:

> Death does not end everything, because it does not end fame, which enjoys more spacious limits than life, without being hidden by the ashes of bodies, nor being incarcerated by the narrow walls of urns or tombs, free from the movement of time or the twists of fate (Guzmán 1612: 4).

The construction of a monument and the production of poetry are explained as activities with the purpose of demonstrating earthly afterlife through *fama*. The catafalque was adorned with 'pedestals, pyramids, and turning columns, and above each a large candle. It had eight pyramids with large candles above the globes' (4). The pyramids symbolised death and the globes eternity, which seems to be the temporal focal point in this construction of cultural memory. The catafalque was presented during mass on the first night and second morning of the New Year in 1612, and was placed in the centre of Córdoba Cathedral. It stretched about a hundred and twenty feet high into the dome of the newly constructed cathedral, creating an immense material spectacle. The monument was perceived as the pride of the people for its grand construction, but, according to Guzmán, what most drew the attention of the participants were the poems on it:

> But what most drew the attention of everyone was the large number of Poetical works, in Vernacular and Latin that occupied part of the columns of the tomb and all of the drapery. The whiteness of the paper created such a pleasurable effect over the black drapery, as did the artifice of their disposition, intermingled with emblems (that the vulgar call Hieroglyphs). It was truly wonderful in its execution, as was the wit of its Epigrams and Sonnets which were written on well-cut cards that invited the numerous audience to try to see and enjoy the rare and admirable thoughts they contained. (6)

This was the material and physical context of the sonnets Góngora composed in 1611 for the *honras funebres* of Queen Margaret. In Guzman's account, the visual and physical display of the poetry, coupled with emblems on the catafalque, seems to have been as important as its content to the contemporary spectators. The poems were cut out on paper cards and hung – along with emblems – on the black drapery of the catafalque, placed in the nave of the cathedral during the procession. The sonnets by Góngora open the book by Guzmán, who affirms that he has followed the order in which they were hung; hence these poems were on top. Interestingly, although focussed on the honour of the late queen, all three of the sonnets evolve around the materiality of death, *vanitas* and *desengaño*. The last of these roughly means 'disillusioned', but comes from the verb *engañar* which means to lie or trick, so *desengaño* is the revealing of a lie and *desengañado* a person with moral insight into the vanity of human striving for possessions and success in earthly life.

The first of these sonnets evokes the splendour of the monument and its geographical placement along the Guadalquivir, relating it to a maritime theme, which gives occasion for the wordplay of Margarita as the pearl of a seashell (*Margarita* means 'pearl' in Latin). The maritime theme, which is present in all three sonnets, speaking of shipwreck and storms, may also be related to the fact that the enormous catafalque with its three-tier system looked like a ship in the church and could further be related to the traditional idea of Christianity as a ship. But the final tercet of the first sonnet turns towards the ashes: 'The ashes now await the final trumpet always resounding for the one, whose memory rather combed disillusion than white hair' (Góngora 2000a: 320). The ashes await the trumpet of the final judgement, and the one in whose memory that sound was always present is St Jerome, constantly brooding on imminent death and resurrection (Salcedo Coronel 1644: 728). This warning by means of *desengaño* – in laudable awareness of human mortality – was generally referred to as *escarmiento*, meaning 'warning', a popular trope in this discursive order. The death of the Queen thereby became a reminder of the mortality of all humankind. Such verses resounded with the architectonic production of the catafalque, which contained a large skeleton as the traditional symbol of death, with the line 'death comes to the fortified castles of kings as well as to the humble houses of the poor' (Andrews 2014: 138).

Baltasar de Gracián quotes the second sonnet with the follwing lines emphasised, and calls it an 'extreme sonnet' in his *Agudeza y Arte del Ingenio* (1648: 64). It ends with a similar turn toward *vanitas* and the last two tercets read:

Splendour of pain you are, a sign not in vain
of our vanity. May the wind confirm
it that owes you, from scents as well as candles,

so much smoke. Oh human ambition,
prudent peacock now with a hundred eyes,
if you turn them to disillusion and to tears.

[Pompa eres de dolor, seña no vana
De nuestra vanidad. Dígalo el viento
Que ya de aromas, ya de luces, tanto

Humo te debe. Ay ambición humana,
Prudente pavón hoy con ojos ciento,
Si al desengaño se los das, y al llanto.]
(Góngora 2000a: 321)

The coffin of the dead queen was perceived as a sign of the vanity of all humans, whose vain ambition deprives them of the moral awareness of their own mortality; vain as the peacock with its beautiful feathers, they are yet incapable of grasping mortality. The *desengaño* and the tears of the peacock turning away from vanity are to be understood as the desired moral effect of this spectacle. The candles and incense of the catafalque here speak to the spectators through the wind, a reference to the material context of the poem that is physical and concrete, as it was placed on the black drapery just below these candles and incense so that a reader of the poem would have smelled and seen what the poem refers to. The spectacle of this huge monument was a fully immersive experience, with hundreds of candles lighting up each part of the construction. The third sonnet begins with the following quatrain:

Funerary edifice, which keeping still,
tells us of the movement of this life,
Pyre, not from any scented grove,
but built for a more glorious Phoenix.

[Machina funeral, que de esta vida
Nos decís la mudanza estando queda,
Pira, no de aromática arboleda,
Si a mas gloriosa Fenix construida.]
(Góngora 2000a: 322).

The words *pira* and *machina* are employed here as synonyms for the catafalque, playing on their associations with classical funeral practices. The pyre is elegantly connected to the Phoenix, in the production of a *memento mori* for the spectator. But in contrast to the Greek pyre, which was constructed of aromatic wood and then burned, this catafalque shall remain, and the Queen/Phoenix shall live again through the *fama* it produces. The sonnet is focussed on the material construction of the catafalque and its effects on the human body.

These poems formed an integral part of the monument, where emblems, statues, light and scents worked together with the manuscript papers attached to the catafalque. The effect of the spectacle can be understood in terms of presence and meaning effects. A reading of the poems that seeks only to attribute meaning will inevitably overlook the presence effects produced by the material artifacts, effects that the poems themselves constantly refer to, so that the boundary between textual and physical is transgressed. The sonnets refer to the smell, light, and materiality of the catafalque, while at the same time forming an integral part of this ephemeral monument by their placement on white paper cards attached to the black drapery.

In 1612, Góngora wrote another sonnet of funerary character which was neither explicitly dedicated to the Queen nor part of the *Relación*. As Robert Jammes has pointed out, however, it may have been written in connection to the three sonnets destined for the catafalque, which he perceives of as 'a meditation on death and the vanity of the world' (Jammes 1967: 232). Giulia Poggi, on the other hand, insists that this poem is a universal meditation on death with no connection to any known chronological circumstance (Poggi 1993: 788). Different commentators have thus interpreted the poem contradictorily. Where some have seen in it as a devotional work, striving to redeem the soul from physical death, others have read it as a rational and almost atheistic meditation on a set of existential terms.

The discursive elements of the poem can be understood in connection to conceptions of memory, death and materiality. The poem revolves around the theme of *vanitas*, *desengaño*, and memory, and is entitled 'To the memory of death and hell'. *Memento mori* is thus already present in the title of this sombre composition:

> May my memories penetrate, without fear,
> plebeian urns, and royal tombs,
> where the executioner of our days
> already with equal foot took unequal steps.
>
> Confront all these signs of death,
> naked bones, and cold ashes, '
> defying the vain, however pious,
> sumptuous Oriental preservations.
>
> Descend then into the abyss, in the depths of which,
> souls blaspheme, and where, in its strong prison,
> one keeps hearing chains, and eternal crying.
>
> If you will, oh memories, at least
> free yourselves from death by means of death,
> and vanquish hell by means of hell.
>
> [Urnas plebeyas, túmulos reales
> Penetrad sin temor memorias mías,
> Por donde ya el verdugo de los días
> Con igual pie dio pasos desiguales.
>
> Revolved tantas señas mortales
> Desnudos huesos, y cenizas frías,

A pesar de las vanas, sino pías
Caras preservaciones Orientales.

Bajad luego al abismo, en cuyos senos
Blasphemán almas, y en su prisión fuerte
Hierros se escuchan siempre, y llanto eterno,

Si queréis, oh memorias, por lo menos
Con la muerte libraros de la muerte,
Y el infierno vencer con el infierno.]
(Góngora 2000a: 333)

The first line echoes the 'death comes to all' theme from the catafalque by the juxtaposition of plebeian urns and royal tombs. The sonnet is built up as a grand *memento mori* with its insistence on material remains, here referred to as 'signs of death'. Naked bones and cold ashes are the material contents of the tombs and urns, and the poet invokes his own memory to penetrate these. The chief difference from the sonnets explicitly dedicated to the Queen's catafalque is the linguistically subjective character of the poem. But we should not assume that it is therefore personal in the sense of subjective experience, a concept that was far less common in the poetics of the era than it would later become during the later course of modernity. Rather, the poem is constructed as an mnemotechnical spiritual exercise, which can be repeated by any reader. When read aloud (as many of these poems were), the poem will refer back to the speaker and invoke mind and memories.

Another important formal feature of the poem is that of the *ars memoria* of inscribing images in the mind to be remembered on a later occasion. According to Frances Yates, if the inventor of this artificial memory was Simonides, then Thomas of Aquino became something like its patron saint (Yates 2001: 82). The widespread idea of this mnemotechnical practice was that 'simple and spiritual intentions slip easily from the memory unless joined to corporeal similitudes'. Yates, who prefers the term 'art of memory' to mnemotechnics, insists on the physicality of this cultural technique, '*seeing* the places, *seeing* the images stored on the places, with a piercing inner vision which immediately brought to his lips the thoughts and words of his speech' (4). According to Yates, the anonymously authored *Ad Herrenium* compiled ca. 86-82 B.C. is the main source for all later arts of memory, including the early modern. In short, the premise of *Ad Herrenium* is that artificial memory is established from places and images, where a *locus* is a place such as a building and images are forms, marks or simulacra of what shall be remembered. By placing an image at a specific place, it can be retrieved as needed, to remember specific things. 'For the places are very much like wax tablets or papyrus, the images like the letters, the arrangement and disposition of the images like the script, and the delivery is like the reading' (7). The author of the treatise explicitly links the art of memory to the cultural technique of writing; they are both practices for storing information, the one internal and the other external. The art of memory depends to a large extent on a simulation of physical presence and material objects. As Mary Carruthers points out, representation 'was understood not in an objective or reproductive sense as often as in a temporal one; signs make something present to the mind by acting on memory. Just as letters, *litterae*, make present the voices (*voces*) and ideas (*res*) of those who are not in fact present, as Isidore said, so pictures serve as present signs of or cues to those same *voces* and *res*' (Carruthers 2008: 274).

In the sonnet 'To the Memory of Death and Hell', the images or objects are the 'naked bones and cold ashes' placed in 'royal tombs and plebeian urns', which produces a descent into hell with its eternal tears and sounds of shackles. The purpose of this technical operation is to produce an authentic *memento mori*, as the poem ends with the hope that the memories may overcome death and hell. In this manner, the poem can be understood as a verbal description of the mental process of *ars memoria* using the objects associated with death to produce the *memento mori*. The problem of *vanitas* is thus solved through the *memento mori* which aims to inscribe and store information so that the subject will not forget death and lead a life in vanity, and will perhaps avoid the eternal suffering of hell. This is the purpose of the *escarmiento*, the warning, produced by this discourse. By storing the proper information through a specific cultural technique, through the art of memory, in writing on parchment or paper, painted images on a canvas, or the construction of material monuments, it seemed possible to neutralise the instability of human life and minimise the risk of oblivion or eternal suffering.

In 1603 Góngora wrote two sonnets on the death of the Duchess de Lerma, the wife of his future protector the Duke of Lerma, to whom the *Relacion de la honras funebres* was also dedicated. These sonnets were composed at the demand of an academy, which was in charge of the funerary preparations of the late Duchess (Jammes 1967: 268). The discursive elements of the poems relate to materiality, memory, and death, in which the religious and the profane coexist:

> Yesterday a human deity, today a little earth,
> altars yesterday, today a tomb, o mortals!
> Feathers, even of Royal eagles,
> are still feathers; whoever ignores it truly errs.
>
> The bones enclosed today by this tomb,
> while not dwelling among oriental aromas,
> display mortal signs of the mortals.
> May reason open what is closed in marble.

This Phoenix, whose Arabia yesterday was Lerma,
is today a worm among ashes,
and a reminder to the wise.

If the Ocean swallows a ship,
what awaits a boat seeing lights through the topsail?
So take, earth, as human being is earth.

[Ayer deidad humana, hoy poca tierra,
Aras ayer, hoy túmulo, ô mortales!
Plumas, aunque de águilas Reales,
Plumas son; quien lo ignora mucho yerra.

Los huesos que hoy este sepulcro encierra,
A no estar entre aromas Orientales,
Mortales señas dieran de mortales.
La razón abra lo que el mármol cierra.

La Fenix que ayer Lerma fue su Arabia
Es hoy entre cenizas un gusano,
Y de consciencia a la persona sabia.

Si una urca se traga el Océano,
Que espera un baxel luces en la gabia?
Tome tierra, que es tierra el ser humano.]
(Góngora 2000a: 209)

This poem similarly sets out to capture the *vanitas* of human beings, as it opens with the transformation of the Duchess from a human deity to a little earth. The second line focusses on the movement from the altar to the tomb, the material counterpart of the human in the preceding line. The last two lines of the quatrain further insist that even royal feathers are feathers, and thus mortal, and whoever ignores this commits a grave error. The feathers function as a metaphor of power and are subsequently associated with the Phoenix by means of negation. The bones that the tomb encloses become signs of mortality for all mortals because they are not embalmed with aromas and will thus become earth. The quatrain ends with an imperative to the mind to perceive the materiality of death contained in the tomb (the *señas mortales*, as in the previous sonnet). The same pattern is produced in the first tercet which describes how the Duchess who was a Phoenix in the Arabia of Lerma (or made happy by her husband, the Duke of Lerma, alluding to the widespread concept of *Arabia Felix*), is now a worm among ashes, a reference to the production of a worm from the ashes of the Phoenix which would give new life, and a reminder of death to wise people. The final tercet revolves around the topos of the shipwreck, rhetorically asking what awaits a small boat if the ocean can swallow a ship (a dialectical *locus a maiore*). According to Salcedo Coronel, the *luces en gabia* of the penultimate line refers to the Star Helena, which when seen through the topsail predicted heavy storms. Rather than an existential meditation on death, the sonnet revolves around its materiality – earth, tomb, bones, coffin, marble, ashes, worm – and regardless of the sources of the imagery (Christian, Greco-Roman etc.) they all refer back to a tangible physical reality that confronted the people in mourning.

The second sonnet written for the same occasion invokes the voice of the deceased Duchess's tomb by means of prosopopeia as an imperative to a passer-by to remember and honour, a recurring feature in the epitaphs of the time (Blanco 1984: 183). By its construction in the first person singular the poem gives voice to the material monument on which it pretends to be inscribed: 'Always royal lily, I was born in Medina'. It ends in a similar fashion as the preceding one with the following lines: 'The softness exhaled by the marble (come closer) comes to the death of Lily, which does not even spare the holy smell of cold ashes'. This last tercet, which echoes the 'cold ashes' in the poem 'Plebeian Urns, Royal Tombs', describes how the marble of the tomb exhales the tenderness of the dead lily in spite of the cold ashes of the dead body (metaphorically called lily throughout the poem), which is perceptible even through the holy smell of incense (Salcedo Coronel 1644: 750). The contemporary historian Luis de Cabrera records that the body of the deceased duchess had to be moved vast distances because of her wishes to be buried in Medinaceli, and when they finally arrived the body had started to decompose and smelled so bad that they had to bury her in secret the night they arrived, without telling anyone during the funerary ceremony the following day (Góngora 1981: 208). The smell of the decomposed body recalls the fact that in spite of the numerous references to ashes in these poems, cremation was strictly prohibited by the Church. The softness that transpires through the marble tomb is understood as a metaphor of how the memory of the deceased will survive through the constellation of its material media.

Memoria Plus Ultra: Epitaphs for El Greco's Tomb

When El Greco died in 1614 both Góngora and Paravicino composed sonnets for his tomb. The one by Góngora has been much discussed and praised, while the one by Paravicino is less well known. The sonnet by Góngora presents itself as an epitaph for El Greco's tomb, constructed as an invitation to a passer-by (*peregrino*) to remember the great painter. Mercedes Blanco has demonstrated that the tomb in the sonnet is exclusively imaginary, while Gene W. Dubois rather unconvincingly tries to prove that the sonnet refers to the Convent of Santo Domingo where El Greco had painted seven majestic altarpieces and where his remains were held (Blanco 2012a: 123; Dubois 2014: 188). The problem comes down to questions of referentiality and materiality. Which tomb and circumstance, if any, do the words in the poem refer to?

Which position should a reader assume in order to attribute meaning to the words? In the case of the sonnets to Queen Margaret's catafalque in Córdoba, such issues are eliminated by access to contemporary sources like the *Relación*, but in the case of the epitaphs for El Greco's tomb the problems of meaning attribution and physical presence are brought to the fore. In short, the problem consists in the incommensurability of the documentary and fictional aspects of poetry. As El Greco's burial was in fact a simple one, Blanco's argument is that Góngora in the sonnet offers him what was *not* awarded him in reality, as a poetic celebration of his memory.

Even if historically imaginary, the tomb that Góngora conceptualises through different materials and cultural techniques is particularly interesting precisely because it reveals what could be imagined within this discursive order. As Blanco notes, this tomb sounds a lot like the one that Michelangelo was awarded in wealthy Florence, which had been described in detail by Vasari and was known in early modern Spain.

> Pilgrim, behold this cold slab's elegance
> this pediment of gleaming porphyry,
> that to the world denies the sweetest brush
> ever to give wood spirit, canvas life.
>
> The name, worthy to be bruited with more
> breath than Fame's trumpets could ever exercise,
> makes this grave marble's face illustrious.
> Pay tribute, and proceed along your path.
>
> Here lies the Greek. Nature has thus
> acquired Art, while Art acquires example,
> Iris color, Phoebus light, and Morpheus shade.
>
> May this great tomb, though in hard stone attired,
> soak up wet tears and fragrances exhaled by the
> costly bark that is from the East conveyed.
> (Góngora 2007: 91)

> [Esta en forma elegante, oh peregrino,
> De pórfido luciente dura llave,
> El pincel niega al mundo, más suave
> Que dio espíritu a leño, vida a lino.
>
> Su nombre, aun de mayor aliento digno
> Que en los clarines de la Fama cabe,
> El campo ilustra de ese mármol grave:
> Venéralo, y prosigue tu camino.

Yace el Griego. Heredó naturaleza
Arte, y el arte, estudio, Iris colores
Febo luces, si no sombras Morfeo.

Tanta urna, a pesar de su dureza
Lágrimas beba, y cuantos suda olores
Corteza funeral de árbol sabeo.]
(Góngora 2000: 425)

This sonnet is constructed as an invitation to a passer-by to stop and remember El Greco, whose remains are laid to rest in the tomb. Funerary epitaphs as inscriptions on tombs are, according to some, the oldest form of literature (Bambacu et al. 2010: 3). Philologists of ancient Greek epitaphs face a problem similar, yet more complicated, than the one faced by the reader of this poem. An epigram such as the one by Góngora may refer deictically to a physical tomb, which may or may not be traceable, and, at the same time, be readable in another material context, such as in a manuscript. In fact, the poem uses this transposition of material context to produce a certain effect of presence, so that the reader is forced to focus attention on the materiality of the supposed tomb.

The invitation to the passer-by to remember can then be read as referring to the reader of the poem, who through the poetical rendering of the tomb and its content can produce the desired perpetuation of memory through words, even if no actual tomb existed. The description of this fictive funerary monument with a coat of arms can be understood as an attempt to elevate the status of the deceased painter by rendering in poetry what was not awarded him physically.

The first quatrain describes how an elegant shining tomb of porphyry denies the world its softest brush. This reference to an instrument of the cultural technique of painting, capable of the magical act of giving spirit to wood and life to canvas, resounds with the sonnets to portraits discussed in the previous chapter. Other than the name, the poem lacks any references to the human subject, who is understood metonymically through the material objects (porphyry, brush, canvas, wood, key, marble, urn). The first quatrain focusses on the instrument, the porphyry tomb, and the physical remains it supposedly contains, as a relic of the deceased painter. The second quatrain proceeds to inform the passer-by/reader that the name of the one who rests in the tomb is greater than what fits the sound of the clarions of *Fama*, a hyperbole typical of both Góngora and the political power of the era (it was the motto of Charles V). The name is said to illuminate the heavy marble, which the passer-by is asked to venerate before continuing on his path.

The next tercet pronounces the name El Greco for the first time, as an inscription on the tomb itself: 'Here lies the Greek'. This sentence, which stands on its own in the poetical construction of the sonnet, is both an utterance of the name and the centre of an inscription for the tomb. The poem thereby refers back to itself as inscription and technography, and the materiality of its stone, which by association stands for the perpetuation of memory, with a storage capacity that exceeds that of the paper on which the poem may be copied. Emilie Bergmann affirms that 'where the epigram is inscribed on stone, or conceived as such, the stone is a material symbol of human memory, crystalizing the dynamic phenomenon. Ultimately, it is the poetry which establishes a relationship between the stone and man through language, and, as the *Greek anthology* demonstrates, the epigram can speak independently of the stone' (Bergmann 1979: 123). This point should be elaborated by adding that the stone is not only a symbol but also an ancient medium for the written word, and it is this storage capacity that associates it with memory in the first place. The epigram can speak independently of stone, but not independently of a material support, whether in paper, parchment, or human memory.

The remaining tercets consist of hyperbole describing the heritage of the painter, turning El Greco into the centre of the sensual world. Nature inherits art from the late painter (and not the other way around), and art inherits his example, Iris his colours, Phoebus his light, and Morpheus his shadows. This list of inheritances accounts for the key technical aspects of the mastery of painting – colour, light and shadow – and reverses the concept of *imitatio* so that the sensual world is understood to emanate from the painter. The last tercet then returns to the materiality of the tomb, which is now animated in a process whereby the hard and heavy urn drinks up the tears of the mourners and exhales the incense associated with the funeral ceremony.

As in other funerary sonnets by Góngora, the focus throughout the poem is on the materiality of death rather than the biography of the deceased. Faced with the problem of death and the need to create a perpetuation of memory, the poet uses the physical and material context so that the poem itself becomes a witness to the monuments of memory. This process could be described as ekphrastic, or be called a form of material imagination, or even ironic, as some scholars have maintained. But with regard to the perpetuation of memory it can also be understood as the imaginary use of various storage media, like paper, marble or stone to construct a form of cultural memory with wider dissemination and longevity. On the one hand, words may outlive plastic artworks, as insisted by Horace in the classical ode, but on the other hand the actors seem aware that in order to survive the words needed a material support as they could no longer be confined to human memory and oral culture alone. The central issue concerns a conception of death that needs memory in order to be supportable, but this historically specific memory culture was becoming less oral and increasingly literal, which gave rise to a focus on the material support of memory.

Paravicino's sonnet on the same subject, in the only and posthumous edition of his work from 1650, carries the epigraph 'To the tomb of this same painter, who was the Greek from Toledo'. According to Mercedes Blanco, the word 'tomb' referred to the catafalques and ephemeral monuments of the type erected in Córdoba for Queen Margaret, which could lead one to think that such a monument would have been erected for El Greco (Blanco 2012a: 126). It is the word employed by Francisco Pacheco in his *Arte de la Pintura* when describing the catafalque erected in Rome for Michelangelo, a monument that he claims many preferred over the one erected for Philip II in Sevilla (to which Cervantes dedicated a sonnet) (Pacheco 1866: 77). When Paravicino died in 1634, Joseph Pellicer composed a book to his memory entitled *Fame, Exclamation, Tomb and Epitaph of Fray Hortensio Felix Paravicino y Arteaga.* The 'tomb' in this book is not a description of a material monument or catafalque but a lengthy poem called 'Tomb of Hortensio's Corpse', which could indicate that there existed a conception of the poem itself as an ephemeral monument. In the catafalque for Queen Margaret in Córdoba, the poetry formed an integral part of the materiality of the monument, so it seems plausible that the poems 'to the tomb' were closely associated with this material construction, and that a manuscript or printed copy of it were understood to function independently as well, by producing a memory of such monuments, which were well known to any reader at the time. El Greco designed a Catafalque for Queen Margaret's death in Toledo at the same time, and Paravicino wrote a sonnet for it.

Paravicino's sonnet for El Greco's tomb shares some features with Góngora´s, and it has been speculated that the former, who was closer to El Greco, sent his poem to the latter along with the news of the artist's decease:

> What could be enclosed of the Greek rests here.
> Piety hides it, faith seals it,
> soft [earth] weighs it down, soft, while
> sapphire is trodden by the part stolen from the knot.
>
> His fame is not reserved for the mute world,
> for any human climate, even if envy tries to obscure
> it from all sides: such a bright star is
> beyond reach for rude horizon's mist.
>
> He worked for a greater century, a greater Apelles,
> not the corrupt applause, and his strangeness
> can only be admired, not imitated, through the ages.
>
> Crete gave him life and brushes;
> Toledo a better fatherland, where he now begins,
> through death, to conquer eternities.
>
> [Del Griego aquí lo que encerrarse pudo
> Yace. Piedad lo esconde, fé lo sella,

Blando le oprime, blando mientras huella
Zafir la parte que se hurtó del nudo.

Su fama el orbe no reserva mudo
Humano clima, bien que a oscurecella
Se arma una envidia y otra: tanta estrella
Nieblas no atiende de horizonte rudo.

Obró a siglo mayor, mayor Apeles,
No el aplauso venal, y su extrañeza
Admirarán, no imitarán edades.

Creta le dio la vida y los pinceles;
Toledo, mejor patria donde empieza
A lograr con la muerte eternidades.]
(Cerdan 2013: 10)

As in Góngora's sonnet, Paravicino employs the epithet Griego rather than the Italian form Greco by which the artist was known in Spain. It has been pointed out that this change emphasises his connection to the *ingenio* associated with ancient Greek culture. Paravicino's sonnet starts out with a deictic reference to the tomb which locks up the remains of the painter, which is then by his earthly virtues held down by the heavy softness of the earth while the soul steals away into heaven. The rest of the poem revolves around El Greco's earthly life, his fame, and the perpetuation of his memory.

The first quatrain describes how his fame extends beyond earthly limits, even if beset by the low envy of the vulgar; a reference to the criticism and lack of appreciation that the painter experienced. His fame, then, is depicted as circulating the orbit of the earth, and El Greco himself as a shining star that cannot be obscured. The first tercet moves on to the temporal aspect of memory by asserting that the artist, working for a better century, became a better painter than Apelles (the Greek archetype of the painter), and did not care for the vulgar praise of his own time; his unique achievements will therefore be admired rather than imitated throughout the ages to come. The last tercet closes the spatial and temporal circle by referring to El Greco's native Crete, which supplied him with life and instruments, and to Toledo as his better homeland, where through his death he conquers eternity. The sonnet captures in its fourteen lines the extension of memory through the dimensions of time and space, and although the first quatrain depicts the traditional Christian concept of the soul transferred into heaven, as is to be be expected in a funerary sonnet by a Royal preacher, its main concern is with earthly memory rather than the salvation of the soul.

The Cardinal's Tomb

In 1616 Góngora wrote a funerary epigram for the tomb of Cardinal Sandoval y Rojas. Unlike El Greco's epitaph, there is no need to speculate on the shape or magnitude of the material referent of this sonnet, as it still stands in the cathedral of Toledo in the Chapel of the Virgin of the Tabernacle, which was built at the order of Sandoval y Rojas, who served as Archbishop of Toledo until his death in 1618. The grand architecture in Herrerian style was constructed by Jorge Manuel Theotocópuli, son of El Greco, and was finished in 1616.

The Cardinal had decided to move the old and famous Virgin of the Tabernacle to this newly constructed chapel where he also constructed his own tomb, and placed those of his relatives. The Virgin is a Roman-style carving, plated in silver in the thirteenth century, which according to legend belonged to the Apostles. To celebrate the installation of this majestic carving in the new chapel, the Cardinal organised a grand eight-day celebration with altar lamps, dances, fireworks, masks, religious processions and orations by the most notable preachers, including a poetic competition in which a large number of poets participated. Góngora's epitaph was written for the newly constructed tomb of the living Cardinal and his dead relatives, as a part of this celebration. The chronological orientation here is partly towards the future death of the Cardinal, which occurred two years later, and it seems to have been natural to focus on the dust into which his body would soon be turned. The tomb of the Cardinal was built according to Roman custom as a sarcophagus, with a pyramid symbolizing death and a ball symbolizing eternity. The symbolic order of the sepulchral architecture is reminiscent of that used for the catafalque of Queen Margaret in Córdoba, although on a much smaller scale.

A book describing the events was printed in the following year, 1617, dedicated to the Duke of Lerma and written by Pedro de Herrera. This codex of eight hundred pages has all the usual marks of an official publication, including dedication, privilege, taxation notice, and introduction. Herrera explains that a previous text of thirty pages was unordered and badly written, and that the Cardinal had asked him to produce a complete description including the orations and poetry, primarily for the Duke of Lerma, who could not participate in the important event. He further explains that it was originally intended to be a manuscript of two or three copies, but that widespread interest obliged him to produce a print run. Mercedes Blanco remarks that a quick look at this codex is enough to understand the importance of events like these for the status and orientation of poetry and preaching during this time. 'Today we tend perhaps to judge the poetry of such events as of minor importance; in the estimation of the contemporaries it was the contrary' (Blanco 2012c: 50).

The Duke of Lerma, to whom this edition was dedicated, was the favourite of Philip III (the same position occupied by Olivares in the court of Philip IV) and the nephew of the Cardinal. He was also the subject of an extensive (but unfinished) panegyric poem by Góngora in that same year. The Duke of Lerma and his closest associate Rodrigo Calderón became protectors of the poet, so the event in Toledo also functioned as an official recognition of the new poetic style of Góngora and represented a key moment in the ongoing debate on his *Soledades* and *Polifemo y Galatea* (Orozco Díaz 1974: 252).

A month before the event, Paravicino, who also contributed orations, produced a notice inviting the best poets to submit work to the competition, and had it displayed in the palaces of Madrid and in Toledo. Paravicino was the head of the poetic competition, appointing judges and deciding the formal aspects. He was appointed Royal Preacher in November that year, just a month after the celebrations, and it is probable that he gained the position as a consequence of his success in Toledo. The production of cultural memory in words and stone – memory of the Cardinal, of the Virgin of the Tabernacle, and of the chapel – was also an important political event. Both Góngora and Paravicino seem to have gained certain positions from it, as a result of the esteem in which their poetry and preaching were held. The description of the event, which presents a selection of the poetry from the competition, comprises about a hundred and forty pages. Herrera reproduces the rules of the competition written by Paravicino; for the sonnet genre, in which Góngora participated, the following guideline applied: 'A sonnet expressing esteem and sorrow, connecting the majesty of the edifice to a proper epitaph directed to the bones of the fathers and brothers of the Cardinal who are already in the urns' (Herrera 1617: 513). Thus the writers had to respect ready-made rules aiming at an epitaph for the edifice and the existing urns containing the bones of the relatives of the Cardinal. Several of the categories of the competition were assigned to a specific material purpose: the sonnet as epitaph on the tomb, a pictogram for the port of the chapel, an epigram in Latin to serve as inscription for the urns. The mechanisms of these operations may be reminiscent of the construction of an edifice, where each part serves a specific purpose. Góngora's sonnet, like several others in the volume, centres on the perpetuation of memory through the materiality of the tomb:

This fabric, which you admire,
this prime pomp of the sculpture, oh wayfarer,
in porphyries rebelling against the diamond,
in metals bitten by the rasp,

is sealed by earth, which earth can never oppress;
if you ignore to whom it belongs, hold back your foot, ignorant
and consult this inscription, which elegantly
informs bronzes and animates marbles.

Generous piety now links beautiful urns
majestically, decorously to the once heroic
and now holy ashes of those who,

leaving five blue stars on a field of gold,
with better steps tread on
golden stars in a blue field.

[Esta, que admiras, fábrica, esta prima
Pompa de la escultura, oh caminante,
En pórfidos rebeldes al diamante,
En metales mordidos de la lima,

Tierra sella que tierra nunca oprima;
Si ignoras cuya, el pie enfrena ignorante,
Y esa inscripción consulta, que elegante
Informa bronces, mármoles anima.

Generosa piedad urnas hoy bellas
Con majestad vincula, con decoro,
A las heroicas ya cenizas santas

De los que, a un campo de oro cinco estrellas
Dejando azules, con mejores plantas,
En campo azul estrellas pisan de oro.]
(Góngora 2000a: 471)

This epitaph addresses both the existing urns of the Cardinal's family members that had just been deposited, and the future urn of the Cardinal himself. The sonnet opens with an imperative to the passer-by to stop and honour the memory of those deposited in the tomb: the *viator* trope customary in Greek sepulchral epitaphs. In ancient Greece, tombs were usually deposited outside the city walls along the road, so a common reader of the epitaphs would be the passer-by, to whom they were addressed (Tueller 2010). In this sonnet, the passer-by has entered the Cathedral of Toledo, but as in the case of archaic and classical Greek epigrams, the reader is fixed in time and place by the deictic reference to the material of the monument. Furthermore, the epitaph serves the documentary purpose of informing the passer-by who is to be remembered.

The first two quatrains describe the materiality of the tomb: its porphyry harder than diamond and its metals prepared by the rasp to make a sculpture of funerary pomp. Its inscription 'informs bronzes' and 'animate marbles', and gives voice to the silent monument, performing the documentary function of informing the passer-by of the contents and purpose of this object. The witty inversion of the earth constructs a movement upwards from the grave by applying the classical tag *sit tibi terra levis*, meaning 'may the earth rest lightly on you', and insists that the ashes shall not be weighed down by the earth covering them, facilitating the ascension to the heavenly sphere described in the last two tercets. This ascension is reconducted towards the earth by the reference to the coat of arms of the Sandovals depicted on the tomb, so that the stars of the sky and the stars of the tomb become interdependent. The five blue stars on a golden field on the coat of arms are inverted through the golden stars on the blue field of heaven. The 'inscription' describes the monument of which it forms part, and taken out of the physical and spatial context of the Cathedral of Toledo, this documentary function will inform any reader of the material and shape of the Cardinal's tomb.

Ashes in an Hour Glass, Papers in a Tomb, and a White Book of Memory

The symbolic value attached to ashes was immense in early modern Spain. It represented mortality and memory alike, constituting a moral imperative to remember in the tradition of the *memento mori*. In Covarrubias's dictionary from 1611 the entry for ashes is several pages long. He explains that:

> Ashes is the fine dust left when matter is consumed by fire: turning things to dust and ashes is reducing them to as little as they can be: and thus in the Holy scripture it means humbleness, dejection, penance: and particularly in man, self-knowledge: because we are foolish, vain and forgetful, our Mother the Holy Church reminds us of this on the Ash Wednesday, putting it on our heads (Covarrubias 540).

Ashes were and still are employed on Ash Wednesday as a reminder of the vanity and mortality of the human being. In the Cathedral of Toledo, just in front of the Chapel where Cardinal Sandoval y Rojas constructed his tomb, Cardinal Portocarro (1635-1709) is buried by a plaque that reads *Hic iacet pulvis, cinis et nihil* meaning 'here lies dust, ashes and nothing': a sober epitaph, reminiscent of Góngora's 'in dust, in shadow, in nothing', although it was probably also inspired by the Capuchin Cardinal Antonio Barberini's epitaph from 1646 in the Santa Maria dell'Immacolata Concezione in Rome.

The Christian symbolism of ashes has a long history, but in early modern Spain it evolved into a historically specific focus on the materiality of memory and death. Interestingly, the Catholic Church's strict prohibition of cremation did not diminish the popularity of pagan references to ashes. The popularity of the Phoenix motif should be understood in connection with this focus on ashes as a symbolic registration of memory and death. The 'holy ashes' (in fact the bones) of the Cardinal became a relic in the Cathedral of Toledo, and although his remains were not visible to visitors, the awareness of their physical presence constituted a material memory and a reminder of mortality. Evidently even an official funerary epitaph to an influential Cardinal could refer to his ashes, so the cultural memory of this pagan burial practice effectively survived the Inquisition. Memory and mortality constitute the perpetuation and finitude of being respectively. Death marks the final limit of a human being's temporality, and memory here is an attempt to overcome this limit in the physical world.

It is perhaps not surprising that the motif of ashes in an hourglass, introduced by the Neo-Latin Italian poet Amalteo, gained popularity in early modern Spanish poetry (Rosales 1966: 47). The idea of keeping the ashes of a beloved and lost person in an hourglass would of course be considered heretical in Catholic countries like Spain where cremation was forbidden. But the symbolic use of the cultural technique of temporal measurement helped to revive ashes as a poetic trope, effectively mixing two key *vanitas* symbols in a kind of double exposure. As Thomas Macho insists, 'time, like numbers, is really an epistemological object which is constituted by concrete cultural techniques and operations, from which it cannot be detached' (Macho 2003: 190). Macho points out the importance of historically specific cultural techniques and operations for the conception of an epistemological object such as time, which is usually understood as universal. Hourglasses, although reminiscent of the ancient *clepsydra* or water-clocks, were introduced and spread throughout Europe in the late middle ages and early modern era. The earliest references to these devices have been found in documents from the first half of the fourteenth century (Dohrn-van Rossum 1996: 118). Along with geared clocks, which were introduced at the same time, they constituted an important instrument for collective time keeping, as their use depended on the introduction of equal hours occurring around the same time. Hourglasses were, like many other time-keeping devices, first used in monastic environments to check the work of public clocks, and in Spain the hours were even struck according to sandglasses. Sandglasses played an important social role in early modern Europe and faciliated the introduction of the new hour-reckoning and new techniques of temporal organization. In line with Macho's argument, we can trace how an instrument for the cultural technique of time measurement enters and constructs the social conception of time in the early modern era, rather than the other way around.

Saavedra Fajardo's *Political Emblems* (1640) uses the hourglass to express the finitude of political power. The hourglass, a historically specific cultural technique of time measurement, became a visual representation of the passage of time itself, which illustrates Macho's observation that the epistemological object of time is formed according to material objects and techniques. The book begins with the birth of the prince and ends with his death, and can be read – through the symbol of the hourglass – as a meditation on the expiration of power. Saavedra Fajardo is deeply occupied with the brevity of human life, the instance of death and the importance of material monuments like tombs as a reminder of this mortality. A few quotes from Saavedra Fajardo may suffice to give an idea of how this discourse is constructed:

> They started in the cradle and end in the tomb. These are the parenthesis of life, which includes a very brief clause of time. I do not know which moment is happier, the one when we open our eyes to the dawn of life, or the one when we close them in the night of death … Fear of the tomb is normal … What is life but a continuous fear of death, with nothing to assure its duration? (Saavedra Fajardo 1988: 674)

Life as a parenthesis between birth and death, or life as constant horror of death; in these conceptions of time the hourglass, showing the fast-approaching end of every hour, reveals the underlying material dimension of the epistemological object of time, which is constructed differently throughout history and depends on the cultural techniques used to measure it. An hourglass expires continually, a geared clock anticipates the future, while the digital watch displays only the past in how much time has passed since the new day begun at midnight.

In poetical discourse, which is not separate but integral to this political discourse, conceptions of time, memory and death formed through cultural techniques and material objects abound. The best-known example comes from Francisco de Quevedo, who dedicated two poems to an hourglass filled with the ashes of a lover:

> You testify, oh happy one, in your ashes
> to the immortal affection of the internal soul;
> As the eternal course is caused by love,
> you perpetuate your days by your yearnings.
>
> As dead, you tyrannise the order of time
> since you measure, repealing its government,
> the hours by the pain of the tender breast,
> the minutes by the happiness you make immortal.
>
> Oh miracle! Oh strange marvel!
> When you violate the laws of nature
> by perpetuating its movement.
>
> You constitute your own destiny:
> since through days, hours, minutes,
> you make your own sentiment eternal.
>
> [Ostentas, ¡oh felice!, en tus cenizas,
> El afecto inmortal del alma interno;

Que como es del amor el curso eterno,
Los días a tus ansias eternizas.

Muerto del tiempo el orden tiranizas,
Pues mides, derogando su gobierno,
Las horas al dolor del pecho tierno,
Los minutos al bien que inmortalizas.

¡Oh milagro! ¡Oh portento peregrino!,
que de lo natural los estatutos
rompes con eternar su movimiento.

Tú mismo constituyes tu destino:
Pues por días, por horas, por minutos,
Eternizas tu proprio sentimiento.]
(Quevedo 2009a: 536)

The poem has rightly been interpreted as an expression of the eternal love that triumphs over time and death. Quevedo constructs a paradox out of the notion of an hourglass filled with ashes, the physical remains of a dead human being. As two primary symbols of death, time and memory, the hourglass and its ashes overcome the destructive power of time and make something eternal. The paradox consists in the shrinking of cosmic space into the narrow borders of the hourglass, where no ascension to heaven is possible, but the laws of nature are overcome on earth in material rather than spiritual form (Cullhed 2005: 296). As in the funerary sonnets of Góngora discussed above, the focus is on the notion of death rather than on the ascension of the soul to heaven, a secularization that retains the symbolic work of ashes, tombs, and marble but seems to omit the salvation which had been the natural endpoint of such epitaphs since the middle ages. The epistemological object of time taken to its extreme point (death) is understood through the symbolic operations of ashes (ancient funerary practice) and hourglass (time measurement). The hourglass 'measures' the hours of pain and the minutes of happiness thereby making them eternal. The cultural technique of measuring time with an hourglass paradoxically becomes a medium of storage, as it cancels the natural order and perpetuates and immortalises that which is already inevitably lost. The ashes flowing through the hourglass perpetuate their own sentiment in this witty inversion of ashes and the technology for measuring the time leading up to death. In metaphorically describing a lover being burnt by the flames of love, Quevedo constructs a paradox consisting in a pagan funeral practice and a current device for time keeping.

In Luis de Ulloa Pereira's sonnet on the same theme, the hourglass becomes a speaking object: 'These mute ashes in a small glass which indicates your years, your hours which you enjoy on loan, is a tongue that tells of *desengaño*' (Ulluoa Perreira 1674: 21). The effect of the object is striking: the transparent urn, by virtue of measuring time, reminds the beholder of his coming death, and thus converts the ashes, although they are mute, into a tongue imposing *desengaño*. The poem describes the imaginary object and gives it a voice to produce a warning (*escarmiento*). Another sonnet on this topic written by Garcia Salcedo Coronel, the commentator on Góngora, can be found in a printed edition of his poetry from 1650. His version, which is presented as a translation of Amalteo's, insists on the exact measurement of the device as the representation of the brevity of human life: 'This dust, which in transparent Glass today offended divides the hours: and diligently suggests, in its repeated course, the brevity of time' (Salcedo Coronel 1650: 9).

A sonnet by Góngora dated 1600 in the Chacon manuscript offers another example of an imaginary inversion of tomb, memory and writing. The poem uses the funerary imagery employed in epitaphs to express sentiment over a lost love. The epigraph reads 'On some papers that a lady had written for him, putting them in a shrine'. The prosaic circumstance of written correspondence is conceptualised here as the physical remains of a dead body:

Here lie the bones entombed
of a friendship that was unique in this world,
either as to the experience of fortune
or as a warning to be cautious.

It was born among thoughts, even if honest,
momentous to love, to many importunate,
so much that it was killed in the cradle
by eyes of envy armed with venom.

A small urn seals them, like bones,
in the end, of an ill-fated creature,
but verses honour them, immortal,

they will live imprinted on the tomb,
the stone being hard Felixmena,
Daliso its sculptor, and a chisel their pains.

[Yacen aquí los huesos sepultados
De una amistad que al mundo será una,
O ya para experiencia de fortuna,
O ya para escarmiento de cuidados.

Nació entre pensamientos, aunque honrados,
Grave al amor, a muchos importuna,
Tanto, que la mataron en la cuna
Ojos de envidia y de ponzoña armados.

Breve urna los sella, como huesos,
Al fin, de malograda criatura,
Pero versos los honran, inmortales,

Que vivirán en el sepulcro impresos,
Siendo la piedra Felixmena dura,
Daliso el escultor, cincel sus males.]
(Góngora 2000a: 181)

The papers, which by virtue of their colour are associated with bones, are metaphorically constructed as the remains of a tomb, which here refers to the shrine. The poet tells the usual story of who these animated objects once were, as they were born from thought and killed by jealousy. The medium of paper thus acquires specific importance, constructing through poetical 'immortalizing' (itself written on paper) a memory of the ephemeral relation and its written correspondence. As in the case of the hourglass, the papers deposited in the shrine become a remainder of something lost and by virtue of this presence construct a memory of it.

Another example of how early modern cultural techniques and objects were poetically conceptualised as storage and memory can be found in an anonymous sonnet found in Ms. 4117 at the Biblioteca Nacional in Madrid. According to the epigraph, the sonnet is dedicated to 'a White book':

White for the letters of my pains
discreet as to the cause for which I owe them,
new lily of the accounts of my soul,
of the loss of blood in my veins,

pages, full of tears from my eyes,
beginning of the receipt where I carry
the hopes which I dare to pay,
end and draft of all others,

discourse of the events of my life,
first chapter of my story,
not well written but deeply felt,

from now on you will be my book of memory,
where for *Celia* to be known,
I shall write the signs of her glory.

[A un libro blanco.
Blanco para las letras de mis penas
Discretas por la causa a quien las debo,

De las cuentas del alma lilio nuevo
Del gasto de la sangre de mis venas,

Hojas, del llanto de mis ojos llenas,
Principio de el recibo donde llevo
Las esperanzas que a pagar me atrevo,
Remate y borrador de las ajenas,

Discurso del succeso de mi vida,
Capitulo primero de mi historia
No bien escrita pero bien sentida,

De hoy mas sereis mi libro de memoria,
Donde, para ser Celia conocida,
Escribire las señas de su gloria.]
(Ms. 4117: 78)

This sonnet is previously unpublished, and the seventeenth-century manuscript contains poetry by Góngora and Quevedo among others. An interesting material feature is that some poetry is completely erased or redacted, probably by the censor. The name 'Celia' could indicate that the author was Luis de Ulloa y Pereira, as that name is mentioned no fewer than twenty-two times in his *Obras de Don Luis de Ulloa Pereira* (1674). (This, however, is not enough to attribute the poem with confidence.) The referent of the poem is a media object that until recently has received little attention from historians. The 'libro de memoria', which explicitly links writing to remembrance, was a small object made of hard, coated leaves on which one could write with a stylus without the need of ink or supporting table, and then erase and reuse as needed. As made clear by Roger Chartier, who convincingly argues that this medium is what Sancho Panza writes the letter to Dulcinea on in *Don Quijote*, the *libro de memoria* was understood to be 'more reliable than memory, because it fixed in writing what might otherwise be forgotten, the *librillo de memoria* was nevertheless not a library or permanent archive. The assumption was that whatever was written in it would be copied onto another medium so that the pages could be restored to their original pristine condition. […] Erasable and reusable, the librillo de memoria is the palimpsest of the Moderns' (Chartier 2007: 22).

This object appears in another canonical work, Shakespeare's *Hamlet*, with a similar function as both metaphor and material support for human memory. When Hamlet has seen his father's ghost, he says: 'Yea, from the table of my Memory, / I'll wipe away all trivial fond records, / All saws of books, all forms, all pressures past, / That youth and observation copied there; / And thy commandment all alone shall live / Within the book and volume of my brain, unmixed with baser matter' (Shakespeare 2006: 219). Thus Hamlet conceptualises his memory through the medium he uses to take notes, that is, the material support of his cognitive memory. Hamlet's conception is similar to the one expressed in the sonnet quoted above, where the white book is written on with the blood of the poet's suffering, leaves filled with his tears (a word play on *hoja/ojo*, meaning 'leaf'/'eye'), while also serving as 'eraser and end of the alien'.

The sonnet also associates the book of memory with accounting, a use for which it was often employed. In the two quatrains the poet seems to erase the debts inscribed in the tablet of his mind and instead writes the signs of the glory of his beloved. The poem may well have been written on such a tablet before being copied into the manuscript where it now survives, just as Hamlet, having referred to his memory as a tablet, says 'My Tables,– meet it is I set it down, / That one may smile, and smile, and be a villain', referring to the material object that the actor would have carried on stage (Stallybrass et al 2004: 380).

This largely forgotten media object appears to have played in important role as a mediator between the fragile human memory and the fixed form of writing in manuscripts and print, which required far more labour and specific tools. Recently, a team of investigators led by Peter Stallybrass found extensive evidence of the widespread use of these objects in early modern England, which had previously not been known by book historians. Stallybrass's team found a small almanac from 1604 with blank leaves of specially treated erasable paper, including instructions on how to erase and clean the pages. Wax tablets had been in use since antiquity but were thought to have disappeared with the introduction of paper throughout Europe in the late middle ages. For this reason, the existence of erasable tablets in the early modern era was thought to have been limited to Northern Europe and especially England, where the introduction of paper was much slower than in Spain. As Chartier points out, however, this particular media object plays an important role in *Don Quijote*. Chartier further traces the existence of such objects to Spanish inventories from the early seventeenth century and notes their occurrence in plays by Lope de Vega, where they serve a similar function as in Shakespeare. Furthermore, it seems plausible that this type of object would have been used by the 'thieves' of which Lope complained, who copied his plays and sold them to printers. The *libro de memoria*, in contrast to accessories such as inkhorn, paper and support, would have been small and discreet enough to use in the audience of a recitation or a play. The title's 'white book'/*libro blanco* is a term for a notebook for registering and accounting, with several occurences in the seventeenth century (the historical database of the Spanish Academy displays six occurences of *libro blanco*, all referring to register books for note taking). Furthermore, the line 'not well written but deeply felt' seems to fit well with this media practice, as does the explicit naming in the last tercet of the 'book of memory'. As in the case of time, memory appears as an epistemological object as well as cognitive function, and its conception is dependent on the cultural techniques used to preserve it.

From Peacock to Phoenix: Execution and Assassination

On 21 October 1621 Rodrigo Calderón, Marquis of Siete Iglesias and Secretary of the Royal Chamber, was beheaded at a public execution on the Plaza Mayor in Madrid. Calderón, who was the favourite of the Duke of Lerma, himself the favourite of Philip III, who had passed away in March the same year, was a controversial character in the Spanish Court. The strong reactions to his death, which seems to have encapsulated much of the tension between vanity and piousness that was so present in the period's discourse around death, may be regarded as emblematic of early modern memory culture.

Calderón had been accused of using witchcraft to kill Queen Margaret, who had died in childbirth in 1611, and of being responsible for the murder of her associate Francisco de Juara, who was undertaking an investigation into Calderon's affairs at the order of the Queen before she died. Calderón was more or less protected as long as Philip III was alive, although he successively lost titles and favour, especially after the fall of Lerma in 1618. He was arrested and sent to prison in 1619 while the investigation into his alleged crimes was undertaken. During the 1610s, Calderón represented the vanity and greed of men in power while the kingdom increasingly suffered from the aggravated financial crisis. After being incarcerated, he was tortured and the public image of him slowly started to change.

Góngora, who was his friend and sought his protection, writes about his compassion for Calderón in a letter dated 20 January 1620 (Góngora 2000b: 345). The former favourite was interrogated about his involvement in the Queen's death, and the interrogators even confronted him with testimonies that the Queen had appeared *post mortem* and accused him of her murder. The process was finally left to the King himself to decide, but he died in March 1621 before Calderón could be absolved. While his connections at Court had protected him from the death sentence until then, the new régime of Philip IV entailed the customary change of ministers and Calderón found himself suddenly without protection. Even if Philip III had agreed to incarcerate and prosecute him, he seemed to want to spare his life. Góngora reports in a letter dated 6 April that on the day of Philip III's death, the new King requested the papers of the process against Calderón and within a week he had questioned the prosecutors three times: 'The same day that his father died the King asked for the process on Siete Iglesias, and since then he has had three hearings with the judges; this affair is strongly pressed and I am afraid it will end badly' (Góngora 2000b: 376). Góngora, who at this point was serving as the Royal Chaplain, was involved in the funerary services for the King's death and composed several poems for them, but his letters reveal his preoccupation with Calderón who, along with Lerma, had been his protector. Góngora's concern about Calderón's fate was obviously well grounded, and he was probably not the only one who could foresee that the death of Philip III would entail the death of the Marquis.

Philip IV and his closest ministers, Baltasar de Zuñiga and the Count of Olivares, wanted to present themselves as the new political masters of the Empire and so blamed the old régime of Calderón and Lerma for corruption and fiscal malfeasance (Boyden 2000: 254). The ministers pressed the judges to pass a death sentence. As John Elliott puts it, 'Zuñiga and Olivares had clearly decided that they needed an exemplary victim' (Elliott 1986: 107). Calderón, who had been the target of much criticism for his excesses and for his questionable ruling methods, became the victim of a political power-play. Calderón was sentenced to public execution on 9 July 1621 for the murder of Francisco Juara and for having obtained royal decrees by foul methods (Boyden 2000: 254). The reasons given for his execution were thus his own violence and his abuse of the bureaucratic apparatus. Góngora writes again to Francisco de Corral in the same month to report on the case of Calderón, who is slowly emerging as a martyr. The poet recounts the calmness with which the former Marquis received the news of his imminent execution, and that he did not say more than 'Praise the Lord; and the Holy Virgin, our Lady' (Góngora 2000b: 389).

James Boyden has described in detail the following development of 'the passion' of Rodrigo Calderón, in which he devoted his remaining time to worshipping Teresa de Avila (Boyden 2000). Quevedo's description of this process captures it quite well: 'he transcended the prospects of this life and began to commune with ultimate realities shorn of the veil of worldly vanities' (Rosales 1964: 80). Calderón turned from a life of vanity and excess to an existence of devotion and meditation on his coming death. He thereby perfectly incarnates the sense of *vanitas* which marked the discourse on life and death in this era. As Boyden puts it, 'Calderon's last thirty-six hours comprise a representation of the good death, intensified by references to martyrdom' (257). When he was finally executed in front of a huge crowd at 12.30 p.m. on 21 October 1621, he displayed a 'calm and bravery' that has entered into the collective memory of Spain. Even today, the expressions 'to conduct oneself more honourably than Don Rodrigo on the scaffold' and 'to be prouder than Don Rodrigo on the gallows' are used to convey bravery in extreme circumstances. Calderon's behaviour embodied the key aristocratic, secular values of honour and courage.

The death of Rodrigo Calderón became an emblematic event in seventeenth-century Spain. The intended staging of a public sacrifice for the new régime failed utterly, instead fuelling criticism of its cruelty. The production of funerary epitaphs was accordingly vast; poems were abundantly copied and circulated. In the collection of manuscripts of the Biblioteca Nacional in Madrid there exist a relatively large number of codices with titles that contain the words 'Calderón' and 'death', many of them presenting poetry, orations, letters and the sentence side by side. Góngora dedicated three sonnets to the death of Calderón, which stand out among the vast corpus of poetry that testifies to the collective trauma of the execution. The first two quatrains of the first sonnet describe the lack of funerary honour awarded Calderón, who had died as an example and sacrifice for the audience:

> Seal the bloody trunk, do not oppress it,
> of the fortunately unfortunate,
> whose changing fate this
> slate can hardly redeem.
>
> Common piety, instead of the sublime
> urn which retribution refused him,
> erects this column in imaginary bronce,
> so that time will wear down its memories in vain.
>
> [Sella el tronco sangriento, no lo oprime,
> De aquel dichosamente desdichado,
> Que de las inconstancias de su hado
> Esta pizarra apenas lo redime,
>
> Piedad común; en vez de la sublime
> Urna, que el escarmiento le ha negado,
> Padrón le erige en bronce imaginado,
> Que en vano el tiempo las memorias lime.]
> (Góngora 1981: 431)

For want of a physical tomb, which Calderón deserved according to his peers – his remains were ordered to be placed in a mass grave for criminals in the church of San Gines, but he was instead secretly buried in a Carmelite House – the poet constructs a tomb from words for the perpetuation of his memory. The sublime urn that was denied Calderón by the public execution is here replaced by a column of imaginary bronze. Covarrubias defines the word *padrón* as 'a column on which is placed some kind of writing, which is public and perpetual'. The poem acts as a technography in drawing attention to its own mediality in constructing a verbal monument that could well be placed on such a column, in a way similar to Góngora's epitaph for El Greco's imaginary tomb. The classical Horatian topos of words outliving plastic art (*aere perennius*) is used here as an argument for the superiority of the poetic tomb over the absent physical monument.

The 'bloody trunk' refers to the decapitated body of Calderón, asking that it not be weighed down, a variation on the *sit tibi terra levis* topos: the wish, common to several funerary sonnets already discussed here, that the earth should not hinder the ascension of the soul from the buried body. The verbal monument produced by the poem aims to produce durable storage for the memory of its subject. Aleida Assmann points out that Egyptians held writing to be the most secure medium of memory: 'they realized that traces of black ink on fragile papyrus represented a more lasting monument than elaborate tombs with lavish furnings' (Assmann 2011: 171). This awareness runs through the poetic production in early modern Spain and appears with striking frequency in the poetry dedicated to actual deaths like Calderón's. Assmann finds similar evidence in Shakespeare's poetry and quotes a sonnet that echoes the one by Góngora: 'Not marble, nor the gilded monuments / Of princes, shall outlive this powerful rhyme' (172). Both poets follow Horace, whose words resound in Góngora's 'imaginary bronze': 'I have finished a monument more lasting than bronze, more lofty than the regal structure of the pyramids'. Here poetry appears as the supreme technique of storage for the perpetuation of memory, in its ability to be copied and disseminated over time.

Góngora's second sonnet to Calderón uses the recurrent motif of the rebirth of the Phoenix to produce an image of the posthumous *fama*, of which the poem itself is a part.

> Your pyre could be elevated,
> made of aromatic wood,
> oh Phoenix in death, if in life
> a bird not even embarrassed by its feet.
>
> Die in happy and consoling peace,
> ascend to the illustrious region,
> because by more eyes than your vanished vain
> feathers had, is your death now bewailed.
>
> The knife purified, instead of the flame,
> your first being, and gloriously,
> reborn from its shed blood,
>
> taking on wings, not of vulgar fame,
> but of Christian valor, of ardent faith,
> shall it owe more to its tomb than its nest.
>
> [Ser pudiera tu pira levantada,
> De aromáticos leños construida,
> Oh Fénix en la muerte, si en la vida
> Ave aun no de sus pies desengañada.
>
> Muere en quietud dichosa y consolada,
> A la región asciende, esclarecida,
> Pues de más ojos que desvanecida
> Tu pluma fue, tu muerte es hoy llorada.

Purificó el cuchillo, en vez de llama,
Tu ser primero, y gloriösamente
De su vertida sangre renacido,

Alas vistiendo, no de vulgar fama,
De cristiano valor sí, de fé ardiente,
Más deberá a su tumba que a su nido.]
(Góngora 2000a: 558)

This sonnet uses the theme of the two symbolic birds, the peacock and the Phoenix, to represent Calderón's transition from a courtier marked by *vanitas* to a Christian martyr who found devotion in death. This contrast seems to have constituted the attraction of Calderón's case for so many contemporary poets – almost everyone who resided in the Court dedicated a poem to the event – as he epitomised the tragic fate of those who aspired to rise in the court; caught between luxurious vanity and hard moral lessons. The first quatrain expresses how, in life, Calderón was like the peacock, a symbol of vanity because, proud of its feathers, it was supposedly unaware of the ugliness of its feet. Indeed, he was not even *desengañado*: the virtue which overcomes *vanitas* in this discourse.

In death, however, Calderón is transformed into the Phoenix, his pyre constructed of aromatic wood. The second quatrain further develops the contrast between a life spent in vain pleasures and a pious death. Calderón dies in reassured and happy peace (because of his devotion and regret), ascending from earth to heaven and the afterlife through his *fama*; more eyes than displayed on the peacock's feathers now weep his death. The tercets develop the theme of the Phoenix, where Calderón's being is purified through the blade which beheaded him (rather than through the flame of the Phoenix), and so is reborn through blood instead of ashes. He is thereby granted wings, not of vulgar fame but of noble fame, for his bravery and faith.

The political context of this sonnet is quite different from that of the death of Queen Margaret, but the imagery used in these poems is similar (Phoenix, pyre). The case of Calderón was a delicate affair, and while they were affected by the cold-bloodedness of his execution, the poets could only praise his Christian devotion and honour in the face of death. Góngora sent this sonnet to Francisco de Corral on 2 November the same year, two weeks after the execution, and asked him to read it to two other associates (one of the few times Góngora mentions his poetry in a letter): 'Please read to both of them this sonnet that I made for the suffering of that unfortunate Marquis and fortunate criminal, with as much modesty as pity, because now is not the time for jokes, and more so for those of us who were his friends, who have renounced *de vehementi*' (Góngora 2000b: 398). Góngora, like many other poets who dedicated sonnets to Calderón, had witnessed the execution of a friend and had to try to produce an expression of 'modesty' and 'pity' at the same time. Publicly, he has to renounce him to protect himself in the new political order, but manuscript poetry here creates the possibility for ambiguous and anonymous expression.

Conde de Villamediana, who is mentioned in the same letter as 'shining greatly, as always', also dedicated several poems to the death of the unfortunate Marquis. Here, like Góngora, he focusses on the transformation of a life worthy of condemnation to a death worthy of memory:

> This one, who in the highest fortune
> did not fit in himself, nor did his fate fit in him,
> seemed worthy of death while living,
> seemed worthy of life while dying.
>
> Oh never grasped Providence,
> superior aid, sturdy notice:
> the smoke into which the applause is turned
> makes the very affront illustrious!
>
> The blade purified the perfect
> parts that watchful religion orders
> to ascend to a greater victory,
>
> and with the causes exchanged for their affects,
> if glories brought him to punishment,
> his punishment restores him to Glory.
>
> [Éste que en la fortuna más subida
> No cupo en sí, ni cupo en él su suerte,
> Viviendo pareció digno de muerte,
> Muriendo pareció digno de vida.
>
> ¡Oh Providencia nunca comprendida,
> auxilio superior, aviso fuerte:
> el humo en que el aplauso se convierte
> hace la misma afrenta esclarecida!
>
> Purificó el cuchillo los perfectos
> Medios que religión celante ordena
> Para ascender a la mayor victoria,
>
> Y trocando las causas sus efectos,
> Si glorias le conducen a la pena,
> Penas restituyen a la Gloria.]
> (Ms. 3906: 100)

This sonnet was, and still is, one of the most famous in Villamediana's production. It circulated in manuscript, like most poetry, and is the first in a printed book from 1622 called *New romance composed of the death of Don Rodrigo Calderón in which is described his imprisonment, sentence and death, and the farewell he took at the time of death.* It opens with a famous sonnet that treats the same matter. It is also included in Gracian's *Agudeza y arte del ingenio*, where it is dubbed 'grand sonnet'. Villamediana wrote numerous satirical sonnets on Calderón, as he was opposed to the reign of Philip III, but here the tone is less satirical and more reflective. The lines of the first quatrain – 'seemed worthy of death while living, / seemed worthy of life while dying' – capture the general sentiment of the public in the various testimonies. Calderón had represented the greed and hunger for power that seemed to cause corruption in the Monarchy, but when faced with death, his noble conduct and regret inspired a collective sentiment of admiration. The death of Calderón became an *escarmiento* – a warning – to the public, and because he died *desengañado*, his fate became instructive as well as admirable. In the second quatrain Villamediana dwells on the apparently contradictory twists of fate, in fact dictated by divine providence.

The first tercet sets out with the word *purificó*, excactly as in Góngora's sonnet on the same topic, while other versions have *calificó* (Rozas 1964). The blade appears as a tool for purification of the Marquis's soul, which can now ascend to heaven in victory; as his earthly glories led to death, death now leads him to heavenly glory. The physical decapitation undertaken publicly on the Plaza Mayor is here integral to the symbolic discourse around death, *vanitas* and *memento mori*. Calderón's execution appears to embody this discourse through the entwining of a violent end and the possibility of salvation.

Many of the numerous poems written to commemorate this event testify to the collective understanding of Calderón's death as a warning, almost as if the spectacle of the execution was in itself a powerful work of art. The staging of it certainly turned it into a spectacle. As John Elliott writes, the new régime had miscalculated the effects of this execution: 'by his proud bearing on the scaffold he redeemed in a few moments the reputation of a lifetime. Instead of the approval it had so confidently expected, the ritual murder planned by the new régime to serve as a symbol of cleansing and regeneration brought only massive condemnation' (Elliott 1986: 107).

The Conde de Villamediana would himself become the object of attention and public grief due to his violent death the following year. The story of Juan de Tassis, second Count of Villamediana and Postmaster General of the Kingdom quickly turned into legend. He was known as a man of excess in money, love, gambling, poetry, and politics alike. Most scholars now believe that he was the inspiration for the myth of Don Juan, as portrayed by Tirso de Molina in *El Burlador de Sevilla* (Marañon 1967; Stradling 1993). Villamediana had been exiled from Philip III's Madrid not once but twice, officially for having cheated in a card game but in reality because of his fearless satire on the Duke of Lerma, Rodrigo Calderón, and the other ministers of Philip III.

As Postmaster General, a title he inherited from his father, he had access to and control over the pivotal medium of the mail, which meant that he could acquire politically sensitive information as well as disseminate his own poetry throughout Europe. Today many of his poems are dispersed in various libraries in Europe, a dissemination which reflects the geopolitical situation of the empire at that time; according to R.A. Stradling they can be found in every major archive in western Europe (Stradling 1993: 13). In the words of Bernhard Siegert, 'the private letter, a compromising of oneself in writing, was the medium of transmission that, alongside the recording media of diaries and autobiographies, assumed the function in an alphabetized Central Europe that confession previously had carried out as the old religious means of control' (Siegert 1999: 38). The title of Postmaster General in a bureaucratic empire that relied to such a large extent on written communication was thus a potentially powerful and dangerous position to hold. Villamediana's father, Juan de Tassis y Acuña, had played in important role in organizing the postal network of Europe, and played a part in 'transforming what had been essentially a royal mail into an efficient public service' (Ettinghausen 2001: 200). By the 1620s, the established postal network made it possible to disseminate any type of sensitive information without it being subjected to the regulations of printed matter.

After Philip III had died and Lerma, Calderón, and others had fallen, the new political régime of the Count-Duke of Olivares recalled Villamediana to the Court in Madrid. As Villamediana had fiercely satirised the old régime, he was considered welcome by the new rulers, although his unpredictable behaviour and satirical writings also made him a dangerous person in a fragile empire that relied on control over the flow of information to exercise its power.

On 23 August, two days after Villamediana's death, Góngora wrote to his friend Cristobal de Heredia to inform him of the events:

> It happened last Sunday in the evening, at the 21st, upon his coming from the palace in his carriage with Don Luis de Haro, oldest son of the Marquis of Carpio, and in Calle Mayor, out of the portals at the sidewalk of San Ginés, there came a man who went over to the left side where the Count was, and with a horrible knife, as the wound showed, he cut him from side to side, causing such a mess that even a bull would be scared. The Count at this point, without stepping from the footrest, fell upon him and put his hand on his sword, but realizing he was too weak, he said 'this is done, confession, gentlemen'. [...] People are cautious when discussing the cause, and justice proceeds with exterior matters, but may God keep the unfortunate in heaven, since I doubt that they will proceed much further. I am as sorry as I am *disillusioned* [desengañado] about all pomp and vanity in life, because this gentleman, after having squandered so much

> [during his lifetime], was buried that night in a wooden coffin taken from San Ginés, due to the haste imposed by the Duke of the *Infantado*, without even being granted a proper sarcophagus. You see now, Your Grace, that I have reason to escape from myself, and even more from this place where I have lost two friends to the steel (Góngora 2000b: 428).

Góngora's letter testifies to the general reaction to Villamediana's violent death as a significant event of the time. He is disillusioned (*desengañado*) with all pomp and vanity of life because of the lack of honour with which Villamediana was buried in a wooden coffin without any funerary processions (a third instance of Góngora reacting to the improper burial of his friends). He has now lost two friends to the steel blade (Calderón and Villamediana), and wants to leave the Court as soon as he can. Góngora's biography aside, the main interest of this event lies in the production of cultural memory of Villamediana's death. Days after the murder the legend starts to crystallise; foreign travellers who resided in the Court would later write of this political murder, reported that the Count-Duke of Olivares and the King himself were responsible. Even today there is no hard evidence of the reason for the murder, but there are a large number of more or less plausible theories, forming part of the cultural memory produced primarily in writing (poetry, letters, theatre, and documents); in this, Villamediana, like Calderón, seems to epitomise some of the core issues of the time: political power, *vanitas*, the symbolic value of death, and control over the flow of information.

Villamediana had been recalled from exile in 1621 after the death of Philip III. Several contemporary sources (among them Joseph Pellicer and Baltasar Gracián) report that the Count appeared at a celebration in Madrid dressed in a coat on which, alluding to the recently introduced silver coin, the *real*, he had written the motto: 'mis amores son reales' (Rosales 1964: 141). This witty wordplay could be taken to mean 'my love is for *reales*' (the coin), but could also be understood as 'my love affairs are royal', implying that he had affairs with members of the royal household. The story reported by foreign travellers in Madrid in subsequent years started building the myth around Villamediana, who, as Antonio de Brunel puts it, 'was the most gallant and most ingenious courtier of Spain' (Rosales 1964: 8). Brunel recounts that Villamediana staged the play *La Gloria de Niquea* in 1622 to celebrate the new king and set fire to the decor, so as to be able to 'rescue' the Queen and carry her in his arms.

The Countess of Aulnoy repeated this story in 1690 in her *Memories of the Court of Spain*, remarking that Villamediana was 'young, good-looking, elegant, brave, lavish, gallant and ingenious', which she obviously had picked up by word of mouth. Both of these travellers report that it was the Count-Duke of Olivares who persuaded the King to have Villamediana assassinated. Aulnoy summarises the attraction of this legend in the following words: 'One could say that the Count of Villamediana was the most perfect gentleman ever seen, and his memory is still venerated among disgraced lovers' (Rozas 1964: 14). The cultural memory of the tragic fate of this lover who got his fingers burned – Villamediana is also associated with Icarus, who burnt the wax of his wings when he flew too close to the sun, and with Phaethon – is in fact the origin of the widespread myth of Don Juan. The fact that Don Juan was Postmaster General and exercised control over the primary medium of affection, the letter, should not be forgotten. The story of how the Count set fire to the theatre decor also appears in one of La Fointaine's *Fables,* published at the same time as Aulnoy's account. As Rosales puts it, 'the Count of Villamediana was converted to a Patron of amorous idealism, to an idol, and all miserable lovers venerated his memory [...] His recklessness made him into a symbol, his idealism into an example' (1964: 18).

As the legend of Villamediana's life and death has been so widely disseminated, forming such an important part of the cultural memory of Spain, it is interesting to return to its conception and construction, in Madrid in 1623, to try to uncover the basic operations that underlie it. In 1928, the investigator Narciso Alonso Cortés found documents in the secret archive of Simancas, which showed that Villamediana was in fact subject to a legal process concerning the *pecado nefando*, the 'abominable sin' of sodomy. Five people were publicly burned alive for the crime of having engaged in homosexual relations shortly after the murder of Villamediana, three of whom were directly linked to his household: two servants and a black slave. Villamediana's name, however, was left out of all the public documents of the process. In secret letters written by Fernando Ramírez Fariña, it is explained that the King had ordered that Villamediana's involvement should be kept secret at all costs, to protect the honour of his memory (Cortés 1928: 81).

The newly founded Council of Castile, in which Olivares was an important actor, had been constituted to reform the morals of the kingdom (it was the same Council that two years later would prohibit the printing of books of entertainment). One of the processes concerned the crime of homosexuality, and evidence was gathered against Villamediana. It is unclear whether the process was initiated before or after his murder, but this circumstance has led several investigators to argue that Villamediana must have been assassinated for his homosexual acts rather than for having had affairs with the Queen or other members of the royal household as per the legend framed from the beginning to protect the legend of Villamediana as a perfect nobleman.

The documents transcribed by Cortés have now been lost from the archive, and Stradling, who tried to locate them in 1986, argues that they were removed to protect the myth of Don Juan that Villamediana is believed to have engendered. As he puts it: 'the accepted prototype of Don Juan, most potent of all myths of heterosexual male seduction, was a promiscuous *homosexual.* [...] At some point after the publication of Cortés' study in 1928 the evidence had been removed [...] A gay Don Juan evidently threatened the integrity of every Spanish male, even the identity of Spain itself. It had to remain a state secret. I had encountered a case of cultural cover-up' (Stradling 1993: 16). In another contribution to the scholarly debate on the death of Villamediana, Frederick A. De Armas argues that it was the staging of Villamediana's play *La Gloria de Niquea*, and more specifically its prologue, consisting of lines from Góngora's poetry (whichsome contemporary sources even claim that Góngora wrote), that had occasioned the death of the Count (De Armas 2001: 439). As interpreted by de Armas, 'the prologue points to certain lines by Góngora, and these lines reveal a hidden message'. The argument is that Villamediana used mythological references to Ganymede – a myth with homoerotic overtones also used by Shakespeare in *As You Like It* – to present himself as cupbearer to the King (Jupiter), a scenario which in turn would have posed a threat to Olivares in his position as the *valido* of the King. Consequently, Villamediana had to be eliminated.

Whether or not one accepts this radical reading of the play as proof of the motive for the murder of Villamediana, the interpretations testify to the long-lasting attraction of the enigma of the death of Villamediana, which even in the twenty-first century continues to give rise to new theories. Philippe Rouached has documented and edited satirical works by and relating to Villamediana, on the basis of which he plausibly argues that the controversial poet was the victim of a political murder staged by the Count-Duke and perhaps involving Philip IV. According to Rouached, the primary cause of the assassination was Villamediana's political satire, although the honour of the King may also have carried significant weight (Rouached 2009: 129).

No other death in early modern Spain gave rise to so much writing, speculation, interpretation, and oral transmission. The conception and construction of the cultural memory of this violent death is therefore highly relevant to the current discussion. Aside from speculating on what really caused Villamediana's murder, the contemporary conception of death and memory in this dramatic case is interesting in and of itself. In Góngora's letter, his understanding is that the case is delicate and will indeed be covered up. Quevedo on the other hand, understands Villamediana's death differently in his account:

> Such was the effect of his quill and the maliciousness of his tongue that those who awaited his death (much attended to, though of scarce honour) while he was alive thought that the knife was well deserved [...] Others said that while he could and should have died in another manner through justice, it happened violently because neither in his life nor in his death was he free of sin. Seeking one's wound and misery at full speed, and the punishment with all of one's body without taking care was like saying: *neither justice nor hate can do greater damage to me than myself* (Rosales 1964: 80).

In Quevedo's opinion, Villamediana brought the death upon himself through his writings and speech. The idea that the Count was murdered because of his poetry was in fact widespread at the time. In many manuscripts we can find poems with epigraphs like 'which caused the death of the Count of Villamediana'. According to the conviction represented by Quevedo, Villamediana would have been executed through some legal process anyway, as there was no part of his life, or death, which was not marked by sin. In short, the fate of the Count was inevitable. Satirical poems written against Villamediana while he was alive represent a similar idea about his heresy: 'If you do not respect God, what end do you expect? In the life you lead, you are in certain danger' (Rosales 1964: 24). This part of the discursive order is important to bear in mind when considering the attraction of Villamediana. Indiscreet writing was understood to be associated with fatal consequences, and the daring image Villamediana constructed of himself was fearless and intrepid, in stark contrast to the Catholic ideals of the period. This aspect can further help to explain the attraction of the medium of the manuscript in which Villamediana's poetry circulated exclusively (as well as the postal system which, as Postmaster General, he oversaw). Many of the contemporary testimonies repeat the idea that silence had been imposed over the death of Villamediana: 'silence was ordered' and 'it was silenced' are recurring phrases (Rozas 1965: 84-87). But Quevedo's insistence that Villamediana sought 'the punishment with all of his body' and that 'neither in his life nor in his death was he free of sin' could be taken to imply that Villamediana was assassinated for his homosexuality.

In brief, Villamediana's contemporaries perceived this violent and tragic death as the culmination of a life of excess, caused either by his love affairs, his sexuality, or his 'ingenuity' – that is, his poetry – or by all of them. Just as in the case of Calderón's death, the event became symbolic as the process of the construction of a cultural memory took place in the transformation of a human being from body to burial as a discursive event.

One of the poems on the occasion of Villamediana's death, attributed to Góngora but disputed by trustworthy sources like Chacon, refers to the circumstances of the murder. The first stanza alludes directly to the cause of the Count's death:

Gossip-bar of Madrid,
tell us; who killed the Count?
No one says and no one hides anything,
so speak without speaking –
They say the Cid killed him
because he was Count Vigorous;
Nonsense! The truth of the matter
is that the killer was Bellido,
and the impulse sovereign.

[Mentidero de Madrid
Decidnos ¿quién mató al Conde?
Ni se dice, ni se esconde,
Sin discurso discurrid:
–Dicen que le mató el Cid
Por ser el Conde Lozano;
¡Disparate chabacano!,
La verdad del caso ha sido
Que el matador fue Bellido
Y el impulso soberano.]
(Rosales 1964: 73)

The poet invokes the gossip shops of Madrid (*mentidero*) to inquire about the murderer of Villamediana, and is told that the King (el Cid) killed him for vengeance, an idea that is refuted in the response that the killer was *Bellido* and the impulse came from the sovereign. These contradictory lines first affirm that it was not the King who killed Villamediana for vengeance and then affirm that it *was* the King or another sovereign. This poem is copied in numerous manuscripts, but some of them present an interesting variant. In manuscript 8252, the last line reads 'death of a courtier' instead of 'impulse sovereign'. As Rosales points out, this version, which instead of accusing simply states the death of a courtier, could be used by the poet to protect himself from any accusations of having written a malicious poem against the King (Rosales 1964: 131). The fact that the poem is attributed to Góngora in numerous manuscripts could indicate that it was a problematic poem, which he could not officially acknowledge in this version. That Góngora's authorship is disputed in the Chacon manuscript, which was dedicated to Olivares, could further be an indication that it was a text that could only exist in a more clandestine medium. If, as Rosales and Rouached argue, Olivares ordered the murder of Villamediana, it would seem natural to disown a poem that accuses him of a crime. The key phrase in the poem, however, is 'No one says and no one hides anything', which means that the cause was not hidden, but was too sensitive to talk about.

A similar poem is attributed to Lope de Vega, which in one manuscript has the epigraph 'response by Lope de Vega in the same consonants' in which he inverts the poem, using the same words to encourage the people not to look for the murderer, as everyone knows who it was, and that it was not the King. According to Rosales, who studied the variants of the epitaphs extensively, many of the poets used double versions of their poems, one innocent and official, the other clandestine and sensitive (Rosales 1964: 129). The death of Villamediana produced an extremely tense situation with regard to poetic writing. Many of the poets were personal friends of the murdered Count and probably saw the warning, or *escarmiento*, that incautious writing could be dangerous. They also needed to obtain the favour of Olivares, who was now the stern ruler of the empire.

Many of the Villamediana epitaphs revolve around the violent nature of the death and how it became a collective memory, representative of the vanity of life and cruelty of death, as well as of the danger of free speech. A poem attributed to Juan Ruiz de Alarcón is quite explicit in this matter: 'Here rests a slanderer, that talked ill even of himself, and whose mortal ashes lie in a decent tomb. He left people with the memory of good and bad living; by steel he came to die, letting everyone understand how a perpetrator of evil things could finish off a speaker of evil things' (Rosales 1965: 98). The mortal ashes of Villamediana, which are now fittingly put in a tomb, have become an example of how an incautious and vain life will end in death by the blade. Several testimonies, in poetry and prose, affirm in a more or less explicit manner the belief that the Count's death was ordered by the palace, either by Olivares or by the King himself.

Góngora also wrote a sonnet on the deaths of Calderón, Villamediana and his protector, the Conde de Lemus. This poem captures the sentiment of these deaths as *desengaño y escarmiento* in typically condensed language built around mythological references:

> I leaned against the trunk of a sturdy oak tree
> that was the vigorous envy of all the wood,
> until one morning the law's stern reaper
> called and left me trembling, bereft of sanctuary.
>
> A laurel whose branches bestowed dignity
> on my poor lyre, unpolished but Castilian
> received one fatal blow whereby its
> vain pomp was blasted (your fault, Calliope).
>
> Green-leaved and white with wisdom
> Minerva's tree the sun destroys as soon as his
> favours cease; its ashes then like dew on the grass you will see.
>
> How false is hope to one whose fate is adverse!
> What disappointments are in store for me?
> What further punishments, what new reverse?
> (Góngora 2007: 99).

> [Al tronco descansaba de una encina
> Que envidia de los bosques fue, lozana,
> Cuando segur legal una mañana
> Alto horror me dejó con su ruïna.

Laurel que de sus ramas hizo dina
Mi lira, ruda sí, mas castellana,
Hierro luego fatal su pompa vana
(Culpa tuya, Calíope) fulmina.

En verdes hojas cano el de Minerva
Árbol culto, del sol yace abrasado,
Aljófar, sus cenizas, de la hierba.

¡Cuánta esperanza miente a un desdichado!
¿A qué más desengaños me reserva,
A qué escarmientos me vincula el hado?]
(Góngora 2000b: 573)

This sonnet is constructed around the idea of Góngora's protectors as mythological trees. Calderón, the subject of the first quatrain, is imagined as a sturdy oak tree, which the poet leaned against, only to see it cut down by the axe of the law, a reference to the public decapitation of Calderón. The next quatrain describes Villamediana as a laurel tree, traditionally associated with poetry and fame, the vain pomp of which was cut down by a knife, a decidedly less explicit way to describe the murder. In the last line of the quatrain it is Calliope, the muse of poetry, who is accused of responsibility for this death, another testimony to the idea that Villamediana was killed because of his satirical poems. Minerva's tree, the olive, is the image for the Count of Lemus, who is burnt to ashes by the sun (the King), as he fell from grace at the end of his life and died shortly thereafter. The last two lines of the poem exclaim how these deaths are *desengaños* and *escarmientos* to the poet. The presence of *vanitas* in this poem on historical deaths is clear, generating a tension between the inevitable fate of the mortal human being and his aspiration to glory. This is one of the last poems that Góngora wrote, and its sombre view on life is reflected in another sonnet 'On human ambition', which ends with the lines: 'You are in danger Licio, if you persist in following shadows and embracing illusions. The hours will not forgive you, hours that count of days, days that are gnawing of years' (Góngora 2007: 103). In this dark sonnet the unforgiving character of time is juxtaposed with the vanity of human ambition, understood as chasing shadows and embracing *engaños* (the opposite of *desengañado*).

Remixing Góngora: the *Funerary Eclogue*

Góngora himself died only four years later, in 1627, without any funerary pomp to celebrate him. However, care for his material memory in manuscripts and printed books involved several actors and projects. The Chacon manuscript, the various printed editions, commentaries, and the further circulation of manuscripts all form part of the poet's posthumous *fama*. When Lope de Vega died in 1634, two volumes of poetry to his memory were produced, involving no fewer than two hundred and fifty poets, in one Spanish and one Italian printed codex. In the case of Góngora, who had occupied such a prominent position during his lifetime, only a few scattered poems were written, one of them by Lope, who had been so opposed to him. His sonnet ends with the following tercets:

> Góngora restores his mortal part
> to time, already his learned lyre
> includes his voice in a final clause.
> He dies and lives, while this holy pyre
> bestows such immortal honour to him
> that he is born a Phoenix where he expires as a swan.
>
> [Góngora ya la parte restituye
> Mortal al tiempo, ya la culta lira
> En cláusula final la voz incluye.
> Ya muere y vive, que esta sacra pira
> Tan inmortal honor le constituye,
> Que nace fénix donde cisne expira.]
> (Cruz Casado 2007: 115)

In 1638, however, the Grenadine poet Martín de Angulo y Pulgar published a small printed book of about fifty pages entitled *Funerary Eclogue to Don Luis de Góngora of verses taken from his works*. As the prologue, by the Carmelite priest Juan de la Plata, explains:

> This is a Cento poem, a composition used by very few people, and not understood by all, so to say what I think of it, I think it is necessary first to give the proper meaning and the translation of the term Cento and the circumstances surrounding it, to make it more intelligible. The ancients used this name for a certain type of Toga, or a robe woven of different threads and colours (Angulo y Pulgar 1638: 4).

The *cento* is thus a patchwork, stitched together from pieces of different origin. Plata goes on to explain the Latin tradition of the *cento* poem in Ausonius, Proba, and others. He admits that its practice requires a strong memory of all the compositions from which the poem is made but insists that it is not only a question of memory, as Ausonius wrote, but also of *ingenuity*: 'Writing verses is such a worn-out exercise, that it is expiring in human appreciation, but ordering Centos made of other Poems is so singular, if not modern, that there are very few who have tried it' (5).

The production of *centos* was rare, then, and could somehow even seem 'modern' to Plata. Today, by contrast, when copy/paste and remix aesthetics prevail in all types of digital writing, we might see it differently. It could be argued that before and after the stabilised authorship of copyright protected printed publications held sacred by the moderns, such practices seemed natural, while during an era of heavily regulated forms of writing, they would seem problematic or impossible. Pulgar's book has been known during the past century, but it has been conspiciously overlooked by modern *gongoristas*. The only scholar who has dedicated a full paper to it concludes, after careful consideration, that the poem may have some literary interest, even though it obviously lacks originality (Cruz Casado 2007).

This *cento* poem was composed at a time when *imitatio* was almost as important as *inventio*, and Pulgar's compilation constitutes in itself an attempt to contribute to the posthumous fame of Góngora using his own voice. Hence, even if the production of *centos*, in the narrow sense, was rare, the practice of cutting and pasting lines from different sources was widespread and generally accepted during this time, as will be clear to anyone who has read the annotated editions of Góngora by Salcedo Coronel and others. Lope even composed a multilingual sonnet with lines from Ariosto, Camoens, Petrarch, Tasso, Horace, Garcilaso de la Vega, and others. Villamediana's play *La Gloria de Niquea*, which was written and staged by order of the Queen to celebrate the King's birthday in 1621, had a prologue made with lines written by Góngora, but presented as if composed by Villamediana. (Pulgar even affirms that it was entirely written by Góngora.)

An interesting aspect of the *cento* is that it was traditionally used to transfer words from a pagan work to a Christian context, the sources being classical authors such as Virgil and Homer (Schottenius Cullhed 2015). Pulgar's take is different in that he uses Góngora's own verses to construct the poet's memory. Hence, it can be read as an exploration of the possibilities of moving information, even if that differs from how Pulgar describes his practice. His words resonate in the discursive order of the early modern era, in that the inspiration came from antiquity, but in the execution of this practice he created something that is particularly interesting with regard to writing, materiality, and memory.

In the front matter, Pulgar further notes, 'I do not cite verses from the printed works because all are not there even if the title claims it, and they are not faithful, even when the prologue boasts that they are; rather they are filled with endless errors, and are of considerable guilt. The quotes from the *Solitudes* are also taken from my own manuscripts' (Angulo y Pulgar 1638: 22). Pulgar thereby repeats the charge expressed in the *Escrutinio*, quoted in the first chapter of this book, as well as in the Estrada manuscript, Pellicer's *Lecciones* and the *Vida* of Góngora in the Chacon manuscript, all of which testify to the idea that years after Góngora had died and several editions had been printed and disseminated, no satisfactory printed book existed, and the only trustworthy storage of his poetic memory was in private manuscripts. These words were written two hundred years after the invention of the printing press and they show how the operations of this cultural technique had still not stabilised the unstable material existence of poetry.

The front matter of Pulgar's book contains further interesting material such as this laudatory sonnet by the priest Luis de Villaverde Ortiz:

> You revoke the echoes in learned song
> of a grand Phoenix, and you write his Life,
> today, with his feathers, so it shall soar more brightly,
> and their echoes inspire awe.
>
> Both echoes and feathers are sweet, and the extent to which
> the matter merits applause
> is only due to your lyre,
> which, in turn, is only due to such a Phoenix.
>
> Echoes, so sweetly revoked,
> feathers out of which you bring forth grave accounts,
> may they belie time, escaping from the flame.
>
> And in such echoes (which you connect so well),
> may his feathers be the flight of your Fame,
> since yours are the echoes of his Fame.
>
> [Los ecos revocais en culto canto
> De un Fenix grave, y le escribis la vida.
> Hoy, con sus plumas, porque mas luzida
> Ella vuele, y aquellos sean espanto.
>
> Ecos, y plumas dulces son, y quanto
> La materia ha de ser mas aplaudida,
> A sola vuestra lira es debida,
> Y ella es debida a solo Fenix tanto.
>
> Ecos tan dulcemente revocados,
> Plumas de quien haceis tan graves sumas
> Niegense al tiempo, hurtense a la llama.
>
> Y en ecos tales (bien por vos ligados)
> De vuestra Fama el vuelo sean sus plumas
> Pues son las vuestras ecos de su Fama.]
> (Angulo y Pulgar 1638: 12)

This straightforward sonnet (at least compared to those by Góngora) uses the Phoenix myth to speak of the *fama* of the poet. The Phoenix here flies again, producing echoes and sweet sounds, in perpetuation of the memory of the poet. The echoes are due to the lyre of Pulgar, who in turn owes his song to the feathers of the Phoenix (Góngora), negating time and escaping from the devouring flame. Finally, as in the case of Pacheco and others, the *fama* of Pulgar will fly with the feathers of Góngora, creating echoes of his *fama*.

The front matter contains a number of poems: a *cento* to the dedicatee of the book, made from lines of Góngora's dedicatory poems, and a *prosopopeia* by Bartolome de Valenzuela, in which Góngora himself thanks Pulgar for this poetic afterlife:

> If Pulgar takes it apart
> to give it new life:
> what miraculous murder[...]
> that destroys and remakes it?
> Because thanks to him it dies and is reborn
> to lament my death.
> Pulgar, since in your argument,
> all words are mine,
> I am the one who is speaking,
> I the one who laments my death...
> and obliges the dead to speak.
>
> [Si Pulgar la hace pedazos
> Para darle nueva vida:
> Tan milagroso homicida...
> Que la destruye, y rehace?
> Pues por el muere, y renace
> Para lamentar mi muerte
> Pulgar, pues de tu argumento
> Es mio qualquier vocablo,
> Yo mismo soy el que hablo,
> Yo el que mi muerte lamento:[...]
> Y obliga a que el muerto hable.]
> (Angulo y Pulgar 1638: 13)

This conception of the *cento* as an act of destruction and resurrection is similar to the idea expressed in many funerary compositions, as well as to the ekphrastic ones, of overcoming death by means of material storage which lets the dead speak to the living. Góngora 'laments his own death', the dead person is 'obliged to speak', in a way that reveals an attempt to transgress the limit between life and death, a problem that runs throughout the poetic production of this era.

The *cento* poem consists of 1200 lines all taken from Góngora's poetic production, whereby an interesting mechanism of contextual change is produced.

> In this volume lives he, who rests
> (ingenious Cordobese) forever glorious,
> in that marble, animated by a brave brush,
> his great name making his field illustrious,
> so that time shall not be able to intent its prescription.
> Here rests Daliso, his ashes seal this seemly urn,
> if not an eminent spire: there, they are at rest,
> and from them, today, he is reborn here,
> like a new Phoenix, in flaming feathers,
> reborn among aromas, of his learned poems,
> vigilant studies, instead of fire, taking on wings,
> not of vulgar fame, but learned beautiful feathers.
>
> [Vive en este volumen el que yace
> (Ingenio Cordobés) siempre glorioso
> En aquel marmol, de pincel valiente
> Animado, su campo ilustra grave
> Su nombre, porque el tiempo
> Su prescripción no intente.
> Yace Daliso, sus cenizas sella
> Esta urna decente,
> Si aguja no eminente;
> Allí tienen reposo,
> I dellas, hoy, el mismo aquí renace,
> Qual nuevo Fenix, en flamantes plumas,
> Renacido, entre aromas,
> De sus poemas cultos,
> El vigilante estudio en vez de llama,
> Alas vistiendo, no de vulgar fama,
> Cultas plumas bellas.]
> (Angulo y Pulgar 1638: 28)

This passage of the poem constructs a poetic memory of Góngora after death using the poems he composed to construct the memory of other deaths. The lines are from the sonnets to Philip II, El Greco's tomb, the Cardinal Sandoval y Rojas tomb, the death of Rodrigo Calderón, and the papers in a shrine, to mention only the poems discussed in this chapter. This change of physical context follows the change brought about by the epigrammatic tradition, whereby a poem to be inscribed on a stone is disentangled from its medium to be evoked in another context (as in the deictic gesture of the *viator* motif).

The *cento* poem ends with a long epitaph, which reuses the deictic gesture to construct the book itself as a tomb for the perpetuation of Góngora's memory:

Pilgrim, behold the elegant form,
of this erected tomb, of Betis,
this prime pediment of gleaming porphyry,
a hard key; earth seals what earth may never oppress;
if you ignore whose, errant, hold back your foot.
This great urn (if small) is mutely telling it.
Here rests Daliso in sweet peace,
since a small marble can hold a lot of Phoenix,
where, today reborn, he owes more to his Pyre
than to his nest. His limbs, which today
(a little human earth), this tomb encloses;
piously Betis bewails, and a small urn seals,
like bones, in the end, of a creature, giving
mortal signs of mortals: but verses honour them,
and will illustriously defeat oblivion.
They will live imprinted on the tomb,
as this volume is the hard stone
(such a work time can never consume)…
Venerate, and continue on your path.
Tell it from people to people,
and walk in peace as the day is ending,
because it is short, even of the sun, in the monarchy.

[Esta, en forma elegante, o peregrino,
Que a levantado, en túmulo de
El Betis, esta prima
De pórfido luciente, dura llave;
Tierra sella, que tierra nunca oprima.
Si ignoras cuya, errante,
El pie enfrena ignorante.
Tanta urna (si breve)
Muda lo esta diciendo. En paz suave
Aquí yace Daliso,
Que en poco mármol mucho Fenix cabe
Donde, hoy renacido,
Mas deberá a su Pira, que a su nido.
Sus miembros, que hoy, (humana poca tierra)
Este sepulcro encierra; Piadoso el Betis llora,
Breve urna los sella, como huesos,
Al fin, de criatura,
Dando mortales señas de mortales:

> Pero versos los honran, que al olvido
> Harán ilustre injuria;
> Que vivirán sobre el sepulcro impressos,
> Siendo la piedra dura este volumen,
> (trabajo tal el tiempo no consuma) [...]
> Venerado, y prosigue tu camino.
> Dilo de gente en gente,
> I antes, camina en paz, que acabe el día
> Porque es breve, aun del sol, la monarquía.]
> (Angulo y Pulgar 1638: 56)

The passer-by (*peregrino*) is offered an extensive description of the funerary monument (the volume) he sees and is then asked to venerate the memory of the one who lies dead (Góngora) and to continue on his path, telling people about the deceased. This construction is in fact well rooted in the archaic and classical Greek epigrammatic tradition, even if – with an early modern twist – the book itself is constructed as a sepulchral marble tomb containing the ashes of a Phoenix being reborn before the reader. As Manuel Baumbach, Andrej Petrovic, and Ivana Petrovic observe, 'the task is to commemorate the words, remove them from the inscription and take them away to spread the news. The passer-by becomes a medium for the epigram and functions as a transmitter on its way to the intended readers' (Baumbach et al. 2011: 17).

Pulgar's cento poem is constructed in eighty-one stanzas, each of which narrates a specific part of Góngora's life in his own words. It thereby presents itself both as a verbal funerary monument in the material form of a printed codex and a biography of the poet it seeks to commemorate. Throughout this poetic biography, not coincidentally, the Phoenix is the most frequently recurring trope, insisting on the eternal perpetuation of memory and fame. Pulgar seems to have been motivated by the two volumes produced for Lope de Vega a few years earlier, and in the commentary on stanzas 50-57 he writes:

> The poets of Spain have imprinted another POSTHUMOUS FAME [for Lope]: celebrating the abundance, clarity and perfection of his verses. And even though I am among them, fol. 131. The sonnet is not mine, neither did I see it after it was printed, nor did I approve of it being printed, I am saying this because it is not mine: not because it is not good. By contrast to this praise stands what Fame herself sings for Don Luis, expressing how his verses are admired, hence nameing some of the grand persons who praised and celebrated Don Luis, and his poems, such as the Cardinals of Rome, among them the Archduke Alberto, our Holy Pope, their Majesties of Philip III and IV. Infante Don Fernando, the Count-Duke, Dukes of Bejar, and of Medina Sidonia. The Duke of Osuna, of Lerma, of Marquess de Ayamonte. The

> Count of Lemos, the Count of Villamediana, the Count of Salinas, and the Marquess of Castelrodrigo, Cardinal Guevara, Bishop Siguenza and the Bishop of Córdoba, historians, and the Royal Preacher Felix Hortensio. On the whole he is praised by all (Angulo y Pulgar 1638: 43-44).

Pulgar contrasts the books printed to the memory of Lope, which he seems to judge as a manifestation of *vulgar fama*, with the lack of any such volume for Góngora. In negating the authority of a sonnet included in that book, it is as if he is trying to distance himself from popular memory and inscribe himself by means of the *cento* within the sphere of Góngora's *fama*. The list of admirers of Góngora's poetry has historical value, even if it cannot be verified, but Pulgar names many of the most influential actors of the early modern Spanish Empire, including two Kings, Popes, and Cardinals of Rome. With such a long list of rich and influential admirers, it may seem ironic that Góngora died a quiet death, poor, and heavily in debt in his hometown of Córdoba. Pulgar gives a hint of the cause of this fate in stanza 60, where he has placed the following lines from Góngora: 'Prudent, in my opinion, without human ambition, of chasing shadows and embracing illusions: but seeing the world's true disillusion; [...] feathers, even of royal eagles, whoever may ignore it will see, are mortal feathers: and even the greatest glory, eventually becomes nothing and turns to earth, dust, smoke and shadow' (50). Here, Góngora's famous *vanitas* becomes an emblem of himself, a *desengañado*, always steadily staring in the face of death.

Conclusion

This book could be described as an investigation of the materiality of early modern poetry. Its purpose has been to focus on physical and concrete aspects in order to create new knowledge of the past. In understanding the poetry of Góngora as a conceptual object resulting from the ontic operations of cultural techniques, I have tried to show how these cultural phenomena were deeply embedded in various spheres held separate by modern institutions. As in the case of philology, however, a driving force has been a longing for presence of cultural objects and a wish to come as close as possible to the lost physical world of that time. I have consulted different manuscripts to obtain as much relevant information as possible, while also building on the important findings of several philologists.

Understanding media as cultural techniques implies a refusal to take things for granted and an attempt to ask fundamental but basic questions about how certain cultural objects were constituted in the first place. A common effect of the cultural techniques investigated here is the production of effects of presence. Papers, for instance, produced the presence of something absent in the case of manuscripts recording ephemeral poetic discourse, but also produced the presence of the sovereign in legal orders and permissions. In both cases, the material object substitutes for the body of a human being, an ability that could also be used to transcend time and space. This is what is meant by *Pellucid Paper* in the lines from Góngora´s *Solitudes* that give this book its title. Paper is written upon, as the stars that were increasningly attracting the attention of cosmographers and scholars in the early modern era were written on the sky, and it allows humans, equipped with feathers or quills, to navigate through space and time.

The media objects of early modern Spain were on the one hand the guarantors of memory after death, and on the other hand integral parts of the symbolic and actual practice of power, as in the case of the Paper King Philip II and his successors. Many of the poems from Golden Age Spain reveal themselves as striking technographies that thematise their own technological production and investigate writing through technology.

As argued, the material existence of the poetry associated with the name 'Góngora' was far from stable. His now-canonical authorship was dispersed throughout a network, and no accepted stable form of material storage of the ephemeral poetic discourse ever existed to his contemporaries. It is as if the object of poetry constantly withdraws itself from human beings, only to come back and reveal its presence. The years after Góngora's death saw competing attempts to create the final form of storage for this important part of cultural memory, but time and again these attempts were frustrated and dismissed as unreliable. The Chacon manuscript was perhaps the one object that could have been accepted as such, but as it was kept in the private library of the Count-Duke of Olivares, and later lost, it had a limited number of readers.

The production of these material objects of storage also connected actors throughout the poetic-political network, where they worked as mediators producing sovereignty and subjectivity in human beings. The projects of printing the poetry of Góngora and producing the Chacon manuscript can be described as attempts at stabilising the unstable, storing the ephemeral in the durable, centralising the decentralised. And what is interesting about these operative sequences is that they all failed to do so. The need for a 'correct' edition reveals an emerging but not yet established notion of authorship that produces a conflict between practices and demands. Author portraits, biographies and verse eulogies as well as the codex itself can be understood as attempts to stabilise and constitute the human subject as a recognizable author of certain pieces of writing. Had a producer of poetry like Góngora adhered to the demand of publishing one authoritative and printed edition the problem might not have occured; it did not in the case of his contemporary Lope de Vega. But the fact that Góngora and the majority of Spanish poets actively refrained from the production of such objects reveals a tension between different media practices at the threshold of the constitution of modernity, in Latour´s sense. The conception of the human being as authoritative subject is essential to the epistemology of the moderns, and as this order today seems to give way to new forms of self-reference it becomes possible to understand it as such.

The absence of authoritative and widely disseminated books has further implications for the poetry itself. When poetry was not written to be published and read by many, how and why *was* it produced? Where did it take place? The dispersed nature of the poetical manuscripts, which presupposed contact with the producer, was mirrored by the dispersed nature of the material and physical referents of the poems. The majority of them were created in a historically specific time and place, with a more or less clear purpose, often pointing with a deictic gesture towards material objects. Throughout this book I have tried to reconstruct and describe such spheres and spaces by letting the poetry act as informant and by juxtaposing it with other historical sources. In this way, I have tried to read the poems not as conceptual objects emanating from the soul of a unified human subject, but as material traces of physical presence.

The poems discussed here often served the documentary purpose of recording an event, a monument or a physical space, and accordingly turn out to display a high degree of contingency. A recurring tendency of this poetry was the employment of concepts and topoi to describe the material components of a given object. It is also in this way that the poems are technographies. In this manner, they reveal a conception of portraits and monuments as objects of storage with the ability to produce effects of presence. Not only does the poetry describe such effects, but they often also direct the attention to how they are being produced through a specific employment of materials and techniques. Thus, a portrait may be understood as producing the presence of an absent human being through the employment of a brush, which transposes colours that the canvas absorbs in forming an image. In the same way, when the poetry becomes self-reflexive, it reveals itself as the product of quills, ink, and paper, which are often associted with mythological entities such as the Phoenix.

The strong rearticulation of the topoi of *vanitas* and *memento mori* around 1600 resulted in a shift toward material storage, *fama*, memory, and earthly afterlife in a reappropriation of Antique phenomena. Books, paintings, tombs, and monuments then became guarantors of presence in absence of a human being turned to 'ashes, dust, shadows, nothing'. Every culture is historically specific and technologically configured, inevitably forming an integral part of the abstract or symbolic concepts through which it comes to be understood. In a time when digitisation may be doing away with the paper-based culture that was so essential to the moderns, entailing several major conceptual shifts, it is important to rememeber that paper could once be pellucid.

Bibliography

Agamben, Giorgio. 2009. *What is an Apparatus? and other Essays*. Palo Alto: Stanford University Press.

Alberti, Leon Battista. 2013. *On Painting: A New Translation and Critical Edition*. Edited and translated by Rocco Sinisgalli. Cambridge: Cambridge University Press.

Alcázar, Baltasar de. 1910. *Poesias*. Madrid: Real Academia Española.

Alonso Cortés, Narciso. 1928. *La muerte de Villamediana*. Valladolid: Imprenta del Colegio Santo.

Alonso, Damaso. 1927. *La lengua poética de Góngora*. Madrid: C.S.I.C.

Alonso, Dámaso. 1978. *Obras Completas V*. Madrid: Gredos.

Álvarez-Ossorio, Antonio. 1999. 'La discreción del cortesano'. In *Edad de Oro XVIII*, edited by Florencio Sevilla Arroyo, 9-46. Madrid: UAM.

Andrews, Jean. 2014. 'The Staging of Góngora's Three Funeral Sonnets for Margarita de Austria Estiria'. In *Spanish Golden Age Poetry in Motion: The Dynamics of Creation and Conversation*, edited by Jean Andrews and Isabel Torres, 131-46. Suffolk: Tamesis.

Angulo y Pulgar, Martin de. 1638. *Egloga funebre A Don Luis de Góngora de versos entresacados de sus obras*. Sevilla.

Arancón, Ana Martínez. 1978. *La Batalla en torno a Góngora*. Barcelona: Casa Editorial.

Argensola, Lupercio and Bartolomé Leonardo de. 1950. *Rimas*, volume 1. Madrid: CSIC.

Armas, Fredrick de. 2001. 'Play's the thing: Clues to a Murder in Villamediana's La Gloria de Niquea'. In *Bulletin of Hispanic Studies* 78: 439-454.

Artigas, Miguel. 1925. *Don Luis de Góngora y Aragote: Biografía y estudio crítico*. Madrid: Tipograf. De la Revista de Archivos.

Assmann, Aleida. 2011. *Cultural Memory and Western Civilization: Functions, Media, Archives*. Cambridge University Press: New York.

Assmann, Jan. 2008. 'Communicative and Cultural Memory'. In *Cultural Memory Studies*, edited by Astrid Eril & Ansgar Nünning, 109-118. New York: De Gruyter.

Assmann, Jan. 2012. *Cultural Memory and Early Civilization: Writing, Remembrance, and Political Imagination.* New York: Cambridge University Press.

Babia, Luis de. 1613. *Quarta parte de la historia pontificial y católica, compuesta y ordenada por el Doctor Luis de Bauia.* Madrid: Luis Sánchez.

Bass, Laura R. 2008. *The Drama of the Portrait: Theater and visual culture in Early Modern Spain.* Pennsylvania: Pennsylvania State University Press.

Baumbach, Manuel, Andrej Petrovic and Ivana Petrovic. 2010. 'Archaic and Classical Greek Epigram: An Introduction'. In *Archaic and Classical Greek Epigram*, edited by Manuel Baumbach, Andrej Petrovic and Ivana Petrovic, 1-20. Cambridge: Cambridge University Press.

Bendala Galán, Manuel. 2003. *Manual del arte español.* Madrid: Silex.

Bennett, Jane. 2010. *Vibrant Matter: A Political Ecology of Things.* Durham: Duke University Press.

Bergmann, Emilie. 1979. *Art inscribed: Essays on Ekphrasis in Spanish Golden Age Poetry.* Cambridge, Mass.: Harvard University Press.

Blair, Ann. 2010. 'The rise of note taking in Early Modern Europe'. *Intellectual History Review* 20: 303-16.

Blanco, Mercedes. 2004. 'Góngora et la peinture'. *LOCVS AMŒNVS* 7: 197-208.

Blanco, Mercedes. 1984. 'L'epitaphe baroque dans l'œuvre poetique de Góngora et Quevedo'. In *Les formes breves: Actes du colloque international de la Baume-les-Aix,* edited by Benito Pelegrin, 179-94. Aix-en-Provence: Publications Université de Provence.

Blanco, Mercedes. 2012. 'Ut poesis, oratio. La oficina poética de la oratoria sacra en Hortensio Félix Paravicino'. *Lectura y Signo* 7: 29-65.

Blanco, Mercedes. 2012. *Góngora heroico: Las Soledades y la tradición épica.* Madrid: CEEH.

Blanco, Mercedes 2012. *Góngora o la invención de una lengua.* Madrid: CEEH.

Blanco, Mercedes. 1992. *Les Rhétoriques de la pointe: Baltasar Gracián et le conceptisme en Europe.* Geneva: Slatkine.

Bolter, Jay David and Michael Gruisin. 1999. *Remediation: Understanding New Media.* Cambridge, Mass.: MIT Press.

Bouza, Fernando. 1989. 'La Biblioteca de El Escorial y el orden de los saberes en el siglo XVI'. In *El Escorial: arte, poder y cultura en la Corte de Felipe II.* Edited by Fernando Checa, 81-99. Madrid: UCM.

Bouza, Fernando. 1994. 'La majestad de Felipe II: Construcción del mito real'. In *La corte de Felipe II*, edited by José Martinez Milan, 37-72. Madrid: Alianza.

Bouza, Fernando. 2011. 'Política del libro del Consejo Real'. In *Poder y Saber: Bibliotecas y bibliofila an la época del conde-duque de Olivares*, edited by Jeremy Lawrence, Oliver Noble Wood and Jeremy Roe, 339-62. Madrid: CEEH.

Bouza, Fernando. 2001. *Corre manuscrito: Una historia cultural del Siglo de Oro*. Madrid: Marcial Pons.

Bouza, Fernando. 1992. *Del Escribano a la biblioteca: La civilización escrita europea en la alta edad moderna*. Madrid: Sintesis.

Bouza, Fernando. 1998. *Imagen y Propaganda. Capítulos de historia cultural del reinado de Felipe II*. Madrid: Akal.

Bouza, Fernando. 2004. *Communication, Knowledge and Memory in Early Modern Spain*, Philadelphia: University of Pennsylvania Press.

Boyden, James M. 2000. 'The Worst Death Becomes a Good Death: the Passion of Don Rodrigo Calderón'. In *The Place of the Dead: Death and Remembrance in Early Modern Europe*. Edited by Bruce Gordon and Peter Marshall, 244-65. Cambridge, Mass.: Cambridge University Press.

Bray, Xavier. 2009. *The Sacred Made Real: Spanish Painting and Sculpture 1600-1700*. New Haven: Yale University Press.

Bredekamp, Horst. 1995. *The Lure of Antiquity and the Cult of the Machine: The Kunstkammer and the Evolution of Nature, Art and Technology*. Princeton: Markus Wiener Pub.

Brendecke, Arndt. 2006. 'Diese Teufel, Meine Papiere: Philipp II von Spanien und das Anwachsen Administrativer Schriftlichkeit'. *Aventinus nova* 6. http://www.aventinus-online.de/no_cache/persistent/artikel/7785/

Brown, Jonathan. 1978. *Images and ideas in Seventeenth-Century Spanish Painting*. Princeton: Princeton University Press.

Brown, Jonathan. 1995. *Kings and Connoiseurs*. London: Yale University Press.

Cabrera, Luis de. 1619. *Felipe segundo, Rey de España*. Madrid: Luis Sanchez.

Cabrera, Luis de. 1857. *Relaciones de las cosas sucedidas en la corte de España desde 1599 hasta 1614*. Madrid: Imprenta de Martín Alegria.

Cacho Casal, Marta. 2007. 'La memoria en el pincel, la fama en la pluma'. *Bulletin Hispanique* 109: 47-65.

Cacho Casal, Marta. 2010. 'The true likeness in Francisco Pacheco's Libro de Retratos'. *Renaissance Studies* 24: 381-401.

Campos y Fernández de Sevilla, Javier. 2009. 'Felipe II el íntimo. El rey y el trabajo personal visto a través de su correspondencia'. *Cuadernos de investigación histórica* 26: 21-58.

Carducho, Vicente. 1633. *Dialogos de la pintura*. Madrid: Francisco Martinez.

Carreira, Antonio. 2012. 'Critica a la edicion critica: Respuesta a Margit Frenk'. *Acta Poetica* 33: 211-21.

Carreira, Antonio. 2004. 'El manuscrito como transmisor de humanidades en la España del Barroco'. In *Barroco*, edited by Pedro Aullón de Haro, 597-618. Madrid: Verbum.

Carreira, Antonio, 2008. 'El sentimiento de la naturaleza en Góngora'. In *Homenaje a Francis Cerdan*. Toulouse: Framespa.

Carreira, Antonio. 2014. 'Presencia de Góngora en la poesía de Quevedo'. In *El universo de Góngora: Origenes, textos y representaciones*, edited by Joaquín Roses, 473-494. Córdoba: Diputación de Córdoba.

Carreira, Antonio. 1998. *Gongoremas*. Barcelona: Peninsula.

Carruthers, Mary. 2014. 'Moving Back in Memory Studies'. *History Workshop Journal* 77: 1-10.

Carruthers, Mary. 2008. *The Book of Memory: A Study of Memory in Medieval Culture*. New York: Cambridge University Press.

Casanova, Joseph de. 1650. *Primera parte del arte de escribir todas formas de letras escrito y tallado por el maestro Joseph de Casanova*. Madrid: Diego Díaz de la Carrera.

Cascales, Francisco. 1634. *Cartas Filologicas*. Murcia: Luis Verós.

Cayuela, Anne. 2011. 'Libros de entretenimiento en la librería de Ana de Arenas: Consecuencias editoriales y literarias de la suspensión de licencias para novelas y comedias (1625-1634)'. In *Poder y Saber: Bibliotecas y Bibliofilia en la época del conde-duque de Olivares*, edited by Jeremy Lawrence, Jeremy Roe, and Oliver Noble Wood, 363-84. Madrid: CEEH.

Cerdan, Francis. 2013. 'Paravicino y El Greco: Un soneto inédito y un retrato desconocido'. *Criticon* 13: 5-28.

Cerquiglini, Bernard. 1999. *In Praise of the Variant: A Critical History of Philology*. Translated by Betsy Wing. Baltimore: John Hopkins University Press.

Cervantes, Miguel de. 2008. *Don Quijote de la Mancha*. Madrid: Punto de Lectura.

Cervantes, Miguel de. 1997-2015. *Don Quijote*. Edited by Francisco Rico. Centro Virtual Cervantes. http://www.cvc.cervantes.es/literatura/clasicos/quijote/edicion/parte1/cap06/cap06_02.htm.

Cervantes, Miguel de. 1613. *Novelas ejemplares*. Madrid: Juan de la Cuesta.

Cervantes, Miguel de. 2003. *Poesias sueltas*. Edited by Rodolfo Schevill and Adolfo Bonilla, Biblioteca Virtual Miguel de Cervantes. http://bib.cervantesvirtual.com/servlet/SirveObras/cerv/12794175 11257162765213/index.htm.

Cervantes, Miguel de. 1615. *Segunda parte del Ingenioso caballero Don Quixote de la Mancha*. Madrid: Juan de la Cuesta.

Cervantes, Miguel de. [1614] 2001. *Viaje del Parnaso*. Edited by Florencio Sevilla Arroyo Alicante. Biblioteca Virtual Miguel de Cervantes. http://www.cervantesvirtual.com/obra/viaje-del-parnaso--0/.

Chaffee-Sorace, Diane. 2010. 'Salómon segundo in Góngora's Sacros, altos, dorados capiteles'. *The South Carolina Modern Language Review* 9: 32-46.

Chartier, Roger. 2007. *Inscription and Erasure*. Philadelphia: University of Pennsylvania Press.

Chartier, Roger. 2013. *The Author's Hand and the Printer's Mind: Transformations of the Written Word in Early Modern Europe*. Philadelphia: University of Pennsylvania Press.

Checa Beltrán, José, ed. 2004. *Pensamiento literario del XVIII español: Antología comentada*. Madrid: Consejo Superior de Investigaciones Científicas.

Chemris, Chrystal. 2014. 'Highlights and issues of the new wave of Góngora studies'. *Revista Canadiense de Estudios Hispánicos* 38: 419-442.

Cicero. 1942. *On the Orator: Books 1-2*. Translated by E.W. Sutton. Loeb Classical Library. Cambrdige, Mass.: Harvard University Press.

Civil, Pierre. 1999. 'Libro y poder real: Sobre algunos frontispicios de la primera mitad del siglo XVII'. In *L'écrit dans l'Espagne du Siecle d'or*, edited by Pedro M. Catedra, 69-84. Salamanca: Ediciones Universidad de Salamanca.

Civil, Pierre. 1996. 'Ut pictura poesis en los preliminares del libro español del Siglo de Oro: El poema al retrato grabado'. *Actas del Congreso de la AISO* 4: 419-32.

Clara Marias Martinez, 2011. 'Poesía en lenguas romances en la biblioteca del conde-duque de Olivares (1627)'. In *Poder y Saber: Bibliotecas y Bibliofilia en la época del conde-duque de Olivares*, edited by Jeremy Lawrence, Jeremy Roe, and Oliver Noble Wood, 479-516. Madrid: CEEH.

Clement, Claude. 1635. *Musei, sive Bibliothecae tam privatae quam publicae extructio, instructio, cura, usus....* Lyon: Lugdini.

Colomer, José Luis. 2002. 'Uso y función de la miniatura en la corte de Felipe IV: Velázquez miniaturista'. *Boletín del Museo del Prado* 20: 65-84.

Connor, Steven. 2016. 'How To Do Things With Writing Machines'. In *Writing, Medium, Machine: Modern Technographies*, edited by Sean Pryor and David Trotter, 18-34. London: Open Humanities Press.

Cotarelo y Mori, Emilio. 1913. *Diccionario biográfico y bibliográfico de calígrafos españoles*. Madrid: Impr. De la revista de Arch., bibliotecas y museos.

Covarrubias, Sebastian. 1611. *Tesoro de la lengua castellana.* Madrid: Luis Sanchez.

Cruz Casado, Antonio. 2007. 'Fama postuma de Góngora: La égloga funebre a Don Luis de Góngora (1638), de Martin de Angulo y Pulgar'. In *Actas del Congreso de la AISO* 15, edited by Beatriz Marisca, 113-25. Monterrey: AIH.

Cruz, Sor Juana Inés de la. 1997. *Poems protest and a dream.* Translated by Margaret Sayers Peden. London: Addison-Wesley.

Cullhed, Anders. 2005. *Quevedo: El instante poético.* Zaragoza: Inst. Fernando el Católico.

Dacosta Kaufmann, Thomas. 2009. *Visual Jokes, Natural History and Still-life Painting.* Chicago: University of Chicago Press.

Dadson, Trevor J. 2012. 'Poesía que vive en variantes: retorno a A. Rodriguez-Moñino de mano del Conde de Salinas'. In *De Re Typographica: Once estudios en homenaje a Jaime Moll*, edited by Victor Infantes and Julián Martín Abad, 73-93. Madrid: Calambur.

Dadson, Trevor J. 2013. 'What the Preliminaries of Early Modern Spanish Books Can Tell Us'. In *Pruebas de imprenta: Estudios sobre la cultura editorial en la España moderna y contemporánea*, edited by Gabriel Sánchez Espinosa, 21-42. Madrid: Iberoamericana.

Deleuze, Gilles. 1991. *Le Pli: Leibniz et le Baroque.* Paris: Éditions Minuit.

Díaz Morante, Pedro. 1631. *Cuarta parte del arte nueva de escribir.* Madrid: Luis Sánchez.

Díaz Morante, Pedro. 1624. *Segunda parte del Arte de Escribir.* Madrid: Luis Sánchez.

Díaz Morante, Pedro. 1629. *Terecera parte del arte nueva de escribir.* Madrid: Luis Sánchez.

Díaz, José Simón. 1983. *El libro español antiguo: Analisis de su estructura.* Kassel: Reichenberger.

Diccionario de la lengua castellana. 1734. Madrid: Imprenta de la Real Academia Española.

Díez Borque, José Maria and Álvaro Bustos Táuler, eds. 2012. *Literatura, bibliotecas y derechos de autor en el Siglo de Oro (1600-1700).* Madrid: Iberoamericana.

Dohrn-Van Rossum, Gerhard. 1996. *History of the Hour: Clocks and Modern Temporal Orders.* Chicago: University of Chicago Press.

Dubois, Gene W. 2014. 'Góngora's sonnet on El Greco's tomb: A reconsideration'. *Romance Notes* 54: 187-94.

Egido, Aurora. 1995. 'Los manuales de escribientes desde el siglo de oro'. *Bulletin Hispanique* 97: 67-94.

Eisenberg, Daniel. 1991. *Estudios Cervantinos*. Barcelona: Sirmio.

Eisenstein, Elizabeth L. 1980. *The Printing Press as an Agent of Change*. Cambridge: Cambridge University Press.

Elliott, John. 1986. *The Count-Duke of Olivares: A Statesman in an Age of Decline*. New Haven: Yale University Press.

Ettinghausen, Henry. 2001. 'Politics and the Press in Spain'. In *The Poitics of Information in Early Modern Europe*, edited by Brendan Dooley and Sabrina A. Baron, 199-215. London: Routledge.

Faria y Sousa, Manuel de. 1646. *Fuente de Aganipe o Rimas varias, divididas en siete partes*. Madrid: C. Sanchez Bravo.

Feijoo, Luis Iglesias. 1983. 'Una carta inédita de Quevedo y algunas noticias sobre los comentaristas de Góngora, con Pellicer al fondo'. *Boletín de la Biblioteca Menéndez Pelayo* 59: 141-203.

Fernández Lopez, José. 1991. *Programas iconográficas de la pintura barroca Sevillana del siglo XVII*. Seville: Universidad de Sevilla.

Flor, Fernando de la. *Barroco. Representación e ideología en el mundo hispanico (1580-1680)*. Madrid: Cátedra.

Foucault, Michel. 1980. *Power, Knowledge: Selected Interviews and Other Writings 1972-1977*. New York: Pantheon.

Frenk, Margit. 2013. 'Réplica a Antonio Carreira'. *Acta Poetica* 34: 211-23.

Frenk, Margit. 2011. 'Un poema en movimiento: *La mas bella niña* de Luis de Góngora'. In *El espacio del poema: Teoria y practica del discurso poetico*, edited by Itziar Lopez Guil and Jenaro Talens, 105-117. Madrid: Biblioteca Nueva.

Fumerton, Patricia. 1991. *Cultural Aesthetics: Renaissance Literature and the Practice of Social Ornament*. Chicago: University of Chicago Press.

Gaillard, Claude. 1988. 'Un inventario de las poesias atribuidas al Conde de Salinas'. *Criticon* 41: 5-66.

Galvez, Marisa. 2012. *Songbook: How Lyrics Became Poetry in Medieval Europe*. Chicago: University of Chicago Press.

García Aguilar, Ignacio. 2009. *Poesia y edición en el Siglo de Oro*. Madrid: Calambur.

Garcia de Salcedo Coronel, José. 1644. *Obras de Don Luis de Góngora comentadas*. Volume 2, 148-59. Madrid: Diego Diaz de la Carrera.

García Salcedo Coronel, José. 1650. *Cristales de Helicona, Rimas de Salzedo Coronel*. Madrid: Diego Diaz de la Carrera.

Gascón Pérez, Jesús. 2009. *El legado de los Argensola*. Zaragoza: Larumbe.

Gaylord, Mary. 1993. 'Góngora and the footprints of the voice'. *MLN* 108: 230-53.

Gere, Charlie. 2016. 'Necromedia by Marcel O. Gorman (review)'. *Technology and Culture* 57: 711-713.

Gitelman, Lisa. 2014. *Paper Knowledge: Toward a Media History of Documents.* Durham: Duke University Press.

Goldsmith, Kenneth. 2011. *Uncreative Writing: Managing Language in the Digital Age.* New York: Columbia University Press.

Góngora, Luis de. 1633. *Todas las obras de don Luis de Góngora en varios poemas.* Edited by Gonzalo de Hozes y Córdoba. Madrid: Alonso Pérez.

Góngora, Luis de. 1921. *Obras Poéticas III*, edited by Raymond Foulché-Delbosc. New York: Hispanic Society of New York.

Góngora, Luis de. 1932. *Obras Completas de Luis de Góngora y Aragote*, edited by Juan and Isabel Millé Giménez. Madrid: Aguilar.

Góngora, Luis de. 1963. *Obras en verso del Homero Español.* Edited by Dámaso Alonso. Madrid: Consejo Superior de Investigaciones Científicas.

Góngora, Luis de. 1981. *Sonetos.* Edited by Birute Ciplijauskaité. Madison: Hispanic Seminary of Medieival Studies.

Góngora, Luis de. 1994. *Soledades.* Edited by Robert Jammes. Madrid: Clasicos Castilia.

Góngora, Luis de. 2000. *Obras completas.* Edited by Antonio Carreira. 2 volumes. Madrid: Biblioteca Castro.

Góngora, Luis de. 2007. *Selected Poems.* Translated by John Dent-Young. Chicago: University of Chicago Press.

Gónzalez García, José María. 1996. 'Flecha del tiempo, rueda de fortuna y reloj barroco'. In *Filosofía moral, educación e historia: Homenaje a Fernando Salmerón.* Edited by Leon Olivé and Luis Villoro, 519-41. Mexico City: Universidad Nacional Autónoma de México.

Gorman, Marcel O. 2015. *Necromedia.* Minneapolis: University of Minnesota Press.

Gornall, J.F.G. 1978. 'Art and nature: Góngora's funerary sonnet for El Greco'. *Bulletin of Hispanic Studies* 55: 115-118.

Gracián, Baltasar. 1648. *Agudeza y Arte del Ingenio.* Madrid: Juan Nogues.

Grant, Erin M. 2013. 'Two views on the Increasing Importance of Library Access in the Seventeenth Century: Gabriel Naudé and Claude Clement'. *Georgia Library Quarterly* 50: 1-6.

Grazia Profeti, Maria. 2004. 'El micro-género de los sonetos de sátira literaria y Quevedo'. *La Perinola* 8: 375-395.

Grebe, Marc-André. 2010. 'Simancas – Ein Archiv um die Welt su regieren? Archivwissen und Verwaltungshandeln zur Zeit Philipps II'. In *Archiv – Macht – Wissen: Organisation und Konstruktion von Wissen und Wirklichkeit in Archiven*, edited by Anja Horstmann and Vanina Kopp 23-37. Frankfurt am Main: Campus.

Gumbrecht, Hans Ulrich. 1988. 'A farewell to interpretation'. In *Materialities of Communication*, edited by Hans Ulrich Gumbrecht and Karl Ludwig Pfeiffer, 389-404. Palo Alto: Stanford University Press.

Gumbrecht, Hans Ulrich. 1990. *Eine Geschichte der Spanischen Literatur*. Berlin: Surhkamp.

Gumbrecht, Hans Ulrich. 2003. *The Powers of Philology: Dynamics of Textual Scholarship*. Chicago: University of Illinois Press.

Gumbrecht, Hans Ulrich. 2004. *Production of Presence: What Meaning Cannot Convey*. Palo Alto: Stanford University Press.

Gumbrecht, Hans Ulrich. 2013. *After 1945: Latency as the Origin of the Present*. Palo Alto: Stanford University Press.

Gumbrecht, Hans Ulrich. 2013. *Explosionen der Aufklärung: Diderot, Goya, Lichtenberg, Mozart*. Jena: Garamond.

Gumbrecht, Hans Ulrich. 2014. 'Media history as the Event of Truth: On the Singularity of Friedrich A. Kittler's Works'. In Friedrich Kittler, *The Truth of the Technological World*, 307-330. Palo Alto: Stanford University Press.

Gumbrecht, Hans Ulrich. 2014. *Our Broad Present: Time and Contemporary Culture*. New York: Columbia University Press,.

Gutiérrez, Carlos M. 2005. *La espada, el rayo y la pluma: Quevedo y los campos literarios y de poder*. West Lafayatte, Indiana: Purdue University Press.

Gúzman, Juan de. 1612. *Relación de las honras que se hicieron en la ciudad de Córdoba a la muerte de la serenissima Reyna Señora nuestra, doña Margarita de Austria*. Córdoba: Viuda de Andrés Barrera.

Hammond, Gerald. 1990. *Fleeting Things: English Poets and Poems 1616-1660*. Cambridge, Ma.: Harvard University Press.

Harman, Graham. 2010. *Towards Speculative Realism: Essays and Lectures*. Winchester: Zero Books.

Hartog, Francois. 2000. 'The invention of history: The pre-history of a concept from Homer to Herodotus'. *History and Theory* 39: 384-395.

Hartog, Francois. 2015. *Regimes of Historicity: Presentism and Experiences of Time*. Translated by Saskia Brown. New York: Columbia University Press.

Heidegger, Martin. 2004. *What Is Called Thinking?* Translated by J. Glenn Gray. New York: Perennial.

Herrera, Pedro de. 1617. *Descripcion de la capilla de N.S. del Sagrario que erigio en la sta iglesia de Toldeo el Illmo Cardenal D. Bernardo de Sandoval y Rojas*. Madrid: Luis Sanchez.

Hidalgo Brinquis, 2006. Maria del Carmen. 'La industria papelera en la España de Cervantes'. In *Imprenta, libros y lectura en la España del Quijote*, edited by José Manuel Lucía Megías, 197-224. Madrid: Ollero y Ramos.

Hills, Helen. 2011. *Rethinking the Baroque*. Surrey: Ashgate.

Homer. *Odyssey*. 1995. Translated by A. T. Murray. Cambridge, Mass: Harvard University Press.

Horace. 2004. *Odes and Epodes*. Translated by Nial Rudd. Cambridge, Mass.: Harvard Univeristy Press.

Horace. 1927. *Satires, Epistles, Ars Poetica*. Translated by H. R. Fairclough. Cambridge, Mass.: Harvard University Press.

Innis, Harold. 1950. *Empire and Communications*. Oxford: Oxford University Press.

Jammes, Robert. 1967. *Études sur l'œuvre poétique de Don Luis de Góngora*. Bourdeaux: Féret et fils.

Jammes, Robert. 2011. 'Góngora en el espacio y en el tiempo (1609-1615)'. In *El poeta soledad: Góngora 1609-1615*. Edited by Begoña Lopez Bueno, 15-32. Zaragoza: Prensas Universitarias de Zaragoza.

Jauregui, Juan de. 1614. *Antídoto contra la pestilente poesía de las soledades*. Madrid.

Jeronimo Collado, Francisco. 1869. *Descripcion del túmulo y relación de las exequias que hizo la ciudad de Sevilla en la muerte del rey Felipe segundo*. Sevilla: José Maria Geofrin.

Jordan, William B. 1982. *El Greco de Toledo*. Madrid: Ministerio de Cultura.

Jordan, William B. 2005. *Juan van der Hamen and the Court of Madrid*. London: Yale Univeristy Press.

Kafka, Ben. 2012. *The Demon of Writing: Powers and Failures of Paperwork*. Cambridge, Mass.: MIT Press.

Kagan, Richard. 1974. *Students and Society in Early Modern Spain*. Baltimore: John Hopkins University Press.

Kittler, Friedrich. 1992. *Discourse Networks 1800/1900*. Translated by Michael Metteer, with Chris Cullens. Palo Alto: Stanford University Press.

Krajewski, Markus. 2011. *Paper Machines: About Cards & Catalogs, 1548-1929*. Cambridge, Mass.: MIT Press.

Krämer, Sibylle and Horst Bredekamp. 2013. 'Culture, Technology, Cultural Techniques: Moving beyond text'. *Theory Culture Society* 30: 20-29.

Kristine Kramer. 2008. 'Mitología y magia óptica: Sobre la relación entre retrato, espejo y escritura en la poesia de Góngora'. *Olivar* 9: 55-86.

Kruse, Christiane. 2010. 'Imagination, Illusion, Repräsentation. Bildbetrachtung als Kulturtechnik'. In *Imagination und Repräsentation: Zwei Bildsphären der Frühen Neuzeit*, edited by Christiane Kruse, Horst Bredekamp and Pablo Schneider, 195-218. Munich: Wilhelm Fink.

Lara Garrido, José. 1987. 'Los retratos de Prometeo'. *Edad de Oro* 6: 133-148.

Lara Garrido, José. 1992. 'Siglo de Oro: considerandos y materiales sobre la historia, sentido y pertinencia de un término'. *Analecta Malacitana* 15: 173-199.

Latour, Bruno. 1986. 'Visualization and Cognition: Drawing things together'. *Knowledge and Society Studies in the Sociology of Culture Past and Present* 6: 1-40.

Latour, Bruno. 1993. *We Have Never Been Modern*. Cambridge, Mass.: Harvard University Press.

Latour, Bruno. 2004. *La Fabrique du Droit: Une Ethnographie du Conseil d'Etat*. Paris: Editions La Découverte,.

Latour, Bruno. 2007. *Re-Assembling the Social: An Introduction to Actor-Network Theory*. Oxford: Oxford University Press.

Latour, Bruno. 2013. *An Inquiry Into Modes of Existence: An Anthropology of the Moderns*. Cambridge, Mass.: Harvard University Press.

Latour, Bruno. 2017. *Facing Gaia: Eight Lectures on the New Climatic Regime*. Cambridge: Polity.

Lawrence, Jeremy. 2011. 'Las Obras de don Luis de Góngora y el Conde-Duque'. In *Poder y Saber: Bibliotecas y Bibliofilia en la época del conde-duque de Olivares*, edited by Jeremy Lawrence, Jeremy Roe, and Oliver Noble Wood, 157-82. Madrid: CEEH.

Lewis Simon L., & Mark A. Maslin. 2015. 'Defining the Anthropocene'. *Nature* 519: 171-80.

Lessig, Lawrence. 2009. *Remix: Making Art and Commerce Thrive in the Hybrid Economy*. London: Penguin Books.

Macho, Thomas. 2003. 'Zeit und Zahl: Kalender- und Zeitrechnung als Kulturtechniken'. In *Bild, Schrift, Zahl*, edited by Sibylle Krämer and Horst Bredekamp, 179-192. Munich: Fink.

Marañon, Gregorio. 1935. 'La biblioteca del Conde-Duque de Olivares', *Boletín de la Real Academia de Historia* 107: 677-92.

Marañon, Gregorio. 1936. *El Conde-Duque de Olivares: La pasión de mandar*. Madrid: Espasa Calpe.

Marañon, Gregrio. 1967. *Don Juan*. Madrid: Espasa Calpe.

Jose Antonio. 2002. *La Cultura del Barroco*. Barcelona: Ariel Editorial.

Menéndez Pelayo, Marcelino. 2010, 'Conceptismo y Gongorismo'. In *Obras completas de Menéndez Pelayo*. Madrid: Fundación Ignacio Larramendi. http://www.larramendi.es/i18n/corpus/unidad.cmd?idUnidad=101381&idCorpus=1000&posicion=1.

Marias, Fernando. 2012. 'El retrato de don Luis de Góngora y Aragote'. In *Góngora: La estrella inextinguible* [exhibition catalogue], 47-59. Madrid: S.E.A.C.

Martín González, Juan José. 1993. *El artista en la sociedad española del siglo XVII*. Madrid: Cátedra.

McLuhan, Marshal. 1962. *The Gutenberg Galaxy: The Making of Typographic Man*. Toronto: University of Toronto Press.

Meillassoux, Quentin. 2008. *After Finitude: An essay on the necessity of contingency*. London: Continuum.

Mitchell, W.J.T. 1996. 'What do pictures really want?' *October* 77: 71-82.

Moll, Jaime. 1974. 'Diez años sin licencias para imprimir comedias y novelas en los reinos de Castilla: 1625-1634'. *Boletin de la Real Academia Española* 54: 97-103.

Moll, Jaime. 1984. 'Las Ediciones de Góngora en el Siglo XVII'. *El Crotalón: Anuario de Filología Española* 1: 921-63.

Moll, Jaime. 1997. 'Notas sobre Obras en verso del Homero Español'. *Voz y letra: Revista de literatura* 8: 29-35.

Moll, Jaime. 2009. 'Problemas bibliográficos del libro del Siglo de Oro'. *Biblioteca Virtual Miguel de Cervantes*. www.cervantesvirtual.com/nd/ark:/59851/bmcvd7c6.

Morán Turina, José Miguel and Fernando Checa Cremades. 1985. *El Coleccionismo en España: De la cámara de maravillas a la galeria de pinturas*. Madrid: Cátedra.

Müller, Lothar. 2012. *Weisse Magie: Die Epoche des Papiers*. Munich: Hanser.

Noble Wood, Oliver J. 2011. 'Vanitas vanitatum, et omnia vanitas: bibliotecas y bibliofilia en la literatura del Siglo de Oro'. In *Poder y Saber: Bibliotecas y Bibliofilia en la época del conde-duque de Olivares*, edited by Jeremy Lawrence, Jeremy Roe, and Oliver Noble Wood, 277-292. Madrid: CEEH.

Noble-Wood, Oliver J. 2014. *A Tale Blazed Through Heaven: Imitation and Invention in the Golden Age of Spain*. Oxford: Oxford University Press.

Nuñez Caceres, Javier. 1974. 'Anotaciones a un soneto de don Luis de Góngora'. *Thesaurus* 39: 539-44.

Ong, Walter. 1982. *Orality and Literacy: The Technologizing of the Word*. London: Routledge.

Orozco Diaz, Emilio. 1974. *Lope y Góngora frente a frente*. Madrid: Gredos.

Osterk, Ludovik. 1999. 'Cervantes y Felipe II'. *Verba Hispanica* 8: 61-69.

Osuna Cabezas, Maria José. 2008. *Las Soledades caminan hacia la corte: Primera fase de la polémica gongorina*. Madrid: Academia del Hispanismo.

Pacheco, Francisco. 1866. *Arte de la Pintura*. Madrid: M. Galliano.

Pacheco, Francisco. 1985. *Libro de descripción de verdaderos retratos de ilustres y memorables varones*. Sevilla: Diputación Provencial.

Page, Carlos. 2009. 'Arquitectura y arte efimera en los funerales reales de Córdoba del Tucuman'. *Hispania Sacra* 61: 423-46.

Parker, Geoffrey. 1978. *Philip II*. Boston: Little Brown.

Parker, Geoffrey. 1998. *The Grand Strategy of Philip II*. New Haven: Yale University Press.

Parker, Geoffrey. 2013. *Global Crisis: War, Climate Change and Catastrophe in the Seventeenth Century*. New Haven: Yale University Press.

Parry, Milman. 1928. *L'epithèt traditionnelle dans Homère* Paris: Société d'éditions

Paz, Amelia de. 2011. 'Góngora en entredicho, o la superstición del codex optimus'. In *El Poeta Soledad: Góngora 1609-1615*, edited by Begoña Lopez Bueno, 57-82. Zaragoza: Prensas Universitarias de Zaragoza.

Paz, Amelia de. 1999. 'Góngora… ¿y Quevedo?' In *Criticón* 75: 29-47.

Paz, Amelia de. 2012. 'Vida del poeta'. In *Góngora: La Estrella inextinguible* [exhibition catalogue], 31-45. Madrid: S.E.A.C.

Pellicer, Joseph. 1630. *Lecciones Solemnes a las Obras de Don Luis de Góngora y Aragote*. Madrid: Imprenta del Reino.

Pérez de Moya, Juan. 1977. *Philosophia secreta de la gentilidad*. Barcelona: Glosa.

Pérez del Barrio, Gabriel. 1613. *Direccion de secretarios de señores*. Madrid: Alonso Martin de Balboa.

Peters, Francis E. 2003. *The Monotheists: Jews, Christians and Muslims in Conflict and Competition*. New Jersey: Princeton University Press.

Peters, John Durham. 2015. *Marvelous Clouds: Toward a Philosophy of Elemental Media*. Chicago: University of Chicago Press.

Plutarch. 2004. *The Life of Alexander the Great*. Translated by John Dryden. New York: The Modern Library.

Poggi, Giulia. 1993. 'Un soneto de Góngora y su fuente italiana'. In *Estado actual de los estudios sobre el Siglo de Oro: Actas del II congreso Internacional de Hispanistas del Siglo de Oro*, edited by Manuel García Martín, 787-793. Salamanca: Ediciones Universidad de Salamanca.

Ponce Cárdenas, Jesus. 2013. 'Cebado los ojos de pintura: Epigrama y retrato en el ciclo Ayamontino'. In *Góngora y el epigrama: Estudios sobre las décimas*, edited by Juan Matas Caballero, José María Mico and Jesus Ponce Cárdenas, 143-66. Pamplona: BAH.

Ponce de Leon, Pedro. 2013. *La Arquitectura del Palacio-Monasterio de Loeches. El Sueño olvidado de un Valido; la Emulación de un Real Retiro*. PhD Thesis. E.T.S. Arquitectura de Madrid. http://oa.upm.es/22388/.

Porreño, Baltasar. 1942. *Dichos y hechos del rey don Felipe II*. Edited by Angel González Palencia. Madrid: Editorial Saeta.

Prendergast, Ryan. 2007. 'Constructing an Icon: The self-referentiality and framing of Sor Juana Inés de la Cruz'. *Journal of Early Modern Cultural Studies* 7: 28-56.

Pryor, Sean, and David Trotter. 2016. *Writing, Medium, Machine: Modern Technographies*. London: Open Humanities Press.

Purdon J. 2018 'Literature—Technology—Media: Towards a new technography'. *Literature Compass* 15: e12423.

Quevedo, Francisco de. 2009. *Obra Poética*. Edited by Jose Manuel Blecua. Madrid: Castalia.

Quevedo, Francisco de. 2009. *Selected Poetry of Francisco de Quevedo: A Bilingual Edition*. Edited and translated by Christopher Johnson. Chicago: The University of Chicago Press.

Rodriguez-Moñino, Antonio. 1965. *Construcción crítica y realidad histórica en la poesia española de los siglos XVI y XVII*. Madrid: Editorial Castilla.

Rodriguez-Moñino, Antonio. 1970. *Diccionario bibliográfico de pliegos sueltos poeticos*. Madrid: Castalia.

Roe, Jeremy. 2014. 'Truthful representation and the limits of artistic licence: A study of the discordance between Pacheco and Carducho's theory and practice of decorum'. In *Imatge, devoció i identitat a l'epoca moderna*, edited by Sílvia Canalda and Cristina Fontcuberta, 33-56. Barcelona: Ediciones de la Universitat de Barcelona.

Rojas Castro, Antonio, Celia Nadal and Amanda Pedraza. 2015. 'Catalogo Bibliographico sobre Góngora: 2000-2014'. *Biblioteca Virtual Miguel de Cervantes*. http://www.cervantesvirtual.es/obra/cabigo--catalogo-bibliografico-sobre-gongora-2000-2014/.

Romanos, Melchora. 2012. 'Góngora atacado, defendido y comentado: manuscritos e impresos de la polémica gongorina y comentarios a su obra'. In *Góngora: La Estrella Inextinguible* [exhibition catalogue], 159-168. Madrid: S.E.A.C.

Rosales, Luis. 1966. *El sentimiento del desengaño en la poesía barroca*. Madrid: Instituto de Cultura Hispánica.

Rosales, Luis. 1964. *Pasión y muerte del Conde de Villamediana*. Madrid: RAE.

Rose, Mark. 1995. *Authors and Owners: The Invention of Copyright*. Cambridge, Mass.: Harvard University Press.

Rosenberg, Daniel. 2003. 'Early Modern Information Overload'. *Journal of the History of Ideas* 64: 1-9.

Roses, Joaquín. 1994. *Una poetica de la oscuridad*. Madrid: Tamesis.

Rouached, Philippe. 2009. *Poésie et combat politique dans l'œuvre du Comte de Villamediana*. PhD Thesis. Paris Sorbonne IV. http://www.e-sorbonne.fr/sites/www.e-sorbonne.fr/files/theses/these-rouached.pdf.

Rozas, Juan Manuel. 1964. 'Los textos dispersos de Villamediana'. *Revista de Filología Española* 47: 341-67.

Rozas, Juan Manuel. 1965. *Cancionero de Mendes Brito: Poesias ineditas del Conde de Villamediana*. Madrid: CSIC.

Ruiz Sanchez, Marcos. 1999. 'El reloj y la angustia del tiempo en dos escritores neolatinos del siglo XVII'. *Myrtia* 14: 187-200.

Saavedra Fajardo, Diego de. 1988. *Empresas politicas: La idea de un Principe Politico Christiano representada en cien empresas*. Barcelona: Planeta.

Sanchez Mariana, Manuel. 1991. 'Historia de los manuscritos'. In Luis de Góngora, *Obras de don Luis de Góngora: El Manuscrito Chacon, Homenaje a Damaso Alonso*. Volume 2, ix-xxxv. Madrid Caja de Ahorros de Ronda.

Sanchéz-Jiménez, Antonio. 2006. *Lope pintado por si mismo: mito e imagen de autor en la poesia de Lope de Vega*. Tamesis, Woodbridge.

Sanchez Robayna, Andrés. 1983. *Tres estudios sobre Góngora*. Barcelona: Ediciones de Mall.

Saunders Magurn, Ruth. 1955. *The Letters of Peter Paul Rubens*. Evanston: Northwestern University Press.

Schneider, Norbert. 2003. *Still Life*. Cologne: Taschen.

Schottenius Cullhed, Sigrid. 2015. *Proba the Prophet*. Leiden: Brill.

Senabre, Ricardo. 1994. 'La sombra alargada de un verso gongorino'. In *Hommage a Robert Jammes III*. Edited by Francis Cerdan, 1089-1098. Toulouse: Presses Universitaires de Mirail.

Serres, Michel. 1982. *The Parasite*. Translated by Laurence R. Schehr. Baltimore: John Hopkins University Press.

Shakespeare, William. 2006. *Hamlet*. London: Arden.

Sieber, Harry. 1998. 'The magnificent fountain: literary patronage in the Court of Philip III'. *Cervantes: Bulletin of the Cervantes Society of America* 18: 85-116.

Siegert, Bernhard. 1999. *Relays: Literature as an Epoch of the Postal System.* Translated by Kevin Repp. Palo Alto: Stanford University Press.

Siegert, Bernhard. 2003. 'Perpetual Doomsday'. In *Europa: Kultur der Sekretäre.* Edited by Bernhard Siegert and Joseph Vogl, 63-78. Berlin: Diaphanes.

Siegert, Bernhard. 2003. *Passage des digitalen: Zeichenpraktiken der neuzeitlichen Wissenschaften 1500-1900.* Berlin: Brinkmann U. Bose.

Siegert, Bernhard. 2003. *Passagiere und Papiere: Schreibakte auf der Schwelle zwischen Spanien und Amerika.* Munich: Wilhem Fink.

Siegert, Bernhard. 2008 'Cacography or communication? Cultural Techniques in German Media Studies'. Translated by Geoffrey Winthrop-Young. *Grey Room* 29: 26-47.

Siegert, Bernhard. 2013. 'Cultural Techniques: Or the End of the Intellectual Postwar Era in German Media Theory'. *Theory, Culture & Society* 30: 48-65.

Siegert, Bernhard. 2015. *Cultural Techniques. Grids, Filters, Doors and Other Articulations of the Real.* Fordham: Fordham University Press.

Silva y Mendoza, Diego de. 1985. *Antologia poetica.* Madrid: Visor,.

Siri, Mercurio. 1722. *Anecdotes du ministère du Comte duc d'Olivares: Tirées & traduites de l'Italien du Mercurio Siry, par Monsieur de Valdory.* Paris: Jean Musier & Francois Barois.

Sliwa, Krzystof. 2004. *Cartas, documentos y escrituras de Luis de Góngora y Argote (1561-1627) y de sus parientes.* Córdoba: Servicio de Publicaciones de la Universidad de Córdoba.

Sloterdijk, Peter. 2011. *Bubbles: Spheres 1: Microspherology.* Translated by Wieland Hoban Cambridge, Mass.: MIT Press.

Stallybrass, Peter, Roger Chartier, John Franklin Mowery and Heather Wolfe. 2004. 'Hamlet's Tables and the Technologies of Writing in Renaissance England'. *Shakespeare Quarterly* 55: 379-419.

Stradling, Robert. 1993. 'The death of Don Juan: Murder, myth and mayhem in Madrid'. *History Today* 43: 11-17.

Svenbro, Jesper. 1993. *Phrasikleia. An Anthropology of Reading in Ancient Greece.* Translated by Janet Lloyd. New York: Cornell University Press.

Tassis y Peralta. 1648. Juan de. *Obras de Don Juan de Tarsis, Conde de Villamediana.* Barcelona: Antonio Lacaballeria.

Tassis y Peralta, Juan de. 1969. *Obras.* Edited by Juan Manuel Rozas. Madrid: Castalia.

Taylor, René. 2006. *Arquitectura y magia: Consideraciones sobre la idea de el Escorial.* Madrid: Siruela.

Toledano Molina, Juana. 2006. 'Tres sonetos de Góngora en su contexto'. In *Actas del Congreso de la AISO 7*. Edited by Anthony Close, 181-90. Cambridge: Asociación Internacional del Siglo de Oro.

Tueller, Michael A. 2010. 'The passer-by in archaic and classical epigram'. In *Archaic and Classical Greek Epigram*. Edited by Manuel Baumbach, Andrej Petrovic and Ivana Petrovic, 42-60. Cambridge: Cambridge University Press.

Ulloa Pereira, Luis de. 1674. *Obras de Luis Ulloa Pereira*. Madrid: Francisco Sanz.

Vega, Lope de. 1965. *Obras de Lope de Vega XIII*. Atlas, Madrid.

Vega, Lope de. 1624. *Rimas humanas y divinas del licenciado Tomé de Burguillos*. Madrid: Luis Sánchez.

Vetrheim, Gjert. 2010. 'Voice in sepulchral epigrams: some remarks on the use of first and second person in sepulchral epigrams, and a comparison with lyric poetry'. In *Archaic and Classical Greek Epigram*. Edited by Manuel Baumbach, Andrej Petrovic and Ivana Petrovic, 61-78. Cambridge: Cambridge University Press.

Villegas, Alonso de. 1589. *Flos sanctorum*. Venice: Felix Valgrisio.

Vismann, Cornelia. 2013. 'Cultural Techniques and Sovereignity'. *Theory, Culture & Society* 30: 83-93.

Vismann, Cornelia. 2000. *Akten: Medientechnik und Recht*. Frankfurt Am Main: S. Fischer.

Vismann, Cornelia. 2008. *Files: Law and Media Technology*. Translated by Geofrrey Winthrop-Young. Palo Alto: Stanford University Press,.

Wagschal, Stephen. 2005. 'From Parmigianino to Pereda: Luis de Góngora on Beautiful Women and Vanitas'. In *Ekphrasis in the Age of Cervantes*, edited by Frederick A. de Armas, 102-23. Lewisburg: Bucknell University Press.

Weber, Alison. 2005. 'Lope de Vega's *Rimas sacras*: Conversion, Clientage, and the performance of Masculinity'. *PMLA* 120: 404-21.

Wheeler, Michael, 'Martin Heidegger', *The Stanford Encyclopedia of Philosophy* (Fall 2017 Edition), Edward N. Zalta (ed.), URL = <https://plato.stanford.edu/archives/fall2017/entries/heidegger/

Winthrop-Young, Geoffrey. 2013. 'Cultural Techniques: Preliminary Remarks'. In *Theory, Culture & Society* 30: 3-19.

Wolf, Hans-Jürgen. 1975. *Geschiche der Druckpressen*. Frankfurt: Interprent.

Woodall, Joanna. 1997. 'Introduction: Facing the Subject'. In *Portraiture: Facing the Subject*, edited by Joanna Woodal, 1-28. Manchester: Manchester University Press.

Yates, Frances. 2001. *The Art of Memory*. Chicago: University of Chicago Press.

Zumthor, Paul. 1972. *Essai de poétique medievale.* Paris: Seuil.

Manuscripts

Ms. RES/45, Biblioteca Nacional Madrid.

Ms. 10409. Biblioteca Nacional Madrid.

Ms. 3913, Bilioteca Nacional Madrid.

Ms. 4117. Biblioteca Nacional Madrid.

Ms. 9/5729. Real Academia de la Historia, Madrid.

Ms. 19.004. Biblioteca Nacional de España.

Ms 17.719. Biblioteca Nacional de España.

Ms. 3906. Biblioteca Nacional de España.

Ms. 2065. Biblioteca de Catalunya.

Index

www.ingramcontent.com/pod-product-compliance
Lightning Source LLC
LaVergne TN
LVHW091122080826
845145LV00008B/2014

* 9 7 8 1 7 8 5 4 2 0 5 4 2 *